(i) Entertainment Directory

GLASGOW
TRAVEL GUIDE

SHOPS, *RESTAURANTS*, **ATTRACTIONS** *& NIGHTLIFE*

⭐⭐⭐⭐⭐

The Most Positively
Reviewed and Recommended
by Locals and Travelers

EGP

GLASGOW
TRAVEL GUIDE
SHOPS, RESTAURANTS, ATTRACTIONS & NIGHTLIFE

GLASGOW TRAVEL GUIDE 2022
Shops, Restaurants, Attractions & Nightlife

© Kim S. Robinson
© E.G.P. Editorial

ISBN-13: 9798748197236

INDEX

SHOPS
Top 500 Shops - 9

RESTAURANTS
Top 500 Restaurants - 53

ATTRACTIONS
Top 500 Attractions - 97

NIGHTLIFE SPOTS
Top 500 Nightlife Spots - 135

GLASGOW TRAVEL GUIDE

Shops, Restaurants, Attractions & Nightlife

*This directory is dedicated to Glasgow Business Owners and Managers
who provide the experience that the locals and tourists enjoy.
Thanks you very much for all that you do and thank for being the "People Choice".*

*Thanks to everyone that posts their reviews online and
the amazing reviews sites that make our life easier.*

*The places listed in this book are the most positively reviewed
and recommended by locals and travelers from around the world.*

*Thank you for your time and enjoy the directory that is
designed with locals and tourist in mind!*

TOP 500 SHOPS

The Most Recommended by Locals & Trevelers
(From #1 to #500)

#1
Princes Square Shopping Centre
Category: Shopping Centre
Average price: Expensive
Area: Buchanan Street, City Centre
Address: 40-48 Buchanan Street
Glasgow G1 3JX
Phone: 0141 221 0324

#2
Monorail
Category: Music & DVDs, Vinyl Records
Average price: Modest
Area: City Centre, Merchant City
Address: 12 Kings Court
Glasgow G1 5RB
Phone: 0141 552 9458

#3
Tam Shepherd's Trick Shop
Category: Hobby Shop
Average price: Modest
Area: City Centre
Address: 33 Queen Street
Glasgow G1 3EF
Phone: 0141 221 2310

#4
Demijohn
Category: Deli, Off Licence, Specialty Food,
Flowers & Gifts
Average price: Modest
Area: Byres Road, Hillhead
Address: 382 Byres Road
Glasgow G12 8AR
Phone: 0141 337 3600

#5
Tiso Glasgow Outdoor Experience
Category: Outdoor Gear
Average price: Modest
Area: City Centre, Cowcaddens
Address: 50 Couper Street
Glasgow G4 0DL
Phone: 0141 559 5450

#6
John Lewis
Category: Department Store
Average price: Expensive
Area: City Centre
Address: 220 Buchanan Street
Glasgow G1 2GF
Phone: 0141 353 6677

#7
Mr Ben
Category: Vintage
Average price: Modest
Area: City Centre, Merchant City
Address: 101 King Street
Glasgow G1 5RB
Phone: 0141 553 1936

#8
New Look
Category: Women's Clothing,
Men's Clothing
Average price: Modest
Area: Buchanan Street, City Centre
Address: 150 Buchanan St
Glasgow G2 2JJ
Phone: 0141 229 5410

#9
Toys 'R' Us
Category: Toy Shop
Average price: Expensive
Area: South Side
Address: 480 Helen Street
Glasgow G51 3HR
Phone: 0141 440 1010

#10
G Force Games
Category: Computers, Electronics
Average price: Modest
Area: City Centre
Address: 77 Union St
Glasgow G1 3TA
Phone: 0141 248 8272

#11
Salvation Army
Category: Charity Shop
Average price: Inexpensive
Area: Partick, West End
Address: 91 Dumbarton Road
Glasgow G11 6PW
Phone: 0141 334 7253

#12
Millers Art Shop
Category: Arts & Crafts
Average price: Modest
Area: City Centre
Address: 28 Stockwell Street
Glasgow G1 4RT
Phone: 0141 553 1660

#13
The Yarn Cake
Category: Knitting Supplies
Average price: Modest
Area: West End
Address: 148 Queen Margaret Drive
Glasgow G20 8NY
Phone: 0141 946 5305

#14
Fopp
Category: Music & DVDs
Average price: Modest
Area: City Centre
Address: 19-27 Union Street
Glasgow G1 3RB
Phone: 0141 285 7190

#15
Gallery Of Modern Art
Category: Art Gallery
Average price: Inexpensive
Area: City Centre
Address: Royal Exchange Square
Glasgow G1 3AH
Phone: 0141 229 1996

#16
Mixed Up Records
Category: Music & DVDs, Vinyl Records
Average price: Modest
Area: West End
Address: 18 Otago Lane
Glasgow G12 8PB
Phone: 0141 357 5737

#17
Forbidden Planet
Category: Toy Shop, Comic Books
Average price: Modest
Area: Buchanan Street, City Centre
Address: 168 Buchanan Street
Glasgow G1 2LW
Phone: 0141 331 1215

#18
Hamleys
Category: Toy Shop
Average price: Modest
Area: City Centre
Address: St Enoch Center
Glasgow G1 4BW
Phone: 0141 227 3040

#19
The Arches Theatre
Category: Art Gallery
Average price: Modest
Area: City Centre
Address: 253 Argyle Street
Glasgow G2 8DL
Phone: 0141 585 1000

#20
Watt Brothers
Category: Department Store,
Women's Clothing
Average price: Inexpensive
Area: City Centre
Address: 119-121 SauchieHalls Street
Glasgow G2 3EL
Phone: 0141 332 5831

#21
Papyrus
Category: Cards & Stationery, Accessories
Average price: Modest
Area: Byres Road, Hillhead
Address: 374 Byres Road
Glasgow G12 8AR
Phone: 0141 334 6514

#22
The Lighthouse
Category: Art Gallery
Average price: Modest
Area: City Centre
Address: 11 Mitchell Lane
Glasgow G1 3NU
Phone: 0141 276 5365

#23
Coast
Category: Women's Clothing, Accessories
Average price: Expensive
Area: Buchanan Street, City Centre
Address: 34 Buchanan Street
Glasgow G1 3LB
Phone: 0141 221 9867

#24
Merchant Square
Category: Shopping Centre
Average price: Expensive
Area: City Centre, Merchant City
Address: Candleriggs
Glasgow G1 1LE
Phone: 0141 552 3452

#25
House of Fraser
Category: Department Store
Average price: Expensive
Area: Buchanan Street, City Centre
Address: 21-45 Buchanan Street
Glasgow G1 3HL
Phone: 0870 160 7243

#26
The Bead Company
Category: Art Supplies
Average price: Modest
Area: Partick, West End
Address: 7 Keith Street
Glasgow G11 6QQ
Phone: 0800 970 5234

#27
Primark
Category: Department Store
Average price: Inexpensive
Area: City Centre
Address: 56 Argyle Street
Glasgow G1 1
Phone: 0141 229 1343

#28
Dunnes Store
Category: Department Store
Average price: Modest
Area: City Centre
Address: 222 SauchieHalls Street
Glasgow G2 3EQ
Phone: 0141 332 9293

#29
Circa Vintage
Category: Vintage
Average price: Modest
Area: West End
Address: 37 Ruthven Lane
Glasgow G12 9BG
Phone: 0141 334 6660

#30
Lush
Category: Beauty & Cosmetics
Average price: Modest
Area: Buchanan Street, City Centre
Address: 116 Buchanan Street
Glasgow G1 3LB
Phone: 0141 243 2522

#31
Pierrot et Coco
Category: Beauty & Cosmetics,
Toy Shop, Jewellery
Average price: Expensive
Area: South Side, Shawlands
Address: 3 Abbot Street
Glasgow G41 3XE
Phone: 0141 649 2489

#32
Oxfam Books
Category: Bookshop
Average price: Modest
Area: Hillhead
Address: 330a Byres Road
Glasgow G12 8AP
Phone: 0141 338 6185

#33
Voltaire & Rousseau
Category: Bookshop, Local Flavour
Average price: Inexpensive
Area: West End
Address: 12-14 Otago Lane
Glasgow G12 8PB
Phone: 0141 339 1811

#34
Zara
Category: Accessories,
Women's Clothing
Average price: Modest
Area: Buchanan Street, City Centre
Address: 12-16 Buchanan Street
Glasgow G1 3LB
Phone: 0141 227 4770

#35
Missing Records
Category: Music & DVDs, Vinyl Records
Average price: Inexpensive
Area: City Centre
Address: 247 Argyle Street
Glasgow G2 8DL
Phone: 0141 248 1661

#36
Vintage Guru
Category: Women's Clothing,
Men's Clothing, Vintage
Average price: Modest
Area: Byres Road, West End
Address: 195 Byres Road
Glasgow G12 8TN
Phone: 0141 339 4750

#37
Love Music
Category: Music & DVDs, Vinyl Records
Average price: Modest
Area: City Centre
Address: 34 Dundas Street
Glasgow G1 2AQ
Phone: 0141 332 2099

#38
Starry Starry Night
Category: Vintage
Average price: Modest
Area: West End
Address: 19 Dowanside Lane
Glasgow G12 9BZ
Phone: 0141 337 1837

#39
Napiers Herbal Health Care
Category: Pharmacy
Average price: Modest
Area: Hillhead
Address: 61 Cresswell Street
Glasgow G12 8AD
Phone: 0141 339 5859

#40
Silverburn Shopping Centre
Category: Shopping Centre
Average price: Modest
Area: South Side, Nitshill
Address: Barrhead Road
Glasgow G53 6QR
Phone: 0141 880 3200

#41
TK Maxx
Category: Fashion
Average price: Modest
Area: SauchieHalls Street, City Centre
Address: 179 SauchieHalls St
Glasgow G2 3ER
Phone: 0141 331 0411

#42
Buchanan Gallery
Category: Shopping Centre
Average price: Modest
Area: Buchanan Street, City Centre
Address: 220 Buchanan Street
Glasgow G1 2FF
Phone: 0141 333 9898

#43
Karen Millen
Category: Women's Clothing
Average price: Expensive
Area: Buchanan Street, City Centre
Address: 36 Buchanan Street
Glasgow G1 3JX
Phone: 0141 243 2136

#44
Galletly & Tubbs Interiors
Category: Furniture Shop, Home Decor
Average price: Expensive
Area: Great Western Road
Address: 439 Great Western Road
Glasgow G4 9JA
Phone: 0141 357 1002

#45
Urban Outfitters
Category: Women's Clothing,
Men's Clothing, Accessories
Average price: Expensive
Area: Buchanan Street, City Centre
Address: 157 Buchanan Street
Glasgow G1 2
Phone: 0141 248 9203

#46
Debenhams
Category: Department Store
Average price: Expensive
Area: City Centre
Address: 97 Argyle Street
Glasgow G2 8AR
Phone: 0844 561 6161

#47
Boots
Category: Pharmacy,
Beauty & Cosmetics
Average price: Modest
Area: City Centre
Address: 200 SauchieHalls St
Glasgow G2 3EN
Phone: 0141 332 1925

#48
The Big Top
Category: Toy Shop
Average price: Modest
Area: Charing Cross, City Centre
Address: 26 Charing Cross Mansions
Glasgow G3 6UJ
Phone: 0141 332 3300

#49
Size?
Category: Shoe Shop, Men's Clothing, Women's Clothing
Average price: Expensive
Area: City Centre
Address: 17 Union St
Glasgow G1 3RB
Phone: 0141 248 8391

#50
Cyber Alternative Clothing Corsetry
Category: Women's Clothing
Average price: Expensive
Area: City Centre, Merchant City
Address: 107 King Street
Glasgow G1 5RB
Phone: 0141 553 0942

#51
Office
Category: Shoe Shop
Average price: Expensive
Area: City Centre
Address: 54-56 Buchanan Street
Glasgow G1 3JL
Phone: 0141 248 8346

#52
Felix and Oscar
Category: Gift Shop, Accessories, Children's Clothing
Average price: Modest
Area: Great Western Road
Address: 459 Great Western Road
Glasgow G12 8HH
Phone: 0141 339 8585

#53
GuitarGuitar
Category: Musical Instruments
Average price: Modest
Area: City Centre, Merchant City
Address: 36 Trongate
Glasgow G1 5ES
Phone: 0141 552 9896

#54
Ollie & Nic
Category: Accessories, Jewellery
Average price: Expensive
Area: Buchanan Street, City Centre
Address: 48 Buchanan Street
Glasgow G1 3JN
Phone: 0141 222 2838

#55
Little Botanica
Category: Gift Shop, Florist
Average price: Modest
Area: South Side
Address: 741 Pollokshaws Road
Glasgow G41 2AA
Phone: 0141 423 3328

#56
Boots
Category: Pharmacy, Beauty & Cosmetics
Average price: Modest
Area: City Centre
Address: Buchanan Gallery
Glasgow G1 2GF
Phone: 0141 333 9306

#57
Merchant City Cameras
Category: Photography Shop
Average price: Expensive
Area: City Centre, Merchant City
Address: 7-11 Parnie Street
Glasgow G1 5
Phone: 0141 552 6823

#58
Bravissimo
Category: Lingerie
Average price: Expensive
Area: City Centre, Merchant City
Address: 229 Ingram Street
Glasgow G1 1DA
Phone: 0141 229 5430

#59
The Disney Store
Category: Toy Shop
Average price: Expensive
Area: City Centre
Address: St Enoch Square
Glasgow G1 4LZ
Phone: 0141 248 1441

#60
Mr Harold & Son
Category: Jewellery
Average price: Expensive
Area: City Centre
Address: 33 Argyll Arcade
Glasgow G2 8BA
Phone: 0141 221 9969

#61
Dower &Halls
Category: Jewellery
Average price: Expensive
Area: Buchanan Street, City Centre
Address: 48 Buchanan Street
Glasgow G1 3JX
Phone: 0141 221 9222

#62
Agent Provocateur
Category: Lingerie, Adult
Average price: Exclusive
Area: City Centre, Merchant City
Address: 213 Ingram Street
Glasgow G1 1DQ
Phone: 0141 221 2538

#63
MAC Cosmetics
Category: Beauty & Cosmetics
Average price: Expensive
Area: Buchanan Street, City Centre
Address: 21-45 Buchanan Street
Glasgow G1 3HL
Phone: 0141 221 4520

#64
Osiris
Category: Accessories, Men's Clothing,
Women's Clothing
Average price: Modest
Area: City Centre
Address: 55 Queen Street
Glasgow G1 3EN
Phone: 0141 243 2400

#65
Young's Interesting Books
Category: Bookshop
Average price: Modest
Area: South Side, Shawlands
Address: 18 Skirving Street
Glasgow G41 3AA
Phone: 0141 649 9599

#66
Bobbi Brown
Category: Beauty & Cosmetics
Average price: Expensive
Area: City Centre
Address: Lister Street
Glasgow G4 0BZ
Phone: 0141 353 6677

#67
The Candle Store
Category: Home Decor
Average price: Modest
Area: South Side, Govan
Address: 23 Robert Street
Glasgow G51 3HB
Phone: 0141 445 1014

#68
The Nancy Smillie Shop
Category: Jewellery, Furniture Shop
Average price: Expensive
Area: Hillhead
Address: 53 Cresswell Street
Glasgow G12 8AE
Phone: 0141 334 4240

#69
Elements
Category: Baby Accessories & Furniture,
Cards & Stationery, Beauty & Cosmetics
Average price: Modest
Area: Hillhead
Address: 5-21 Cresswell Lane
Glasgow G12 8AA
Phone: 0141 357 2983

#70
A1 Toys & A1 Comics
Category: Toy Shop, Comic Books
Average price: Modest
Area: City Centre, Merchant City
Address: 31-35 Parnie Street
Glasgow G1 5RJ
Phone: 0141 552 6692

#71
Andersons
Category: Wholesaler, Greengrocer
Average price: Modest
Area: West End
Address: 92 Queen Margaret Drive
Glasgow G20 8NZ
Phone: 0141 946 9843

#72
Shelter
Category: Charity Shop
Average price: Inexpensive
Area: Great Western Road, Hillhead
Address: 679 Great Western Road
Glasgow G12 8RA
Phone: 0141 357 4347

#73
Cycle Lane
Category: Bicycles
Average price: Modest
Area: South Side
Address: 193 Clarkston Road
Glasgow G44 3BS
Phone: 0141 637 2439

#74
Next
Category: Fashion
Average price: Modest
Area: City Centre, Merchant City
Address: 70-76 Argyle Street
Glasgow G2 8AG
Phone: 0870 386 5374

#75
Ann Summers
Category: Lingerie, Adult
Average price: Expensive
Area: SauchieHalls Street, City Centre
Address: 55-57 SauchieHalls Street
Glasgow G2 3AT
Phone: 0141 331 0272

#76
Accessorize
Category: Accessories
Average price: Modest
Area: City Centre
Address: 220 Buchanan Street
Glasgow G1 2GF
Phone: 0141 354 0133

#77
Remnant Kings Central
Category: Haberdashery & Fabrics
Average price: Inexpensive
Area: Buchanan Street, City Centre
Address: 146 Argyle Street
Glasgow G2 8BL
Phone: 0141 221 2220

#78
Illuminati
Category: Cards & Stationery
Average price: Modest
Area: Buchanan Street, City Centre
Address: 42 Buchanan Street
Glasgow G1 3JX
Phone: 0141 221 8787

#79
Brazen Studio
Category: Jewellery
Average price: Expensive
Area: City Centre, Merchant City
Address: 58 Albion Street
Glasgow G1 1LH
Phone: 0141 552 4551

#80
Marks & Spencer
Category: Department Store
Average price: Modest
Area: City Centre
Address: 172 SauchieHalls Street
Glasgow G2 3EE
Phone: 0141 332 6097

#81
Bhs
Category: Department Store,
Women's Clothing
Average price: Modest
Area: City Centre
Address: 67-81 SauchieHalls Street
Glasgow G2 3DA
Phone: 0141 332 0401

#82
H & M
Category: Women's Clothing,
Accessories, Men's Clothing,
Children's Clothing
Average price: Inexpensive
Area: City Centre
Address: 55 St Enoch Square
Glasgow G1 4BW
Phone: 0141 204 3900

#83
Nancy Smillie Jewellery Studio
Category: Jewellery
Average price: Modest
Area: Great Western Road
Address: 425 Great Western Road
Glasgow G4 9JA
Phone: 0141 334 0055

#84
Slater Menswear
Category: Men's Clothing
Average price: Modest
Area: City Centre, Merchant City
Address: 165 Howard Street
Glasgow G1 4HF
Phone: 0141 552 7171

#85
Rainbow Room International
Category: Hairdressers,
Beauty & Cosmetics
Average price: Expensive
Area: Great Western Road, Hillhead
Address: 607 Great Western Road
Glasgow G12 8HX
Phone: 0141 337 3370

#86
CC Music
Category: Musical Instruments
Average price: Modest
Area: Great Western Road
Address: 33 Otago Street
Glasgow G12 8JJ
Phone: 0141 339 7766

#87
Caledonia Books
Category: Bookshop
Average price: Modest
Area: Great Western Road
Address: 483 Great Western Road
Glasgow G12 8HL
Phone: 0141 334 9663

#88
Superdrug
Category: Pharmacy, Beauty & Cosmetics,
Sandwiches
Average price: Inexpensive
Area: City Centre
Address: 66 Argyle Street
Glasgow G2 8AG
Phone: 0141 221 9644

#89
Barnardo's
Category: Charity Shop
Average price: Modest
Area: City Centre, Merchant City
Address: 54 Wilson Street
Glasgow G1 1HD
Phone: 0141 552 9581

#90
Bose
Category: Electronics
Average price: Exclusive
Area: City Centre, Merchant City
Address: 136 Ingram Street
Glasgow G1 1EJ
Phone: 0141 552 7333

#91
Achilles Heel
Category: Shoe Shop, Sports Wear
Average price: Expensive
Area: Great Western Road, Hillhead
Address: 593 Great Western Road
Glasgow G12 8HX
Phone: 0141 342 5722

#92
Game
Category: Videos & Video Game Rental
Average price: Modest
Area: City Centre
Address: 43 Union Street
Glasgow G1 3RB
Phone: 0141 204 3005

#93
Space NK
Category: Beauty & Cosmetics
Average price: Expensive
Area: Buchanan Street, City Centre
Address: 48 Buchanan Street
Glasgow G1 3JN
Phone: 0141 248 7931

#94
Cancer Research UK
Category: Charity Shop
Average price: Modest
Area: Byres Road, West End
Address: 315 Byres Rd
Glasgow G12 8UQ
Phone: 0141 334 9717

#95
The City Retro Fashion
Category: Men's Clothing,
Women's Clothing
Average price: Modest
Area: City Centre, Merchant City
Address: 41 King Street
Glasgow G1 5RA
Phone: 0141 201 7400

#96
Pippens Toys
Category: Toy Shop
Average price: Modest
Area: Gallowgate
Address: 36 Gallowgate
Glasgow G1 5AB
Phone: 0141 552 8083

#97
Barras Market
Category: Antiques
Average price: Inexpensive
Area: Parkhead
Address: Gallowgate
Glasgow G31 4
Phone: 0141 552 4601

#98
Slanj Kilts
Category: Men's Clothing
Average price: Modest
Area: City Centre
Address: 80 Saint Vincent Street
Glasgow G2 5UB
Phone: 0141 248 5632

#99
HMV
Category: Music & DVDs
Average price: Modest
Area: City Centre, Merchant City
Address: 6 Argyle Street
Glasgow G2 8AA
Phone: 0141 204 4787

#100
Rub A Dub
Category: Vinyl Records
Average price: Modest
Area: City Centre
Address: 35 Howard Street
Glasgow G1 4BA
Phone: 0141 221 9657

#101
Argos
Category: Department Store
Average price: Inexpensive
Area: City Centre
Address: 40 Stockwell Street
Glasgow G1 4RT
Phone: 0141 552 8161

#102
Acqua Di Parma
Category: Beauty & Cosmetics
Average price: Expensive
Area: City Centre, Merchant City
Address: 21-45 Buchanan Street
Glasgow G1 3HL
Phone: 0141 221 4520

#103
B&M Bargains
Category: Hobby Shop
Average price: Inexpensive
Area: South Side, Shawlands
Address: 84-88 Kilmarnock Rd
Glasgow G41 3NN
Phone: 0141 649 9110

#104
Annan Gallery
Category: Art Gallery
Average price: Expensive
Area: Woodlands, West End
Address: 164 Woodlands Road
Glasgow G3 6LL
Phone: 0141 332 0028

#105
Alba Second-Hand Printed Music
Category: Bookshop, Vintage
Average price: Inexpensive
Area: West End
Address: 55 Otago Street
Glasgow G12 8PQ
Phone: 0141 357 1795

#106
Thistle Books
Category: Bookshop
Average price: Inexpensive
Area: West End
Address: 55 Otago Street
Glasgow G12 8PQ
Phone: 0141 334 8777

#107
Cancer Research UK
Category: Charity Shop
Average price: Inexpensive
Area: Partick, West End
Address: 458 Dumbarton Road
Glasgow G11 6SE
Phone: 0141 339 8858

#108
Home Bargains
Category: Department Store
Average price: Inexpensive
Area: South Side, Govan
Address: Govan Road
Glasgow G51 3UL
Phone: 0141 445 6158

#109
Hyndland Bookshop
Category: Bookshop
Average price: Modest
Area: West End
Address: 143 Hyndland Road
Glasgow G12 9JA
Phone: 0141 334 5522

#110
Richer Sounds
Category: Electronics
Average price: Modest
Area: City Centre
Address: 57 Jamaica Street
Glasgow G1 4NN
Phone: 0141 226 5551

#111
Nevisport
Category: Sporting Goods
Average price: Modest
Area: SauchieHalls Street, City Centre
Address: 261 SauchieHalls St
Glasgow G2 3EZ
Phone: 0141 332 4814

#112
Schuh
Category: Shoe Shop
Average price: Modest
Area: City Centre
Address: 118-120 Argyle Street
Glasgow G2 8BH
Phone: 0141 248 7331

#113
Poundland
Category: Beauty & Cosmetics,
Toy Shop, Kitchen & Bath
Average price: Inexpensive
Area: City Centre, Merchant City
Address: 187 Trongate
Glasgow G1 5HF
Phone: 0141 553 2631

#114
Geoffrey Tailor Highland Crafts
Category: Fashion
Average price: Exclusive
Area: SauchieHalls Street, City Centre
Address: 309 SauchieHalls St
Glasgow G2 3HW
Phone: 0141 331 2388

#115
Arran Aromatics
Category: Beauty & Cosmetics
Average price: Modest
Area: City Centre
Address: 48 Buchanan Street
Glasgow G1 3JN
Phone: 0141 248 5242

#116
Christo's
Category: Art Gallery
Average price: Expensive
Area: Great Western Road, Hillhead
Address: 595 Great Western Road
Glasgow G12 8HX
Phone: 0141 579 0004

#117
Molton Brown
Category: Beauty & Cosmetics,
Skin Care
Average price: Expensive
Area: Buchanan Street, City Centre
Address: 59 Buchannan St
Glasgow G1 3HR
Phone: 0141 248 9488

#118
Monsoon
Category: Accessories,
Women's Clothing
Average price: Expensive
Area: Buchanan Street, City Centre
Address: 57 Buchanan Street
Glasgow G1 3HL
Phone: 0141 226 5357

#119
Italian Centre
Category: Shopping Centre
Average price: Exclusive
Area: City Centre, Merchant City
Address: 7 John Street
Glasgow G1 1HP
Phone: 0141 552 6368

#120
River Island
Category: Accessories, Men's Clothing,
Women's Clothing
Average price: Expensive
Area: Buchanan Street, SauchieHalls
Street, City Centre
Address: 220 Buchanan Street
Glasgow G1 2GF
Phone: 0141 331 2449

#121
The Forge Market
Category: Department Store
Average price: Inexpensive
Area: Parkhead
Address: 1201 Duke St
Glasgow G31 5NZ
Phone: 0141 554 1395

#122
Thomas Sabo
Category: Jewellery
Average price: Expensive
Area: City Centre
Address: 220 Buchanan Street
Glasgow G1 2FF
Phone: 0141 332 1899

#123
Static Games
Category: Toy Shop
Average price: Modest
Area: City Centre, Merchant City
Address: 35-39 King St
Glasgow G1 5RA
Phone: 0141 552 9785

#124
Cosy Camper
Category: Outdoor Gear
Average price: Expensive
Area: Buchanan Street, City Centre
Address: 220 Buchanan St
Glasgow G2 1
Phone: 0141 333 9898

#125
Merchant City Music
Category: Musical Instruments
Average price: Modest
Area: Gallowgate
Address: 60 London Road
Glasgow G1 5NB
Phone: 0141 552 6290

#126
St Enoch Shopping Centre
Category: Shopping Centre
Average price: Modest
Area: City Centre
Address: 55 St Enoch Sq
Glasgow G1 4LZ
Phone: 0141 204 3900

#127
La Coco
Category: Cards & Stationery, Jewellery
Average price: Modest
Area: Partick, West End
Address: 16 Merkland Street
Glasgow G11 6DB
Phone: 0141 337 6333

#128
Barry's Convenience Store
Category: Supermarket, Tobacconists
Average price: Modest
Area: South Side
Address: 18 Clarkston Road
Glasgow G44 4EH
Phone: 0141 633 3948

#129
All Kinds of Everything
Category: Cards & Stationery, Jewellery
Average price: Modest
Area: Duke Street, Dennistoun
Address: 469 Duke Street
Glasgow G31 1DL
Phone: 0141 554 4060

#130
Marks & Spencer
Category: Department Store
Average price: Expensive
Area: City Centre, Merchant City
Address: 2-12 Argyle Street
Glasgow G2 8AA
Phone: 0141 552 4546

#131
Mind The Gap
Category: Art Supplies, Toy Shop
Average price: Modest
Area: Hillhead
Address: 5 Cresswell Ln
Glasgow G12 8AA
Phone: 0141 334 2144

#132
Rhythm Base
Category: Musical Instruments
Average price: Expensive
Area: South Side, Tradeston
Address: 7-9 Commerce Street
Glasgow G5 8AB
Phone: 0141 429 3799

#133
Boxwood
Category: Flowers & Gifts
Average price: Expensive
Area: Byres Road, Hillhead
Address: 388 Byres Rd
Glasgow G12 8AR
Phone: 0141 357 6642

#134
H Samuel
Category: Jewellery
Average price: Modest
Area: City Centre
Address: 15-18 Argyll Arcade
Glasgow G2 8BA
Phone: 0141 221 8281

#135
MacGregor & MacDuff
Category: Fashion
Average price: Modest
Area: City Centre
Address: 41 Bath Street
Glasgow G2 1HW
Phone: 0141 332 0299

#136
Montana Tan
Category: Tanning, Beauty & Cosmetics
Average price: Inexpensive
Area: SauchieHalls Street, City Centre
Address: 142 west nile street
Glasgow G1 2RQ
Phone: 0800 644 0525

#137
Boux Avenue
Category: Lingerie, Swimwear
Average price: Modest
Area: Buchanan Street, City Centre
Address: Buchanan Street
Glasgow G1 2FF
Phone: 0141 332 7234

#138
Niche Optical Tailor
Category: Eyewear & Opticians
Average price: Modest
Area: City Centre, Merchant City
Address: 119 Candleriggs
Glasgow G1 1NP
Phone: 0141 553 2077

#139
Catani Of Anniesland
Category: Hardware Store
Average price: Inexpensive
Area: Great Western Road, Anniesland
Address: 1549 Great Western Road
Glasgow G13 1HL
Phone: 0141 954 6300

#140
Glasgow Bike Station
Category: Bicycles, Mountain Biking
Average price: Inexpensive
Area: Finnieston, West End
Address: 65 Haugh Road
Glasgow G3 8TX
Phone: 0141 248 5409

#141
Butterfly Kisses
Category: Women's Clothing,
Children's Clothing
Average price: Modest
Area: South Side, Shawlands
Address: 8 Skirving Street
Glasgow G41 3AA
Phone: 0141 649 3552

#142
Recoat Gallery
Category: Art Gallery
Average price: Modest
Area: West End
Address: 323 North Woodside Road
Glasgow G20 6ND
Phone: 0141 341 0069

#143
Phones 4U
Category: Mobile Phones
Average price: Modest
Area: Byres Road, Hillhead
Address: 276-280 Byres Road
Glasgow G12 8AW
Phone: 0141 357 4584

#144
Pink Poodle
Category: Women's Clothing
Average price: Expensive
Area: Byres Road, West End
Address: 181-183 Byres Road
Glasgow G12 8TS
Phone: 0141 357 3344

#145
Granny Would be Proud
Vintage and Craft Fair
Category: Arts & Crafts, Vintage
Average price: Modest
Area: Hillhead
Address: 17 Vinicombe Street
Glasgow G12 8
Phone: 0141 576 1700

#146
Bike Love
Category: Bicycles, Sports & Leisure
Average price: Modest
Area: West End
Address: 120 Queen Margaret Drive
Glasgow G20 8NZ
Phone: 0141 945 0999

#147
Greaves Sports
Category: Sporting Goods,
Average price: Exclusive
Area: City Centre
Address: 23 Gordon St
Glasgow G1 3PW
Phone: 0141 221 3322

#148
Boots
Category: Pharmacy,
Beauty & Cosmetics
Average price: Modest
Area: Partick, West End
Address: 50 Crow Road
Glasgow G11 7
Phone: 0141 334 6183

#149
Superdrug
Category: Pharmacy
Average price: Inexpensive
Area: SauchieHalls Street, City Centre
Address: 167 SauchieHalls Street
Glasgow G2 3ER
Phone: 0141 332 4284

#150
Fat Buddha
Category: Fashion, Hobby Shop, Bookshop
Average price: Modest
Area: City Centre
Address: 73 St Vincent Street
Glasgow G2 5TF
Phone: 0141 226 8972

#151
Retro
Category: Vintage
Average price: Modest
Area: Great Western Road
Address: 8 Otago Street
Glasgow G12 8JH
Phone: 0141 576 0165

#152
Reiss
Category: Fashion
Average price: Expensive
Area: City Centre
Address: 1-3 Royal Exchange Square
Glasgow G1 3AH
Phone: 0141 248 4141

#153
Jigsaw
Category: Women's Clothing
Average price: Expensive
Area: City Centre, Merchant City
Address: 177 Ingram Street
Glasgow G1 1DA
Phone: 0141 552 7639

#154
Beauty Store
Category: Beauty & Cosmetics
Average price: Modest
Area: City Centre, Merchant City
Address: 45 Virginia Court
Glasgow G1 1TS
Phone: 0141 204 2244

#155
Laura Mercier
Category: Beauty & Cosmetics
Average price: Expensive
Area: City Centre, Merchant City
Address: 21-45 Buchanan Street
Glasgow G1 3HL
Phone: 0141 221 4520

#156
The Real Deal
Category: Antiques
Average price: Modest
Area: Finnieston, West End
Address: 1022 Argyle St
Glasgow G3 5DN
Phone: 07564 205553

#157
Strung Out Guitars
Category: Musical Instruments
Average price: Modest
Area: City Centre, Merchant City
Address: 93 King Street
Glasgow G1 5RB
Phone: 0141 552 4848

#158
Sloan's Market
Category: Flea Market
Average price: Modest
Area: Buchanan Street, City Centre
Address: Argyle Arcade
Glasgow G2 8BG
Phone: 07879 935498

#159
Newsbox
Category: Newsagent
Average price: Inexpensive
Area: City Centre
Address: 26 Renfrew St
Glasgow G2 3BW
Phone: 0141 333 9754

#160
Fabric Bazaar
Category: Haberdashery & Fabrics
Average price: Inexpensive
Area: Gallowgate
Address: 171-177 London Road
Glasgow G1 5BX
Phone: 0141 552 5085

#161
The Glasgow Vintage
Category: Vintage
Average price: Modest
Area: Great Western Road
Address: 453 Great Western Road
Glasgow G12 8HH
Phone: 0141 338 6633

#162
Steamer Trading Cookshop
Category: Kitchen & Bath
Average price: Modest
Area: City Centre
Address: 35-39 Gordon Street
Glasgow G1 3PF
Phone: 0141 204 4141

#163
TJ Hughes
Category: Department Store,
Beauty & Cosmetics
Average price: Inexpensive
Area: City Centre, Merchant City
Address: 127-135 Trongate
Glasgow G1 5HF
Phone: 0141 548 8400

#164
Gamestation
Category: Computers
Average price: Modest
Area: SauchieHalls Street, City Centre
Address: 83 SauchieHalls St
Glasgow G2 3DD
Phone: 0141 332 6850

#165
Neon Gecko
Category: Hobby Shop, Pet Shop
Average price: Modest
Area: Gallowgate
Address: 204 London Road
Glasgow G40 1PB
Phone: 0141 552 1252

#166
Vallance Discount Carpets
Category: Home Decor
Average price: Modest
Area: South Side
Address: 49-61 Clarkston Road
Glasgow G44 3BQ
Phone: 0141 637 0848

#167
Oxfam
Category: Charity Shop
Average price: Inexpensive
Area: South Side
Address: 437 Victoria Road
Glasgow G42 8RW
Phone: 0141 423 4317

#168
Stevenson's Jewellers
Category: Jewellery, Watches
Average price: Modest
Area: Byres Road, West End
Address: 257 Byres Road
Glasgow G12 8UB
Phone: 0141 334 1899

#169
Rosie Cheeks
Category: Baby Accessories & Furniture
Average price: Modest
Area: Woodlands, Great Western Road
Address: 415 Great Western Road
Glasgow G4 9JA
Phone: 0141 237 4407

#170
Semichem
Category: Beauty & Cosmetics,
Skin Care
Average price: Inexpensive
Area: Partick, West End
Address: 92 Dumbarton Road
Glasgow G11 6RZ
Phone: 0141 357 4169

#171
Authentics Antiques
Category: Antiques
Average price: Modest
Area: Great Western Road
Address: 12 Otago Street
Glasgow G12 8JH
Phone: 0141 334 2848

#172
Primark
Category: Men's Clothing,
Women's Clothing, Children's Clothing
Average price: Inexpensive
Area: SauchieHalls Street, City Centre
Address: 171 SauchieHalls St
Glasgow G2 3ER
Phone: 0141 332 6960

#173
The Magpie's Nest
Category: Charity Shop
Average price: Inexpensive
Area: South Side, Govan
Address: 47 Burleigh Street
Glasgow G51 3LA
Phone: 0141 440 1008

#174
Spoiled For Choice
Category: Cards & Stationery
Average price: Inexpensive
Area: Partick, West End
Address: 399 Dumbarton Road
Glasgow G11 6BE
Phone: 0141 334 7059

#175
Fabric Creations
Category: Furniture Shop
Average price: Modest
Area: South Side
Address: 277 Clarkston Road
Glasgow G44 3DT
Phone: 0141 637 3883

#176
Scribbler
Category: Cards & Stationery
Average price: Modest
Area: Buchanan Street, City Centre
Address: 176 Buchanan Street
Glasgow G1 2LW
Phone: 0141 353 1015

#177
Poundstretcher
Category: Pound Shop
Average price: Modest
Area: South Side, Shawlands
Address: Shawlands Arcacde
Glasgow G41 3YN
Phone: 0141 636 0224

#178
Paradise of Flowers
Category: Florist
Average price: Modest
Area: South Side, Mount Florida
Address: 196 Battlefield Road
Glasgow G42 9HN
Phone: 0141 637 7870

#179
Record Fayre
Category: Music & DVDs
Average price: Modest
Area: City Centre, Merchant City
Address: 13-15 Chisholm Street
Glasgow G1 5HA
Phone: 0141 552 5696

#180
Mango
Category: Fashion
Average price: Expensive
Area: City Centre
Address: 220 Buchanan Street
Glasgow G1 2FF
Phone: 0141 332 9260

#181
Tesco Extra
Category: Department Store
Average price: Modest
Area: Springburn
Address: Cobden Road
Glasgow G21 1YL
Phone: 0845 677 9309

#182
French Connection
Category: Accessories, Men's Clothing,
Women's Clothing
Average price: Expensive
Area: Buchanan Street, City Centre
Address: Princes Square
Glasgow G1 3JX
Phone: 0141 248 7565

#183
Stuff
Category: Adult, Flowers & Gifts
Average price: Modest
Area: City Centre
Address: 100 Union Street
Glasgow G1 3QW
Phone: 0141 248 3401

#184
Oxfam Music
Category: Vinyl Records, Charity Shop
Average price: Modest
Area: Byres Road, West End
Address: 171 Byres Road
Glasgow G12 8TS
Phone: 0141 334 7669

#185
Hobbs
Category: Fashion
Average price: Expensive
Area: Buchanan Street, City Centre
Address: 127 Buchanan Street
Glasgow G1 2JA
Phone: 0141 248 3978

#186
The North Face
Category: Outdoor Gear
Average price: Expensive
Area: Buchanan Street, City Centre
Address: 153-155 Buchanan St
Glasgow G1 2JX
Phone: 04414 1221 3302

#187
Gear Bikes
Category: Bicycles
Average price: Expensive
Area: West End
Address: 19 Gibson Street
Glasgow G12 8NU
Phone: 0141 339 1179

#188
Isis
Category: Women's Clothing,
Beauty & Cosmetics
Average price: Modest
Area: City Centre
Address: 255 Argyle St
Glasgow G2 DL
Phone: 0141 248 1211

#189
Play It Again Records
Category: Vinyl Records
Average price: Inexpensive
Area: West End
Address: 47 Ruthven Ln
Glasgow G12 9BG
Phone: 0141 339 7777

#190
Gap
Category: Fashion
Average price: Expensive
Area: City Centre
Address: 16 Buchanan Gallery
Glasgow G1 2GF
Phone: 0141 331 2636

#191
Mountain Warehouse
Category: Outdoor Gear
Average price: Modest
Area: SauchieHalls Street, City Centre
Address: 97 SauchieHalls St
Glasgow G2 3DD
Phone: 0141 333 9890

#192
Glasgow Art Club
Category: Art Gallery, Music Venues
Average price: Modest
Area: City Centre
Address: 185 Bath Street
Glasgow G2 4HU
Phone: 0141 248 5210

#193
The Works
Category: Bookshop, Cards & Stationery
Average price: Inexpensive
Area: SauchieHalls Street, City Centre
Address: 84 SauchieHalls St
Glasgow G2 3DE
Phone: 0141 332 2885

#194
HMV
Category: Music & DVDs, Electronics
Average price: Modest
Area: Buchanan Street, SauchieHalls Street,
City Centre
Address: 235 Buchanan Street
Glasgow G1 2NG
Phone: 0843 221 0203

#195
Hellfire
Category: Men's Clothing,
Women's Clothing
Average price: Modest
Area: City Centre
Address: 46 Queen Street
Glasgow G1 3DN
Phone: 0141 204 2825

#196
Millets
Category: Outdoor Gear
Average price: Modest
Area: SauchieHalls Street, City Centre
Address: SauchieHalls St
Glasgow G2 3ER
Phone: 0141 332 5617

#197
Claire's Accessories
Category: Accessories
Average price: Modest
Area: City Centre
Address: 29g Buchanan Gallery
Glasgow G1 2FF
Phone: 0141 332 1800

#198
Peace & Jam
Category: Children's Clothing
Average price: Expensive
Area: Great Western Road
Address: 407 Great Western Road
Glasgow G4 9JA
Phone: 0141 339 8599

#199
Victor Morris
Category: Musical Instruments,
Vinyl Records
Average price: Exclusive
Area: City Centre
Address: 340 Argyle Street
Glasgow G2 8LY
Phone: 0141 221 8958

#200
The Number 1 Bead Shop
Category: Hobby Shop, Jewellery
Average price: Modest
Area: Finnieston, West End
Address: 121-127 Lancefield St
Glasgow G3 8HZ
Phone: 0141 229 0544

#201
Cath Kidston
Category: Accessories,
Women's Clothing
Average price: Expensive
Area: City Centre
Address: 18 Gordon St
Glasgow G1 3
Phone: 0141 433 0171

#202
Cooper Hay Rare Books
Category: Bookshop
Average price: Expensive
Area: City Centre
Address: 185 Bath Street
Glasgow G2 4HU
Phone: 0141 221 3922

#203
Roger Billcliffe Gallery
Category: Art Gallery
Average price: Exclusive
Area: SauchieHalls Street, City Centre
Address: 134 Blythswood Street
Glasgow G2 4EL
Phone: 0141 332 4027

#204
St. Tropez Salon
Category: Tanning, Beauty & Cosmetics
Average price: Modest
Area: City Centre
Address: 97 Argyle St
Glasgow G2 8AR
Phone: 0141 225 3445

#205
Orange
Category: Mobile Phones
Average price: Modest
Area: Buchanan Street, City Centre
Address: 128 Buchanan St
Glasgow G1 2JW
Phone: 0870 376 3837

#206
Ness
Category: Women's Clothing
Average price: Expensive
Area: City Centre
Address: Unit 271
Glasgow G1 4BW
Phone: 0141 221 0345

#207
Angelique Lamont
Category: Bridal, Accessories
Average price: Modest
Area: City Centre, Merchant City
Address: 181-185 Howard Street
Glasgow G1 4HF
Phone: 0141 552 6800

#208
Fantasie Flowers
Category: Gardening Centre
Average price: Expensive
Area: South Side, Gorbals
Address: 37 Bridge Street
Glasgow G5 9JB
Phone: 0141 429 8880

#209
Clarins Spa
Category: Beauty & Cosmetics,
Skin Care
Average price: Inexpensive
Area: City Centre
Address: 220 Buchanan Street
Glasgow G1 2GF
Phone: 0141 354 0417

#210
Belstaff
Category: Fashion
Average price: Exclusive
Area: City Centre
Address: 48 Buchanan Street
Glasgow G1 3
Phone: 0141 222 2371

#211
Hector Russell Kiltmaker
Category: Fashion
Average price: Modest
Area: Buchanan Street, City Centre
Address: 110 Buchanan Street
Glasgow G1 2JN
Phone: 0141 221 0217

#212
Loud & Clear Scotland
Category: Electronics
Average price: Expensive
Area: Charing Cross, Finnieston
Address: 520 St Vincent St
Glasgow G3 8XZ
Phone: 0141 221 0221

#213
Sarah Louise Bridal
Category: Fashion, Bridal
Average price: Modest
Area: City Centre
Address: 176 Hope St
Glasgow G2 2TU
Phone: 0141 332 6060

#214
Volcanic Tongue
Category: Music & DVDs
Average price: Exclusive
Area: Finnieston, West End
Address: 1103 Argyle Street
Glasgow G3 8ND
Phone: 0141 204 3322

#215
Cotton Print Factory Shop
Category: Haberdashery & Fabrics
Average price: Inexpensive
Area: South Side, Kinning Park
Address: 58 Admiral Street
Glasgow G41 1HU
Phone: 0141 420 1855

#216
Greaves Sports
Category: Sports Wear
Average price: Modest
Area: SauchieHalls Street, City Centre
Address: 82 SauchieHalls Street
Glasgow G2 3DF
Phone: 0141 333 0030

#217
Whistles
Category: Women's Clothing
Average price: Expensive
Area: Buchanan Street, City Centre
Address: 48 Buchanan Street
Glasgow G1 3JN
Phone: 0141 226 5259

#218
Accessorize
Category: Accessories
Average price: Modest
Area: Buchanan Street, City Centre
Address: 48 Buchanan Street
Glasgow G1 3JN
Phone: 0141 221 3164

#219
Boots
Category: Pharmacy,
Beauty & Cosmetics
Average price: Modest
Area: Buchanan Street, City Centre
Address: 220 Buchanan St
Glasgow G2 1GF
Phone: 0141 333 9306

#220
Dwell
Category: Furniture Shop, Home Decor
Average price: Expensive
Area: Buchanan Street, City Centre
Address: 3-5 Princes Square
Glasgow G1 3JN
Phone: 0845 675 9082

#221
Maplin Electronics
Category: Electronics
Average price: Modest
Area: City Centre
Address: 30 St Enoch Square
Glasgow G1 4DB
Phone: 0141 248 6572

#222
Cessnock Newsagent
Category: Newsagent
Average price: Inexpensive
Area: South Side, Kinning Park
Address: 359 Paisley Road West
Glasgow G51 1LX
Phone: 0141 427 4926

#223
Deichmann Shoes
Category: Shoe Shop
Average price: Inexpensive
Area: City Centre
Address: 250-252 SauchieHalls St
Glasgow G2 3EQ
Phone: 0141 332 4110

#224
Laptops Direct
Category: Computer Repair, Computers
Average price: Modest
Area: Partick, West End
Address: 119-121 Dumbarton Rd
Glasgow G11 6PR
Phone: 0141 533 2596

#225
Blooms
Category: Florist
Average price: Modest
Area: Partick, West End
Address: 182 Dumbarton Road
Glasgow G11 6XE
Phone: 0141 334 8552

#226
JoJo Maman Bébé
Category: Baby Accessories & Furniture
Average price: Modest
Area: Hillhead
Address: 170-174 Great George St
Glasgow G12 8AJ
Phone: 0141 357 7386

#227
Emmaus Glasgow
Category: Charity Shop
Average price: Inexpensive
Area: Partick, West End
Address: 576-580 Dumbarton Road
Glasgow G11 6RH
Phone: 0141 342 4089

#228
S & S Argento
Category: Jewellery
Average price: Modest
Area: Byres Road, Hillhead
Address: 284 Byres Road
Glasgow G12 8AW
Phone: 0141 337 1717

#229
Insight Opticians
Category: Eyewear & Opticians
Average price: Expensive
Area: Byres Road, West End
Address: 303 Byres Road
Glasgow G12 8UQ
Phone: 0141 334 5655

#230
Build a Bear
Category: Toy Shop
Average price: Modest
Area: Buchanan Street, City Centre
Address: 220 Buchanan Street
Glasgow G2 1
Phone: 0141 331 2173

#231
Florresters
Category: Florist
Average price: Modest
Area: Duke Street, Dennistoun
Address: 447 Duke St
Glasgow G31 1RD
Phone: 0141 550 0001

#232
Cats Protection Charity Shop
Category: Charity Shop
Average price: Inexpensive
Area: Partick, West End
Address: 440 Dumbarton Rd
Glasgow G11 6SE
Phone: 0141 334 6907

#233
Cult
Category: Fashion
Average price: Expensive
Area: City Centre
Address: 63-67 Queen Street
Glasgow G1 3EN
Phone: 0141 226 6822

#234
Savoy Shopping Centre
Category: Shopping Centre
Average price: Inexpensive
Area: SauchieHalls Street, City Centre
Address: 140 SauchieHalls St
Glasgow G2 3
Phone: 0141 333 9507

#235
Eden Home & Gift Boutique
Category: Flowers & Gifts
Average price: Expensive
Area: South Side
Address: 9 Sinclair Dr
Glasgow G42 9PR
Phone: 0141 632 4163

#236
Southside Art
Category: Art Gallery
Average price: Modest
Area: South Side
Address: 26-28 Battlefield Road
Glasgow G42 9QH
Phone: 0141 649 8888

#237
Forge Shopping Centre
Category: Shopping Centre
Average price: Modest
Area: Parkhead
Address: 1221 Gallowgate
Glasgow G31 4EB
Phone: 0141 556 6661

#238
WH Smith
Category: Bookshop, Office Equipment
Average price: Modest
Area: City Centre
Address: 53-55 Argyle Street
Glasgow G2 8AH
Phone: 0141 204 0636

#239
Argos
Category: Department Store
Average price: Inexpensive
Area: City Centre
Address: 200 SauchieHalls St
Glasgow G2 3EF
Phone: 0845 640 2020

#240
Poundland
Category: Pound Shop
Average price: Inexpensive
Area: Parkhead
Address: 1221 Gallowgate
Glasgow G31 4EB
Phone: 0141 237 2830

#241
Spirito
Category: Flowers & Gifts
Average price: Expensive
Area: Partick, West End
Address: 319 Crow Road
Glasgow G11 7BU
Phone: 0141 337 3307

#242
Ark Acts Of Random Kindness
Category: Flowers & Gifts
Average price: Modest
Area: South Side
Address: 1484 Paisley Road West
Glasgow G52 1SP
Phone: 0141 882 2662

#243
All Saints
Category: Children's Clothing,
Men's Clothing, Women's Clothing
Average price: Exclusive
Area: Buchanan Street, City Centre
Address: 98 Buchanan St
Glasgow G1 3BA
Phone: 0141 285 0931

#244
Govan Cross Shopping Centre
Category: Shopping Centre
Average price: Inexpensive
Area: South Side, Govan
Address: 795 Govan Rd
Glasgow G51 3JW
Phone: 0141 440 2555

#245
Opal Moon
Category: Hobby Shop
Average price: Modest
Area: West End
Address: 136 Queen Margaret Dr
Glasgow G20 8NY
Phone: 0141 576 0113

#246
Homebase
Category: Hardware Store
Average price: Modest
Area: South Side
Address: 222 Nether Auldhouse Road
Glasgow G43 1LS
Phone: 0141 649 2120

#247
Celtic Store
Category: Sports Wear, Bookshop
Average price: Expensive
Area: City Centre
Address: 154 Argyle St
Glasgow G2 8BX
Phone: 0141 204 1588

#248
Moss
Category: Men's Clothing
Average price: Modest
Area: City Centre
Address: 25 Renfield St
Glasgow G2 5AJ
Phone: 0844 847 9260

#249
Clinton Cards
Category: Cards & Stationery
Average price: Inexpensive
Area: SauchieHalls Street, City Centre
Address: 165 SauchieHalls Street
Glasgow G2 3EW
Phone: 0141 331 0352

#250
Radley
Category: Accessories
Average price: Expensive
Area: City Centre
Address: 14 Royal Exchange Square
Glasgow G1 3AB
Phone: 0141 248 7896

#251
Adventure 1
Category: Outdoor Gear
Average price: Modest
Area: City Centre
Address: 38 Dundas St
Glasgow G1 2AQ
Phone: 0141 353 3788

#252
Arty Party Shop
Category: Party Supplies, Fancy Dress
Average price: Expensive
Area: Charing Cross, Woodlands
Address: 73 St Georges Road
Glasgow G3 6JA
Phone: 0141 331 0707

#253
Bumblebee @ Paul Hodgkiss Designs
Category: Kitchen & Bath, Jewellery, Home Decor
Average price: Expensive
Area: South Side
Address: 200 Clarkston Road
Glasgow G44 3DN
Phone: 0141 571 0207

#254
Shelter Kelvinbridge Shop
Category: Charity Shop
Average price: Inexpensive
Area: Great Western Road, West End
Address: 214 Great Western Rd
Glasgow G4 9EJ
Phone: 0141 332 8505

#255
The Carphone Warehouse
Category: Mobile Phones
Average price: Modest
Area: Byres Road, Hillhead
Address: 276-278 Byres Rd
Glasgow G12 8AW
Phone: 0870 168 2385

#256
Ae Fond Kiss
Category: Arts & Crafts
Average price: Modest
Area: West End
Address: 112 Queen Margaret Dr
Glasgow G20 8NZ
Phone: 0141 945 0100

#257
Waterstones
Category: Bookshop
Average price: Modest
Area: City Centre
Address: 174-176 Argyle St
Glasgow G2 8BT
Phone: 0141 248 4814

#258
Claire's Accessories
Category: Accessories
Average price: Modest
Area: City Centre
Address: 169 Argyle Street
Glasgow G2 8BU
Phone: 0141 249 9994

#259
Wish
Category: Women's Clothing
Average price: Expensive
Area: City Centre
Address: 266 Clyde Street
Glasgow G1 4JH
Phone: 0141 226 2426

#260
Oddbins
Category: Tobacconists
Average price: Expensive
Area: City Centre
Address: 93 Mitchell St
Glasgow G1 3LN
Phone: 0141 221 4760

#261
Arteries Gallery
Category: Art Gallery
Average price: Exclusive
Area: SauchieHalls Street, City Centre
Address: 127 Douglas Street
Glasgow G2 4JX
Phone: 0141 333 0999

#262
New Look
Category: Fashion
Average price: Modest
Area: City Centre
Address: 125-130 SauchieHalls St
Glasgow G2 3DH
Phone: 0141 332 3696

#263
Body Care
Category: Pharmacy
Average price: Inexpensive
Area: City Centre
Address: 136 SauchieHalls St
Glasgow G2 3
Phone: 0141 333 9930

#264
Laura Ashley
Category: Women's Clothing, Furniture Shop, Home Decor
Average price: Expensive
Area: City Centre
Address: 36 W George St
Glasgow G2 1DA
Phone: 0871 223 1479

#265
Ted Baker
Category: Men's Clothing,
Women's Clothing
Average price: Expensive
Area: Buchanan Street, City Centre
Address: 48 Buchanan Street
Glasgow G1 3JN
Phone: 0141 221 9664

#266
Dune Footwear
Category: Shoe Shop, Accessories
Average price: Expensive
Area: Buchanan Street, City Centre
Address: 105 Buchanan Street
Glasgow G1 3HF
Phone: 0141 226 8873

#267
Lego
Category: Toy Shop
Average price: Expensive
Area: City Centre
Address: Unit 37 220 Buchanan Street
Glasgow G1 2FF
Phone: 0141 353 3503

#268
Cards Galore
Category: Cards & Stationery
Average price: Modest
Area: City Centre
Address: Glasgow Central Station
Glasgow G1 3SQ
Phone: 0141 248 0142

#269
Folli Follie
Category: Accessories, Jewellery
Average price: Expensive
Area: City Centre
Address: Unit 241
Glasgow G1 4BW
Phone: 0141 221 7730

#270
Teeshirtnation
Category: Women's Clothing,
Men's Clothing
Average price: Modest
Area: City Centre, Merchant City
Address: 91 King St
Glasgow G1 5RB
Phone: 0141 553 1777

#271
Park Road Pharmacy
Category: Pharmacy
Average price: Modest
Area: Woodlands, Great Western Road
Address: 405 Great Western Road
Glasgow G4 9HY
Phone: 0141 339 5979

#272
Rug Room
Category: Home & Garden
Average price: Expensive
Area: Great Western Road
Address: 29-37 Otago St
Glasgow G12 8JJ
Phone: 0141 337 2845

#273
Farmfoods
Category: Supermarket, Pound Shop
Average price: Inexpensive
Area: Partick, Byres Road, West End
Address: 22 Byres Road
Glasgow G11 5JY
Phone: 0141 357 5380

#274
Superdrug
Category: Pharmacy,
Beauty & Cosmetics
Average price: Inexpensive
Area: Byres Road, Hillhead
Address: 326 Byres Road
Glasgow G12 8AP
Phone: 0141 334 8180

#275
Flowers By Andersons
Category: Florist
Average price: Modest
Area: West End
Address: 94 Queen Margaret Drive
Glasgow G20 8NZ
Phone: 0141 946 6006

#276
Pricebusters
Category: Hardware Store
Average price: Modest
Area: Partick, West End
Address: 296 Dumbarton Road
Glasgow G11 6TD
Phone: 0141 339 2555

#277
Past Times
Category: Antiques, Cards & Stationery
Average price: Modest
Area: South Side
Address: Barrhead Rd
Glasgow G53 6QR
Phone: 0141 881 4137

#278
Hallsford Antiques
Category: Antiques, Furniture Shop
Average price: Expensive
Area: Partick, West End
Address: 371 Dumbarton Rd
Glasgow G11 6BA
Phone: 0141 334 2240

#279
**Cocoberry Ladies
Fashion Boutique**
Category: Women's Clothing
Average price: Expensive
Area: Duke Street, Dennistoun
Address: 348 Duke Street
Glasgow G31 1RB
Phone: 0141 556 3353

#280
**Cassiopeia Home
and Gift Boutique**
Category: Flowers & Gifts
Average price: Expensive
Area: West End
Address: 165 B Hyndland Road
Glasgow G12 9HT
Phone: 0141 357 7374

#281
Barrett
Category: Newsagent
Average price: Modest
Area: Byres Road, West End
Address: 263 Byres Road
Glasgow G12 8TL
Phone: 0141 339 0488

#282
Cake Clothing
Category: Fashion
Average price: Expensive
Area: Partick, West End
Address: 90 Dumbarton Rd
Glasgow G11 6NX
Phone: 0141 576 6900

#283
HMV
Category: Books, Mags, Music & Video
Average price: Modest
Area: City Centre
Address: Argyle Street
Glasgow G2
Phone: 0843 221 0201

#284
Central News
Category: Newsagent
Average price: Expensive
Area: City Centre
Address: 61 Union St
Glasgow G1 3QS
Phone: 0141 248 1677

#285
Long Tall Sally
Category: Fashion
Average price: Expensive
Area: City Centre
Address: 43 West Nile Street
Glasgow G1 2PT
Phone: 0141 221 8474

#286
Henderson The Jewellers
Category: Jewellery, Watch Repair
Average price: Expensive
Area: SauchieHalls Street, City Centre
Address: 217 SauchieHalls St
Glasgow G2 3EX
Phone: 04133 12569

#287
Jack Wills
Category: Fashion
Average price: Modest
Area: Buchanan Street, City Centre
Address: 137 Buchanan Street
Glasgow G1 2JA
Phone: 0141 221 5192

#288
River Island Clothing
Category: Fashion
Average price: Expensive
Area: City Centre, Merchant City
Address: 20-24 Argyle Street
Glasgow G2 8AD
Phone: 0844 395 1006

#289
Clintons
Category: Gift Shop
Average price: Modest
Area: City Centre
Address: 55 St Enoch Square
Glasgow G1 4BW
Phone: 0141 204 2459

#290
Ralph Lauren
Category: Fashion
Average price: Expensive
Area: City Centre, Merchant City
Address: 208 Ingram St
Glasgow G1 1DG
Phone: 0141 242 6000

#291
Orro Jewellers
Category: Jewellery
Average price: Exclusive
Area: City Centre, Merchant City
Address: 12 Wilson Street
Glasgow G1 1SS
Phone: 0141 552 7888

#292
Swatch
Category: Watches
Average price: Expensive
Area: City Centre
Address: St Enoch Shopping Centre
Glasgow G1 4BW
Phone: 0141 221 7486

#293
Goodd
Category: Furniture Shop
Average price: Expensive
Area: Gallowgate
Address: 11 James Morrison Street
Glasgow G1 5PE
Phone: 0141 552 6777

#294
Cards Galore
Category: Gift Shop
Average price: Modest
Area: City Centre
Address: Central Station
Glasgow G1 3SL
Phone: 0141 248 0141

#295
Ted Baker Glasgow
Category: Men's Clothing,
Women's Clothing
Average price: Exclusive
Area: Buchanan Street, City Centre
Address: 45 Buchanan Street
Glasgow G1
Phone: 0141 204 3182

#296
Negotiate Now
Category: Pound Shop
Average price: Inexpensive
Area: City Centre
Address: 69 Buchanan Street
Glasgow G1 3HL
Phone: 0141 314 3592

#297
Lush
Category: Beauty & Cosmetics
Average price: Expensive
Area: Buchanan Street, City Centre
Address: 95 Buchanan Street
Glasgow G1 3HF
Phone: 0141 243 2522

#298
Welcome Home
Category: Art Gallery
Average price: Modest
Area: City Centre
Address: 350 SauchieHalls Street
Glasgow G2 3JD
Phone: 0141 334 9598

#299
Churchill Opticians
Category: Eyewear & Opticians
Average price: Expensive
Area: City Centre
Address: 73 Renfield Street
Glasgow G2 1LP
Phone: 0141 332 5279

#300
John Smith & Son
Category: Books, Mags, Music & Video
Average price: Expensive
Area: City Centre, Cowcaddens
Address: 70 Cowcaddens Rd
Glasgow G4 0BA
Phone: 0141 332 8778

#301
Pretavoir Sunglasses
Category: Eyewear & Opticians
Average price: Inexpensive
Area: City Centre, Merchant City
Address: 153 Howard Street
Glasgow G1 4
Phone: 0141 237 7375

#302
Fireplace Gallery
Category: Home & Garden,
Building Supplies
Average price: Exclusive
Area: West End
Address: 1300 Argyle Street
Glasgow G3 8AB
Phone: 0141 339 9269

#303
The Virginia Gallery
Category: Art Gallery
Average price: Modest
Area: City Centre, Merchant City
Address: 45 Virginia Street
Glasgow G1 1TS
Phone: 0141 552 5699

#304
Powerhouse Fitness
Category: Sporting Goods,
Sports & Leisure
Average price: Inexpensive
Area: City Centre, Merchant City
Address: 100 Stockwell Street
Glasgow G1 4HR
Phone: 0141 552 7628

#305
Debra
Category: Furniture Shop
Average price: Modest
Area: City Centre, Merchant City
Address: 15-17 Argyle Street
Glasgow G2 8HA
Phone: 0141 548 1083

#306
Timberland
Category: Fashion
Average price: Expensive
Area: Buchanan Street, City Centre
Address: 61 Buchanan Street
Glasgow G1 3HL
Phone: 0141 229 1717

#307
The Hemphouse
Category: Tobacconists
Average price: Expensive
Area: City Centre, Merchant City
Address: 8 Parnie Street
Glasgow G1 5LR
Phone: 0141 552 5666

#308
Original Levi Store
Category: Men's Clothing,
Women's Clothing
Average price: Expensive
Area: Buchanan Street, City Centre
Address: 45 Buchanan St
Glasgow G1 3HL
Phone: 0141 332 7139

#309
Aldo
Category: Shoe Shop, Accessories
Average price: Modest
Area: Buchanan Street, City Centre
Address: 64 Buchanan Street
Glasgow G1 3JE
Phone: 0141 248 7041

#310
Bang & Olufsen Merchant City
Category: Electronics
Average price: Expensive
Area: City Centre, Merchant City
Address: 153 Ingram St
Glasgow G1 1DW
Phone: 0141 552 5552

#311
**Great Western Newsagent
& Off Licence**
Category: Newsagent
Average price: Inexpensive
Area: Woodlands, Great Western Road
Address: 375 Great Western Rd
Glasgow G4 9HY
Phone: 0141 337 2635

#312
Billy Bilsland Cycles
Category: Bicycles
Average price: Modest
Area: City Centre
Address: 176 Saltmarket
Glasgow G1 5LA
Phone: 0141 552 0841

#313
Market on the Green
Category: Charity Shop
Average price: Inexpensive
Area: City Centre
Address: 174 Saltmarket
Glasgow G1 5LA
Phone: 0141 237 9694

#314
TK Maxx
Category: Accessories, Home & Garden
Average price: Inexpensive
Area: City Centre
Address: 5 St Enoch Centre
Glasgow G1 4BW
Phone: 0141 221 9393

#315
Fast News
Category: Newsagent, Print Media
Average price: Inexpensive
Area: City Centre, Merchant City
Address: 53 High Street
Glasgow G1 1LX
Phone: 0141 552 8264

#316
Ernest Jones
Category: Jewellery
Average price: Expensive
Area: City Centre
Address: 220 Buchanan Street
Glasgow G1 2GF
Phone: 0141 353 1087

#317
A Violin Shop
Category: Music & DVDs
Average price: Modest
Area: West End
Address: 7-11 Blackie Street
Glasgow G3 8TN
Phone: 0141 339 8083

#318
Willy Bains Bicycle Repairs
Category: Bicycles
Average price: Modest
Area: South Side
Address: 359 Pollokshaws Road
Glasgow G41 1QT
Phone: 0141 423 9010

#319
Miss Selfridge
Category: Women's Clothing, Accessories
Average price: Modest
Area: City Centre
Address: 220 Buchanan Street
Glasgow G1 2GF
Phone: 0141 354 0104

#320
Glasgow Antiques & Collectables Market
Category: Antiques
Average price: Modest
Area: Gallowgate
Address: 233 London Road
Glasgow G40 1PE
Phone: 0141 552 6989

#321
Quiksilver
Category: Sports Wear
Average price: Modest
Area: Buchanan Street, City Centre
Address: 220 Buchanan St
Glasgow G2 1
Phone: 0141 332 6941

#322
Oliver Bonas
Category: Home & Garden, Accessories
Average price: Modest
Area: Byres Road, West End
Address: 243-245 Byres Road
Glasgow G12 8UB
Phone: 0131 226 6809

#323
Visitor Centre
Category: Gift Shop
Average price: Modest
Area: West End
Address:
Glasgow University
Glasgow G12 8QQ
Phone: 0141 330 5511

#324
W2 Store
Category: Fashion
Average price: Expensive
Area: West End
Address: 10 Ruthven Lane
Glasgow G12 9BG
Phone: 0141 339 2315

#325
Busy Bees Craft Studio
Category: Arts & Crafts, Kids Activities
Average price: Modest
Area: South Side
Address: 82-84 Niddrie Road
Glasgow G42 8PU
Phone: 0141 433 9506

#326
**Hunterian Art Gallery
and The Mackintosh House**
Category: Art Gallery, Museum
Average price: Modest
Area: Hillhead
Address: 82 Hillhead Street
Glasgow G12 8QQ
Phone: 0141 330 5431

#327
By Distinction Art
Category: Art Gallery
Average price: Expensive
Area: Partick, Byres Road, West End
Address: 100 Byres Road
Glasgow G12 8TB
Phone: 07973 315460

#328
Hollywood Nails & Beauty
Category: Beauty & Cosmetics,
Nail Salon, Beautician& Day Spa
Average price: Modest
Area: Hillhead
Address: 14 Vinicombe Street
Glasgow G12 8BG
Phone: 0141 334 0093

#329
Marie Curie Cancer Care
Category: Charity Shop
Average price: Inexpensive
Area: Partick, West End
Address: 383 Dumbarton Road
Glasgow G11 6BE
Phone: 0141 341 0258

#330
City Centre Comics
Category: Comic Books
Average price: Inexpensive
Area: Byres Road, Hillhead
Address: 37 Ruthven Lane
Glasgow G12
Phone: 07570 117057

#331
Cancer Research UK
Category: Charity Shop
Average price: Inexpensive
Area: South Side, Shawlands
Address: 1073 Pollokshaws Rd
Glasgow G41 3YG
Phone: 0141 632 4961

#332
Asda Store
Category: Department Store
Average price: Inexpensive
Area: South Side, Govan
Address: 500 Helen St
Glasgow G51 3HR
Phone: 0141 445 4257

#333
Love It Again
Category: Children's Clothing
Average price: Expensive
Area: Partick, West End
Address: 33 Hyndland St
Glasgow G11 5QF
Phone: 0141 339 8920

#334
Hip Hop Shop
Category: Jewellery,
Men's Clothing, Accessories
Average price: Modest
Area: City Centre
Address: 249 Argyle St
Glasgow G2 8DL
Phone: 0141 248 2097

#335
The Wee Handmade Gallery
Category: Gift Shop
Average price: Expensive
Area: South Side, Shawlands
Address: 167 Deanston Drive
Glasgow G41
Phone: 07962 133766

#336
Burnside Mcphee
Category: Eyewear & Opticians
Average price: Modest
Area: South Side
Address: 94 Battlefield Road
Glasgow G42 9JN
Phone: 0141 636 1123

#337
J P Mackie
Category: Pharmacy
Average price: Modest
Area: South Side
Address: 41 Sinclair Drive
Glasgow G42 9PR
Phone: 0141 632 0690

#338
Tool Station
Category: Hardware Store
Average price: Inexpensive
Area: Parkhead
Address: Alma Street
Glasgow G31
Phone: 0808 100 7211

#339
Vodafone
Category: Mobile Phones
Average price: Expensive
Area: Buchanan Street, City Centre
Address: 84-90 Buchanan St
Glasgow G1 3HA
Phone: 0870 070 0191

#340
Cyril Gerber Fine Art
Category: Art Gallery
Average price: Exclusive
Area: City Centre
Address: 148 West Regent Street
Glasgow G2 2RQ
Phone: 0141 221 3095

#341
Futureshock
Category: Comic Books
Average price: Modest
Area: Woodlands, West End
Address: 200 Woodlands Rd
Glasgow G3 6LN
Phone: 0141 332 7785

#342
Bathstore
Category: Kitchen & Bath
Average price: Expensive
Area: South Side
Address: 310 Clarkston Road
Glasgow G44 3EG
Phone: 0141 637 9070

#343
Isabella's Wardrobe
Category: Vintage
Average price: Modest
Area: Partick, West End
Address: 318 Crow Road
Glasgow G11 7HS
Phone: 0141 337 3877

#344
Oxfam Charity Shop
Category: Charity Shop
Average price: Modest
Area: Byres Road, West End
Address: 231 Byres Road
Glasgow G12 8UD
Phone: 0141 339 3111

#345
Candy Box
Category: Newsagent
Average price: Inexpensive
Area: South Side
Address: 348 Holmlea Road
Glasgow G44 4BX
Phone: 0141 637 5519

#346
Focus Skateboard Store
Category: Shoe Shop, Sports Wear
Average price: Modest
Area: City Centre
Address: 220 Argyle St
Glasgow G2 8HA
Phone: 0141 248 2446

#347
Kenny's music
Category: Musical Instruments
Average price: Modest
Area: City Centre
Address: 61-67 Jamaica Street
Glasgow G1 4NN
Phone: 0141 204 0322

#348
Newsbox
Category: Newsagent
Average price: Modest
Area: SauchieHalls Street, City Centre
Address: 297 SauchieHalls Street
Glasgow G2 3HQ
Phone: 0141 572 1393

#349
Aye-Aye Books
Category: Bookshop
Average price: Modest
Area: City Centre
Address: 350 SauchieHalls Street
Glasgow G2 3JD
Phone: 07946 643757

#350
St Georges Tron Parish Church
Category: Church, Bookshop
Average price: Modest
Area: City Centre
Address: 163 Buchanan Street
Glasgow G1 2JX
Phone: 0141 221 2141

#351
Art Store At The Art School
Category: Arts & Crafts
Average price: Modest
Area: City Centre
Address: 167 Renfrew Street
Glasgow G3 6RQ
Phone: 0141 331 1277

#352
Monsoon
Category: Accessories,
Women's Clothing
Average price: Expensive
Area: Buchanan Street, City Centre
Address: 48 Buchanan Street
Glasgow G1 3JN
Phone: 0141 221 8783

#353
Ortak Jewellery
Category: Jewellery, Home Decor
Average price: Modest
Area: City Centre
Address: 220 Buchanan Street
Glasgow G1 2NB
Phone: 0141 332 5255

#354
Chest, Heart and Stroke Scotland
Category: Charity Shop
Average price: Modest
Area: South Side
Address: 103 Clarkston Road
Glasgow G44 3BL
Phone: 0141 633 0473

#355
Merrylee Pharmacy
Category: Pharmacy
Average price: Modest
Area: South Side
Address: 213-215 Clarkston Rd
Glasgow G44 3DS
Phone: 0141 637 3747

#356
Merkland Street Furnishers
Category: Antiques, Furniture Shop
Average price: Modest
Area: Partick, West End
Address: 21 Vine St
Glasgow G11 6
Phone: 0141 579 5557

#357
Catherines Of Partick
Category: Women's Clothing
Average price: Exclusive
Area: Partick, West End
Address: 106-110 Dumbarton Road
Glasgow G11 6NY
Phone: 0141 339 1351

#358
Stables Gallery
Category: Home Decor, Antiques
Average price: Expensive
Area: Great Western Road, Hillhead
Address: 625 Great Western Rd
Glasgow G12 8RE
Phone: 0141 334 9623

#359
J P Mackie
Category: Pharmacy
Average price: Modest
Area: South Side
Address: 1795 Paisley Road West
Glasgow G52 3SS
Phone: 0141 882 8535

#360
Man's World
Category: Men's Clothing, Children's
Clothing, Sports Wear
Average price: Modest
Area: Byres Road, West End
Address: 157 Byres Road
Glasgow G12 8TS
Phone: 0141 357 0400

#361
Clarks Shoes
Category: Shoe Shop
Average price: Modest
Area: Byres Road, West End
Address: 319-321 Byres Road
Glasgow G12 8UQ
Phone: 0141 339 8512

#362
Au Naturale
Category: Home Decor
Average price: Inexpensive
Area: City Centre
Address: Argyle Street
Glasgow G2 8AH
Phone: 0141 221 1655

#363
Evans
Category: Fashion
Average price: Expensive
Area: City Centre
Address: 137-143 Argyle Street
Glasgow G2 8BX
Phone: 0141 204 3902

#364
Love From...
Category: Flowers & Gifts
Average price: Modest
Area: South Side
Address: 423 Clarkston Road
Glasgow G44 3LL
Phone: 0141 637 8382

#365
Diesel Jeans
Category: Fashion
Average price: Expensive
Area: Buchanan Street, City Centre
Address: 116-120 Buchanan St
Glasgow G1 2JW
Phone: 0141 221 5255

#366
Rage Hyndland
Category: Women's Clothing
Average price: Expensive
Area: West End
Address: 133 Hyndland Road
Glasgow G12 9JA
Phone: 0141 337 2803

#367
The Maxie Richards Foundation
Category: Furniture Shop, Charity Shop
Average price: Expensive
Area: Partick, West End
Address: 568 Dumbarton Rd
Glasgow G11 6RH
Phone: 0141 334 7799

#368
Glasgow Pram Centre
Category: Baby Accessories & Furniture
Average price: Expensive
Area: Dennistoun, Gallowgate
Address: 25-29 Mcfarlane St
Glasgow G4 0TL
Phone: 0141 552 3998

#369
La Senza
Category: Lingerie
Average price: Expensive
Area: City Centre
Address: 220 Buchanan Street
Glasgow G1 2GF
Phone: 0141 353 6515

#370
Mr News
Category: Newsagent
Average price: Inexpensive
Area: City Centre
Address: 540 SauchieHalls Street
Glasgow G2 3LX
Phone: 0141 332 4731

#371
Maia
Category: Cards & Stationery,
Home Decor, Gift Shop
Average price: Modest
Area: City Centre
Address: 21 Bath Street
Glasgow G2 1HW
Phone: 0141 333 1356

#372
Next Clearance
Category: Men's Clothing,
Women's Clothing
Average price: Inexpensive
Area: Parkhead
Address: 2 Forge Retail Park
Glasgow G31 4BH
Phone: 0141 550 7280

#373
Alliance Pharmacy
Category: Pharmacy
Average price: Modest
Area: South Side
Address: 50 Hillington Road South
Glasgow G52 2AA
Phone: 0141 882 8829

#374
Dunnes Store
Category: Department Store
Average price: Modest
Area: Parkhead
Address: 1221 Gallowgate
Glasgow G31 4EB
Phone: 0141 554 4332

#375
The Good Spirits Co.
Category: Tobacconists
Average price: Modest
Area: City Centre
Address: 23 Bath Street
Glasgow G2 1HW
Phone: 0141 258 8427

#376
Shawlands Arcade
Shopping Centre
Category: Shopping Centre
Average price: Modest
Area: South Side, Shawlands
Address: 104 Kilmarnock Road
Glasgow G41 3NN
Phone: 0141 636 8550

#377
Glasgow City Antiques Centre
Category: Antiques
Average price: Expensive
Area: Finnieston, West End
Address: 121-127 Lancefield Street
Glasgow G3 8HZ
Phone: 0141 248 7914

#378
The Body Shop
Category: Beauty & Cosmetics
Average price: Expensive
Area: City Centre
Address: 46 St Enoch Centre
Glasgow G1 4BW
Phone: 0141 204 4275

#379
Black & Lizars
Category: Eyewear & Opticians
Average price: Expensive
Area: City Centre
Address: 42 Gordon St
Glasgow G1 3PU
Phone: 0141 221 8062

#380
Mappin & Webb
Category: Jewellery
Average price: Exclusive
Area: Buchanan Street, City Centre
Address: 28 Buchanan Street
Glasgow G1 3LB
Phone: 0141 221 7683

#381
Curves and Lace
Category: Lingerie
Average price: Expensive
Area: Buchanan Street, City Centre
Address: 48 Buchanan Street
Glasgow G1 3JN
Phone: 0141 226 2233

#382
Specsavers
Category: Eyewear & Opticians
Average price: Inexpensive
Area: City Centre, Merchant City
Address: 187 Trongate
Glasgow G1 5HF
Phone: 0141 552 2776

#383
Clinton Cards
Category: Cards & Stationery
Average price: Inexpensive
Area: City Centre
Address: 220 Buchanan St
Glasgow G1 2FF
Phone: 0141 354 0264

#384
Cruise
Category: Women's Clothing,
Men's Clothing, Accessories
Average price: Exclusive
Area: City Centre, Merchant City
Address: 180 Ingram Street
Glasgow G1 1DN
Phone: 0141 229 0000

#385
Art Exposure Gallery
Category: Art Gallery
Average price: Modest
Area: City Centre, Merchant City
Address: 19 Parnie Street
Glasgow G1 5
Phone: 0141 552 7779

#386
The Aga Shop
Category: Kitchen & Bath
Average price: Exclusive
Area: Great Western Road, West End
Address: 130-132 Great Western Rd
Glasgow G4 9AD
Phone: 0141 332 8486

#387
Maplin Electronics
Category: Electronics, Computers
Average price: Expensive
Area: Great Western Road, West End
Address: 264-266 Great Western Road
Glasgow G4 9EJ
Phone: 0141 353 3323

#388
Beautique Skincare
Category: Beauty & Cosmetics
Average price: Inexpensive
Area: Woodlands, Great Western Road
Address: 257 Great Western Road
Glasgow G4 9EG
Phone: 0141 332 5624

#389
Marks & Spencer
Category: Department Store
Average price: Expensive
Area: South Side, Nitshill
Address: Barrhead Rd
Glasgow G53 6QR
Phone: 0141 302 2000

#390
Lloyds Pharmacy
Category: Pharmacy
Average price: Modest
Area: Great Western Road, West End
Address: 147 Great Western Rd
Glasgow G4 9
Phone: 0141 332 1478

#391
Carpet Monkeys
Category: Shoe Shop,
Children's Clothing
Average price: Expensive
Area: Woodlands, Great Western Road
Address: 9 Park Road
Glasgow G4 9JD
Phone: 0141 334 0995

#392
Marie Brown At Home
Category: Cards & Stationery
Average price: Modest
Area: South Side
Address: 10 Kildrostan St
Glasgow G41 4LU
Phone: 0141 423 4307

#393
American Apparel
Category: Men's Clothing,
Women's Clothing
Average price: Modest
Area: City Centre
Address: Nelson Mandela Place
Glasgow G2 1QY
Phone: 0141 221 9593

#394
PC World
Category: Computer Repair, Computers
Average price: Expensive
Area: Finnieston, West End
Address: 30 Finnieston St
Glasgow G3 8JU
Phone: 0870 242 0444

#395
Boots The Chemist
Category: Pharmacy
Average price: Inexpensive
Area: West End
Address: 80 Queen Margaret Dr
Glasgow G20 8NZ
Phone: 0141 946 3333

#396
1LevelUp
Category: Videos & Video Game Rental
Average price: Inexpensive
Area: City Centre
Address: 34 St Enoch Square
Glasgow G1 4DF
Phone: 0141 221 3337

#397
Gamestation
Category: Computers
Average price: Inexpensive
Area: Partick, West End
Address: 2 Merkland Court
Glasgow G11 6BZ
Phone: 0141 337 6895

#398
Games Workshop
Category: Toy Shop, Hobby Shop
Average price: Modest
Area: City Centre
Address: 81-83 Union St
Glasgow G1 3TA
Phone: 0141 221 1673

#399
Celtic
Category: Sporting Goods
Average price: Modest
Area: SauchieHalls Street, City Centre
Address: 215 SauchieHalls Street
Glasgow G2 3EX
Phone: 0141 353 1488

#400
Clarks Shoes
Category: Shoe Shop
Average price: Modest
Area: City Centre
Address: 104-114 SauchieHalls Street
Glasgow G2 3DE
Phone: 0141 332 7947

#401
Bo Concept
Category: Furniture Shop, Fashion
Average price: Expensive
Area: SauchieHalls Street, City Centre
Address: 257 SauchieHalls Street
Glasgow G2 3EZ
Phone: 0141 341 4920

#402
Forever 21
Category: Women's Clothing
Average price: Modest
Area: Buchanan Street, City Centre
Address: Buchanan Street
Glasgow G1 2JA
Phone: 0141 353 3249

#403
Jane Norman
Category: Women's Clothing, Accessories
Average price: Expensive
Area: City Centre
Address: 220 Buchanan St
Glasgow G1 2FF
Phone: 0141 332215

#404
Outdoor World
Category: Outdoor Gear
Average price: Modest
Area: City Centre
Address: 42-66 New City Rd
Glasgow G4 9JT
Phone: 0141 332 5014

#405
Fat Face
Category: Fashion
Average price: Expensive
Area: City Centre
Address: 69 Queen St
Glasgow G1 3BZ
Phone: 0141 226 2256

#406
Bhs
Category: Department Store,
Home Decor
Average price: Inexpensive
Area: City Centre
Address: 55 St Enoch Square
Glasgow G1 4BW
Phone: 0141 221 4944

#407
The Maxie Richards Foundation
Category: Charity Shop
Average price: Modest
Area: West End
Address: 1079 Maryhill Road
Glasgow G20 9AX
Phone: 0141 946 0209

#408
USC
Category: Fashion
Average price: Expensive
Area: Buchanan Street, City Centre
Address: 71-77 Buchanan Street
Glasgow G1 3HL
Phone: 0141 221 4560

#409
Superdrug
Category: Pharmacy
Average price: Inexpensive
Area: South Side, Shawlands
Address: 80-82 Kilmarnock Rd
Glasgow G41 3NN
Phone: 0141 632 9338

#410
Co-op
Category: Supermarket
Average price: Modest
Area: Woodlands, Great Western Road
Address: 285 Great Western Road
Glasgow G4 9HR
Phone: 0141 339 6370

#411
Morton's T Shirts
Category: T-Shirts
Average price: Inexpensive
Area: Woodlands, Great Western Road
Address: 72 South Woodside Rd
Glasgow G4 9HG
Phone: 0141 337 1441

#412
Battlefield Pharmacy
Category: Pharmacy
Average price: Modest
Area: South Side, Mount Florida
Address: 168a Battlefield Rd
Glasgow G42 9JT
Phone: 0141 632 1364

#413
Creative Computing
Category: Computer Repair, Computers
Average price: Modest
Area: South Side
Address: 1429-1433 Pollokshaws Road
Glasgow G41 3RQ
Phone: 0141 649 7577

#414
John Smith Bookshop
Category: Bookshop
Average price: Expensive
Area: West End
Address: Fraser Bldg
Glasgow G12 8QQ
Phone: 0141 330 7000

#415
Barnardo's Store
Category: Charity Shop
Average price: Inexpensive
Area: Partick, West End
Address: 116 Dumbarton Rd
Glasgow G11 6NY
Phone: 0141 357 4165

#416
St. Margaret of Scotland Hospice Shop
Category: Charity Shop
Average price: Inexpensive
Area: Partick, West End
Address: 116 Dumbarton Rd
Glasgow G11 6NY
Phone: 0141 357 4165

#417
Fat Face
Category: Fashion, Outdoor Gear
Average price: Expensive
Area: Byres Road, Hillhead
Address: 310 / 312 Byres Rd
Glasgow G12 8AW
Phone: 0141 357 6452

#418
Oddbins
Category: Tobacconists
Average price: Modest
Area: South Side, Shawlands
Address: 7 Skirving Street
Glasgow G41 3AB
Phone: 0141 632 1172

#419
Age Scotland
Category: Arts & Crafts, Charity Shop
Average price: Modest
Area: City Centre
Address: 113 Union Street
Glasgow G1
Phone: 0845 152 9732

#420
Cos
Category: Women's Clothing, Men's Clothing
Average price: Modest
Area: City Centre
Address: Princes Square
Glasgow G1 3JX
Phone: 0141 223 0020

#421
The White Co.
Category: Furniture Shop
Average price: Expensive
Area: Buchanan Street, City Centre
Address: 123 Buchanan St
Glasgow G1 2JA
Phone: 0141 221 6884

#422
Jack Brown Eyecare
Category: Eyewear & Opticians
Average price: Modest
Area: City Centre
Address: 35 Bath Street
Glasgow G2 1HW
Phone: 0141 332 1977

#423
Levi's
Category: Fashion
Average price: Expensive
Area: Buchanan Street, City Centre
Address: Buchannan St
Glasgow G1 2GF
Phone: 0141 332 7139

#424
British Heart Foundation Furniture and Electrical
Category: Charity Shop,
Furniture Shop, Appliances
Average price: Expensive
Area: City Centre, Merchant City
Address: 26 Stockwell St
Glasgow G1 4RZ
Phone: 0844 248 9135

#425
Optimax
Category: Eyewear & Opticians,
Optometrists, Laser Eye Surgery/Lasik
Average price: Expensive
Area: Charing Cross, Woodlands
Address: 18 Charing Cross Mansions
Glasgow G3 6UJ
Phone: 0800 093 1110

#426
Big Ideas
Category: Women's Clothing
Average price: Expensive
Area: City Centre, Merchant City
Address: 10 John Street
Glasgow G1 1HP
Phone: 0141 552 2722

#427
All That Is Solid
Category: Accessories
Average price: Modest
Area: City Centre, Merchant City
Address: 60 Osborne Street
Glasgow G1 5QH
Phone: 0141 271 4700

#428
Glasgow Print Studio
Category: Theatre, Art Gallery
Average price: Modest
Area: City Centre, Merchant City
Address: 48 King Street
Glasgow G1 5QT
Phone: 0141 552 0704

#429
Mcmillen Stage Costume Hire
Category: Fancy Dress, Fashion
Average price: Modest
Area: City Centre
Address: 19 Bridgegate
Glasgow G1 5HX
Phone: 0141 552 2544

#430
Waddells Models
Category: Toy Shop
Average price: Modest
Area: City Centre, Merchant City
Address: 56 Bell Street
Glasgow G1 1LQ
Phone: 0141 552 8044

#431
Republic Retail
Category: Fashion
Average price: Inexpensive
Area: City Centre
Address: 220 Buchanan Street
Glasgow G1 2GF
Phone: 0141 333 1050

#432
Dales Cycles
Category: Bicycles, Bicycle Rentals
Average price: Modest
Area: City Centre, Cowcaddens
Address: 150 Dobbies Loan
Glasgow G4 0JE
Phone: 0141 332 2705

#433
The Red Book Shop
Category: Bookshop
Average price: Inexpensive
Area: Gallowgate
Address: 137 London Road
Glasgow G1 5
Phone: 0141 221 7470

#434
W Crumb & Son
Category: Domestic Appliances
Average price: Modest
Area: Merchant City
Address: 233 High St
Glasgow G4 0QR
Phone: 0141 552 8383

#435
Staples
Category: Cards & Stationery
Average price: Modest
Area: City Centre
Address: 34 Baird St
Glasgow G4 0PT
Phone: 0141 552 4153

#436
Otago Studio
Category: Art Gallery
Average price: Modest
Area: Great Western Road
Address: 39b Otago St
Glasgow G12 8JJ
Phone: 0141 334 1159

#437
Zico
Category: Fashion
Average price: Modest
Area: West End
Address: 37 Ruthven Ln
Glasgow G12 9BG
Phone: 0141 339 1970

#438
News Plus Group
Category: Newsagent
Average price: Inexpensive
Area: Partick, West End
Address: 240 Dumbarton Road
Glasgow G11 6TU
Phone: 0141 337 3906

#439
Rue Lafayette Knitwear
Category: Women's Clothing
Average price: Expensive
Area: City Centre
Address: ST. Enoch Square
Glasgow G1 4BW
Phone: 0141 204 4631

#440
**Buchanan & Campbell
Pharmacy**
Category: Pharmacy,
Beauty & Cosmetics
Average price: Inexpensive
Area: Partick, West End
Address: 364a Dumbarton Road
Glasgow G11 6RZ
Phone: 0141 334 0353

#441
Deans Supersaver
Category: Hardware Store
Average price: Inexpensive
Area: South Side, Govan
Address: 2 Govan Cross Shopping Centre,
Glasgow G51 3JW
Phone: 0141 445 6366

#442
Boudoir
Category: Lingerie
Average price: Inexpensive
Area: Partick, West End
Address: 6 Merkland Street
Glasgow G11 6DB
Phone: 0141 334 6282

#443
John Smith & Son Glasgow
Category: Bookshop
Average price: Expensive
Area: City Centre
Address: 100 Cathedral Street
Glasgow G4 0RD
Phone: 0141 552 3377

#444
Academy News
Category: Newsagent
Average price: Inexpensive
Area: South Side, Shawlands
Address: 1117a Pollokshaws Road
Glasgow G41 3YH
Phone: 0141 636 6954

#445
Daniel Footwear
Category: Shoe Shop
Average price: Exclusive
Area: West End
Address: 193 Hyndland Road
Glasgow G12 9HT
Phone: 0141 339 3773

#446
Brenda Muir
Category: Women's Clothing
Average price: Expensive
Area: West End
Address: 157 Hyndland Road
Glasgow G12 9JA
Phone: 0141 334 5985

#447
Cheaper Laptops UK
Category: Computer Repair, Computers
Average price: Modest
Area: South Side, Shawlands
Address: 77 Deanston Drive
Glasgow G41 3AQ
Phone: 0141 649 8733

#448
Paper Plane
Category: Gift Shop
Average price: Expensive
Area: South Side, Shawlands
Address: 12 Skirving Street
Glasgow G41 3AA
Phone: 0141 649 5450

#449
G-Star Raw Store Glasgow
Category: Men's Clothing,
Women's Clothing
Average price: Modest
Area: City Centre
Address: 135 Argyle Street
Glasgow G2 8BX
Phone: 0141 221 9446

#450
Hugo Boss
Category: Men's Clothing
Average price: Exclusive
Area: Buchanan Street, City Centre
Address: 55 Buchanan Street
Glasgow G1 3HL
Phone: 0141 221 7168

#451
Pollokshaws Newsagent
Category: Newsagent
Average price: Modest
Area: South Side, Shawlands
Address: 1309 Pollokshaws Road
Glasgow G41 3RP
Phone: 0141 649 2497

#452
Life Charity Shop
Category: Charity Shop, Vintage
Average price: Inexpensive
Area: South Side, Shawlands
Address: 1315 Pollokshaws Road
Glasgow G41 3RP
Phone: 0141 636 9240

#453
Menkind
Category: Toy Shop, Electronics
Average price: Modest
Area: City Centre
Address: Buchanan St
Glasgow G1 2FF
Phone: 0141 332 3325

#454
Oasis
Category: Women's Clothing, Accessories
Average price: Modest
Area: City Centre
Address: Buchanan Street
Glasgow G1 2GF
Phone: 0141 332 4463

#455
Envy
Category: Women's Clothing,
Men's Clothing
Average price: Modest
Area: City Centre
Address: 220 Buchanan Street
Glasgow G1 2FF
Phone: 0141 332 2679

#456
**The Treasure Bunker
Militaria Shop**
Category: Gift Shop
Average price: Expensive
Area: City Centre, Merchant City
Address: 21 King Street
Glasgow G1 5QZ
Phone: 0141 552 8164

#457
Marks & Spencer
Category: Department Store
Average price: Modest
Area: Dennistoun, Parkhead
Address: 941 Gallowgate
Glasgow G31 4BW
Phone: 0141 556 5216

#458
Adorn Supplies
Category: Luggage
Average price: Expensive
Area: South Side, Tradeston
Address: 38 Bridge St
Glasgow G5 9HU
Phone: 0141 420 1726

#459
Hardware Hut
Category: Hardware Store
Average price: Inexpensive
Area: Dennistoun
Address: 660 Alexandra Parade
Glasgow G31 3BU
Phone: 0141 554 5504

#460
Mountain Warehouse
Category: Sporting Goods
Average price: Modest
Area: City Centre
Address: 7 Gordon St
Glasgow G1 3PL
Phone: 0141 248 9290

#461
Birthdays
Category: Cards & Stationery
Average price: Inexpensive
Area: SauchieHalls Street, City Centre
Address: 133 SauchieHalls Street
Glasgow G2 3EW
Phone: 0141 331 1256

#462
Dorothy Perkins
Category: Women's Clothing
Average price: Modest
Area: City Centre
Address: 55 St Enoch Square
Glasgow G1 4BW
Phone: 0141 226 4440

#463
Game
Category: Computer Repair,
Videos & Video Game Rental
Average price: Modest
Area: City Centre
Address: 55 St Enoch Square
Glasgow G1 4BW
Phone: 0141 221 3491

#464
D2
Category: Fashion
Average price: Expensive
Area: City Centre
Address: 43 St Enoch Square
Glasgow G1 4LZ
Phone: 0141 204 5051

#465
Mulberry
Category: Accessories
Average price: Expensive
Area: City Centre, Merchant City
Address: 204-207 Ingram St
Glasgow G1 1DG
Phone: 0141 248 6456

#466
Replay
Category: Fashion
Average price: Expensive
Area: City Centre, Merchant City
Address: 162-166 Ingram Street
Glasgow G1 1DN
Phone: 0141 552 8000

#467
Docherty Chemists
Category: Pharmacy
Average price: Inexpensive
Area: South Side, Shawlands
Address: 224 Kilmarnock Road
Glasgow G43 1TY
Phone: 0141 632 3356

#468
Antique Cave
Category: Antiques
Average price: Expensive
Area: Woodlands, West End
Address: 188 Woodlands Rd
Glasgow G3 6LL
Phone: 0141 332 7150

#469
East
Category: Fashion
Average price: Expensive
Area: City Centre
Address: 220 Buchanan Street
Glasgow G1 2FF
Phone: 0141 354 0151

#470
Station Flowers
Category: Florist
Average price: Inexpensive
Area: South Side, Shawlands
Address: 282 Kilmarnock Road
Glasgow G43 2XS
Phone: 0141 571 0017

#471
Asda
Category: Pharmacy, Department Store
Average price: Modest
Area: Parkhead
Address: Unit 22a
Glasgow G31 4EB
Phone: 0141 414 1510

#472
Rite Price Grocers
Category: Newsagent
Average price: Modest
Area: South Side
Address: 2 Holmlea Road
Glasgow G44 4AH
Phone: 0141 632 7006

#473
The Record Tape
& Compact Disc Exchange
Category: Music & DVDs
Average price: Inexpensive
Area: South Side, Queen's Park
Address: 918 Pollokshaws Rd
Glasgow G41 2ET
Phone: 0141 636 6686

#474
Boots
Category: Pharmacy,
Beauty & Cosmetics
Average price: Modest
Area: Byres Road, West End
Address: 277 Byres Road
Glasgow G12 8TL
Phone: 0141 339 1954

#475
Mansfield Park Gallery
Category: Art Gallery
Average price: Expensive
Area: Partick, West End
Address: 5 Hyndland Street
Glasgow G11 5QE
Phone: 0141 342 4124

#476
Bellissimo Kidz
Category: Children's Clothing
Average price: Modest
Area: Partick, West End
Address: 283-285 Dumbarton Road
Glasgow G11 6AB
Phone: 0141 338 6199

#477
British Heart Foundation
Category: Charity Shop,
Furniture Shop, Appliances
Average price: Inexpensive
Area: Partick, West End
Address: 467 Dumbarton Road
Glasgow G11 6EJ
Phone: 0844 499 4151

#478
Au Naturale
Category: Flowers & Gifts
Average price: Inexpensive
Area: Partick, West End
Address: 4b Crow Road
Glasgow G11 7RY
Phone: 0141 357 6731

#479
Harry Corry
Category: Shades & Blinds,
Home Decor
Average price: Modest
Area: South Side
Address: Cogan Street
Glasgow G43 1AP
Phone: 0141 616 6700

#480
Carpetright
Category: Home & Garden
Average price: Modest
Area: South Side
Address: Cogan Street
Glasgow G43 1AP
Phone: 0141 632 8051

#481
Park Stationery
Category: Cards & Stationery
Average price: Inexpensive
Area: South Side, Govan
Address: 851 Govan Rd
Glasgow G51 3DL
Phone: 0141 445 2686

#482
Jasmine
Category: Accessories,
Women's Clothing
Average price: Expensive
Area: West End
Address: 171 Hyndland Road
Glasgow G12 9HT
Phone: 0141 339 6575

#483
Ralph Leslie Pharmacy
Category: Pharmacy
Average price: Modest
Area: South Side
Address: 111 Clarkston Road
Glasgow G44 3BL
Phone: 0141 637 2638

#484
Flowerhaven
Category: Florist
Average price: Modest
Area: West End
Address: 1133 Maryhill Rd
Glasgow G20 9AZ
Phone: 0141 946 9419

#485
B Mccall
Category: Newsagent
Average price: Modest
Area: South Side
Address: 221 Clarkston Road
Glasgow G44 3DS
Phone: 0141 633 2834

#486
Toska Florist
Category: Florist
Average price: Modest
Area: South Side
Address: 17 Tinto Rd
Glasgow G43 2AP
Phone: 0141 633 0550

#487
Lloyds Pharmacy
Category: Pharmacy
Average price: Modest
Area: South Side
Address: 1851 Paisley Road West
Glasgow G52 3SX
Phone: 0141 882 1513

#488
Revo-I.T.
Category: Computer Repair, Computers
Average price: Modest
Area: South Side
Address: 317 Clarkston Road
Glasgow G44 3EJ
Phone: 0141 637 9694

#489
Clark's Factory Shop
Category: Shoe Shop
Average price: Modest
Area: Parkhead
Address: 1221 Gallowgate
Glasgow G31 4EB
Phone: 0141 556 5290

#490
Schuh
Category: Shoe Shop
Average price: Modest
Area: SauchieHalls Street, City Centre
Address: 9 SauchieHalls Street
Glasgow G2 3AT
Phone: 0141 353 1990

#491
Knox Opticians
Category: Eyewear & Opticians
Average price: Modest
Area: South Side
Address: 403-405 Clarkston Road
Glasgow G44 3JN
Phone: 0141 633 3922

#492
Sole Trader
Category: Shoe Shop
Average price: Expensive
Area: Buchanan Street, City Centre
Address: 164a Buchanan St
Glasgow G1 2LW
Phone: 0141 353 3022

#493
A S Electrics
Category: Electricians, Hardware Store
Average price: Inexpensive
Area: Charing Cross, City Centre
Address: 71 St Georges Rd
Glasgow G3 6JA
Phone: 0141 331 1957

#494
Savers
Category: Pound Shop
Average price: Inexpensive
Area: SauchieHalls Street, City Centre
Address: 104-114 SauchieHalls St
Glasgow G2 3DE
Phone: 0141 333 0332

#495
Strawberry Fields
Category: Children's Clothing
Average price: Expensive
Area: Great Western Road, Anniesland
Address: 517 Great Western Rd
Glasgow G12 8HN
Phone: 0141 339 1121

#496
Muirend Picture Framers
Category: Framing
Average price: Modest
Area: South Side
Address: 519 Clarkston Road
Glasgow G44 3PN
Phone: 0141 633 3606

#497
Lost Chord
Category: Music & DVDs
Average price: Expensive
Area: Woodlands, Great Western Road
Address: 11 Park Rd
Glasgow G4 9JD
Phone: 0141 334 5528

#498
Sandalwood Shoes
Category: Shoe Shop
Average price: Expensive
Area: Byres Road, West End
Address: 149 Byres Rd
Glasgow G12 8TS
Phone: 0141 334 4777

#499
Miss Diva
Category: Shoe Shop, Accessories
Average price: Modest
Area: City Centre, Merchant City
Address: 43-41 Argyle St
Glasgow G1 1
Phone: 0141 222 2857

#500
WH Smith
Category: Stationery, Books
Average price: Expensive
Area: City Centre, Cowcaddens
Address: Killermont Street
Glasgow G2 3NP
Phone: 0141 332 4872

TOP 500 RESTAURANTS

The Most Recommended by Locals & Trevelers

(From #1 to #500)

#1
Mother India's Café
Cuisines: Indian
Average price: £11-25
Area: West End
Address: 1355 Argyle Street
Glasgow G3 8AD
Phone: 0141 339 9145

#2
The Butchershop Bar & Grill
Cuisines: Steakhouse,
Breakfast & Brunch
Average price: £26-45
Area: SauchieHalls Street West
Address: 1055 SauchieHalls Street
Glasgow G3 7UD
Phone: 0141 339 2999

#3
Where The Monkey Sleeps
Cuisines: Coffee & Tea,
Sandwiches, Bagels
Average price: Under £10
Area: City Centre
Address: 182 West Regent Street
Glasgow G2 4RU
Phone: 0141 226 3406

#4
Ubiquitous Chip
Cuisines: British
Average price: £26-45
Area: Hillhead, West End
Address: 8-12 Ashton Lane
Glasgow G12 8SJ
Phone: 0141 334 5007

#5
Gamba
Cuisines: Seafood, British
Average price: £26-45
Area: City Centre
Address: 225a West George Street
Glasgow G2 2ND
Phone: 0141 572 0899

#6
Banana Leaf
Cuisines: Malaysian, Chinese
Average price: £11-25
Area: City Centre
Address: 67 Cambridge Street
Glasgow G3 6QX
Phone: 0141 333 9994

#7
Café Gandolfi
Cuisines: British, Cafe
Average price: £11-25
Area: City Centre, Merchant City
Address: 64 Albion Street
Glasgow G1 1NY
Phone: 0141 552 6813

#8
Stereo
Cuisines: Bar, Cafe
Average price: Under £10
Area: City Centre
Address: 20 Renfield Lane
Glasgow G2 6PH
Phone: 0141 222 2254

#9
Martha's
Cuisines: Breakfast & Brunch, Salad
Average price: Under £10
Area: City Centre
Address: 142A St Vincent Street
Glasgow G2 5LQ
Phone: 0141 248 9771

#10
The Dhabba
Cuisines: Indian
Average price: £26-45
Area: City Centre, Merchant City
Address: 44 Candleriggs
Glasgow G1 1LE
Phone: 0141 553 1249

#11
Number 16 Restaurant
Cuisines: British
Average price: £11-25
Area: Partick, Byres Road, West End
Address: 16 Byres Road
Glasgow G11 5JY
Phone: 0141 339 2544

#12
Babu Bombay Street Kitchen
Cuisines: Indian, Coffee & Tea,
Fast Food & Takeaway
Average price: Under £10
Area: City Centre
Address: 186 W Regent Street
Glasgow G2 4RU
Phone: 0141 204 4042

#13
The Butterfly & The Pig
Cuisines: Gastropub
Average price: £11-25
Area: City Centre
Address: 153 Bath Street
Glasgow G2 4SQ
Phone: 0141 221 7711

#14
The Tiki Bar & Kitsch Inn
Cuisines: Bar, British, Thai
Average price: £26-45
Area: City Centre
Address: 214 Bath Street
Glasgow G2 4HW
Phone: 0141 332 1341

#15
Cocktail & Burger
Cuisines: American, Burgers,
Cocktail Bar
Average price: Under £10
Area: SauchieHalls Street, City Centre
Address: 323 SauchieHalls Street
Glasgow G2 3HW
Phone: 0141 353 0953

#16
Avenue G Café
Cuisines: Coffee & Tea,
Breakfast & Brunch, Cafe
Average price: Under £10
Area: Byres Road, West End
Address: 291 Byres Road
Glasgow G12 8TL
Phone: 0141 339 5336

#17
Smile Café
Cuisines: Breakfast & Brunch, Cafe
Average price: Under £10
Area: West End
Address: 102 Queen Margaret Drive
Glasgow G20 8NZ
Phone: 07528 661275

#18
Stravaigin
Cuisines: Gastropub
Average price: £11-25
Area: West End
Address: 28 Gibson Street
Glasgow G12 8NX
Phone: 0141 334 2665

#19
Thai Lemongrass
Cuisines: Thai
Average price: £11-25
Area: City Centre
Address: 24 Renfrew Street
Glasgow G2 3BW
Phone: 0141 331 1315

#20
Kember & Jones
Cuisines: Breakfast & Brunch,
Bakeries, Cafe
Average price: £11-25
Area: Great Western Road, West End
Address: 134 Byres Road
Glasgow G12 8TD
Phone: 0141 337 3851

#21
Dumpling Monkey
Cuisines: Dim Sum,
Fast Food & Takeaway
Average price: Under £10
Area: Partick, West End
Address: 121 Dumbarton Road
Glasgow G11 6PR
Phone: 0141 583 8300

#22
Pinto Mexican
Cuisines: Mexican
Average price: Under £10
Area: City Centre, Merchant City
Address: 138 Queen Street
Glasgow G1 3BX
Phone: 0141 221 9330

#23
Guy's Restaurant and Bar
Cuisines: British, Italian
Average price: £26-45
Area: City Centre, Merchant City
Address: 24 Candleriggs
Glasgow G1 1LD
Phone: 0141 552 1114

#24
The 78
Cuisines: Bar, Vegan
Average price: Under £10
Area: Finnieston, West End
Address: 10-14 Kelvinhaugh Street
Glasgow G3 8NU
Phone: 0141 576 5018

#25
Battlefield Rest
Cuisines: Italian, Brasserie
Average price: £11-25
Area: South Side
Address: 55 Battlefield Road
Glasgow G42 9JL
Phone: 0141 636 6955

#26
Trans-Europe Café
Cuisines: European, Cafe
Average price: £11-25
Area: City Centre, Merchant City
Address: 25 Parnie Street
Glasgow G1 5RJ
Phone: 0141 552 7999

#27
Chinaski's
Cuisines: Pub, Gastropub
Average price: £11-25
Area: Charing Cross, SauchieHalls Street
West, West End
Address: 239 North Street
Glasgow G3 7DL
Phone: 0141 221 0061

#28
House For An Art Lover
Cuisines: European, Historical Building
Average price: £11-25
Area: South Side
Address: 10 Dumbreck Road
Glasgow G41 5BW
Phone: 0141 353 4770

#29
Nanakusa
Cuisines: Japanese, Sushi Bar
Average price: £11-25
Area: Charing Cross, SauchieHalls Street
Address: 441-449 SauchieHalls Street
Glasgow G2 3LG
Phone: 0141 332 6303

#30
The Left Bank
Cuisines: Gastropub
Average price: £11-25
Area: West End
Address: 35 Gibson Street
Glasgow G12 8NU
Phone: 0141 339 5969

#31
Two Fat Ladies
Cuisines: Seafood
Average price: £26-45
Area: Partick, West End
Address: 88 Dumbarton Road
Glasgow G11 6NX
Phone: 0141 339 1944

#32
Celino's
Cuisines: Deli, Italian, Ice Cream
Average price: £11-25
Area: Dennistoun
Address: 620-624 Alexandra Parade
Glasgow G31 3BT
Phone: 0141 554 0523

#33
The Sisters
Cuisines: British
Average price: £11-25
Area: West End
Address: 36 Kelvingrove St
Glasgow G3 7SA
Phone: 0141 564 1157

#34
Demijohn
Cuisines: Deli, Specialty Food
Average price: £11-25
Area: Byres Road, Hillhead, West End
Address: 382 Byres Road
Glasgow G12 8AR
Phone: 0141 337 3600

#35
Shish Mahal
Cuisines: Indian, Pakistani
Average price: £11-25
Area: Woodlands, West End
Address: 66-68 Park Road
Glasgow G4 9JF
Phone: 0141 339 8256

#36
Little Italy
Cuisines: Italian, Coffee & Tea
Average price: Under £10
Area: Byres Road, West End
Address: 205 Byres Road
Glasgow G12 8TN
Phone: 0141 339 6287

#37
13th Note
Cuisines: Bar, Vegan
Average price: £11-25
Area: City Centre, Merchant City
Address: 50-60 King Street
Glasgow G1 5QT
Phone: 0141 553 1638

#38
Cail Bruich West
Cuisines: Scottish, British
Average price: £11-25
Area: Great Western Road, Hillhead
Address: 725 Great Western Road
Glasgow G12 8QX
Phone: 0141 334 6265

#39
University Cafe
Cuisines: Coffee & Tea, British
Average price: £11-25
Area: Partick, Byres Road, West End
Address: 87 Byres Road
Glasgow G11 5HN
Phone: 0141 339 5217

#40
Mono
Cuisines: Bar, Vegan
Average price: £11-25
Area: City Centre, Merchant City
Address: 12 Kings Court
Glasgow G1 5RB
Phone: 0141 553 2400

#41
La Fiorentina
Cuisines: Italian
Average price: £26-45
Area: South Side, Kinning Park
Address: 2 Paisley Road W
Glasgow G51 1LE
Phone: 0141 420 1585

#42
The Flying Duck
Cuisines: Bar, Club, Vegan
Average price: Under £10
Area: City Centre
Address: 142 Renfield Street
Glasgow G2 3AU
Phone: 0141 564 1450

#43
The Wee Curry Shop
Cuisines: Indian
Average price: Under £10
Area: Partick, Byres Road, West End
Address: 41 Byres Road
Glasgow G11 5RG
Phone: 0141 339 1339

#44
The Chippy Doon The Lane
Cuisines: Fish & Chips, Seafood
Average price: £11-25
Area: City Centre
Address: 23 Royal Exchange Square
Glasgow G1 3AJ
Phone: 0141 225 5612

#45
Cherry & Heather
Cuisines: Fast Food & Takeaway
Average price: Under £10
Area: South Side, Kinning Park
Address: 7 N Gower Street
Glasgow G51 1PW
Phone: 0141 427 0272

#46
Crabshakk
Cuisines: Seafood
Average price: £26-45
Area: Finnieston, West End
Address: 1114 Argyle Street
Glasgow G3 8TD
Phone: 0141 334 6127

#47
Firebird
Cuisines: Italian, Pizza, Pub
Average price: £11-25
Area: West End
Address: 1321 Argyle Street
Glasgow G3 8TL
Phone: 0141 334 0594

#48
Bibi's
Cuisines: Mexican
Average price: £11-25
Area: Partick, West End
Address: 599 Dumbarton Road
Glasgow G11 6HY
Phone: 0141 579 0179

#49
Hotel Du Vin
Cuisines: Hotel, European
Average price: Above £46
Area: Great Western Road, Hyndland
Address: 5 Devonshire Garden
Glasgow G12 0UX
Phone: 0141 339 2001

#50
Opium
Cuisines: Dim Sum, Asian Fusion
Average price: £11-25
Area: City Centre
Address: 191 Hope Street
Glasgow G2 2UL
Phone: 0141 332 6668

#51
North Star Café & Bistro
Cuisines: Bistro, Cafe
Average price: Under £10
Area: West End
Address: 108 Queen Margaret Drive
Glasgow G20 8NZ
Phone: 0141 946 5365

#52
Cafezique
Cuisines: Deli, Breakfast & Brunch
Average price: £11-25
Area: Partick, West End
Address: 70-72 Hyndland Street
Glasgow G11 5PT
Phone: 0141 339 7180

#53
McPhabbs
Cuisines: Pub, British
Average price: £11-25
Area: Charing Cross, West End
Address: 23 Sandyford Place
Glasgow G3 7NG
Phone: 0141 221 8176

#54
Enjoy
Cuisines: Breakfast & Brunch,
Bistro, Mediterranean
Average price: Under £10
Area: Great Western Road, Kelvinbridge
Address: 393-395 Great Western Road
Glasgow G4 9HY
Phone: 0141 334 6622

#55
Nando's
Cuisines: Flame-Grilled,
Fast Food & Takeaway
Average price: £11-25
Area: City Centre
Address: St Enoch Centre
Glasgow G1 4BW
Phone: 0141 221 5768

#56
The Wee Curry Shop
Cuisines: Indian, Pakistani
Average price: £11-25
Area: Hillhead, West End
Address: 29 Ashton Lane
Glasgow G12 8SJ
Phone: 0141 357 5280

#57
Thai Siam
Cuisines: Thai
Average price: £11-25
Area: Finnieston, West End
Address: 1191-1193 Argyle Street
Glasgow G3 8TQ
Phone: 0141 229 1191

#58
Gandolfi Fish
Cuisines: Seafood
Average price: £26-45
Area: City Centre, Merchant City
Address: 84-86 Albion Street
Glasgow G1 1NY
Phone: 0141 552 9475

#59
Charcoals
Cuisines: Indian
Average price: £11-25
Area: City Centre
Address: 26a Renfield Street
Glasgow G2 1LU
Phone: 0141 221 9251

#60
La Vallee Blanche
Cuisines: French
Average price: £26-45
Area: Byres Road, Hillhead, West End
Address: 360 Byres Road
Glasgow G12 8AW
Phone: 0141 334 3333

#61
Dining In with Mother India
Cuisines: Indian
Average price: £11-25
Area: West End
Address: 1347 Argyll Street
Glasgow G3 8AD
Phone: 0141 334 3815

#62
The Grill Room
Cuisines: Scottish, Steakhouse
Average price: Above £46
Area: City Centre
Address: 29 Royal Exchange Square
Glasgow G1 3AJ
Phone: 0141 225 5615

#63
Thairiffic
Cuisines: Thai
Average price: £11-25
Area: SauchieHalls Street, City Centre
Address: 303 SauchieHalls Street
Glasgow G2 3HQ
Phone: 0141 332 3000

#64
McCune Smith
Cuisines: Sandwiches, Deli
Average price: £11-25
Area: Duke Street, Dennistoun
Address: 3-5 Duke Street
Glasgow G4 0UL
Phone: 0141 548 1114

#65
Two Fat Ladies
Cuisines: Seafood
Average price: £26-45
Area: City Centre
Address: 118a Blythswood Street
Glasgow G2 4EG
Phone: 0141 847 0088

#66
The Rio Café
Cuisines: Cafe
Average price: Under £10
Area: Partick, West End
Address: 27 Hyndland Street
Glasgow G11 5QF
Phone: 0141 334 9909

#67
Bar Soba
Cuisines: Pub, Japanese
Average price: £11-25
Area: City Centre
Address: 11 Mitchell Lane
Glasgow G1 3NU
Phone: 0141 204 2404

#68
Two Fat Ladies at The Buttery
Cuisines: Seafood
Average price: £26-45
Area: Finnieston, West End
Address: 652-654 Argyle St
Glasgow G3 8UF
Phone: 0141 221 8188

#69
The Grill On the Corner
Cuisines: Steakhouse, Seafood
Average price: £26-45
Area: City Centre
Address: 21-25 Bothwell Street
Glasgow G2 6NL
Phone: 0141 248 6262

#70
Russian Cafe-Gallery Cossachok
Cuisines: Russian, Ukrainian
Average price: £26-45
Area: City Centre, Merchant City
Address: 10 King Street
Glasgow G1 5QP
Phone: 0141 553 0733

#71
Ad Lib
Cuisines: Bar, American
Average price: £11-25
Area: City Centre
Address: 111 Hope Street
Glasgow G2 6LL
Phone: 0141 248 6645

#72
India Quay
Cuisines: Indian
Average price: £11-25
Area: Finnieston, West End
Address: 181 Finnieston Street
Glasgow G3 8HE
Phone: 0141 221 1616

#73
Oran Mor
Cuisines: Pub, Scottish
Average price: £26-45
Area: Great Western Road, Hillhead
Address: 731 Great Western Road
Glasgow G12 8QX
Phone: 0141 357 6200

#74
La Lanterna
Cuisines: Italian
Average price: £26-45
Area: City Centre
Address: 35 Hope Street
Glasgow G2 6AE
Phone: 0141 221 9160

#75
Brel
Cuisines: Belgian, Bar
Average price: £11-25
Area: Hillhead, West End
Address: 39 Ashton Lane
Glasgow G12 8SJ
Phone: 0141 342 4966

#76
Paradise
Cuisines: Persian/Iranian
Average price: £11-25
Area: Great Western Road, Kelvinbridge
Address: 411-413 Great Western Road
Glasgow G4 9JA
Phone: 0141 339 2170

#77
The Squid & Whale
Cuisines: Pub, American, Mexican
Average price: £11-25
Area: Great Western Road, West End
Address: 372-374 Great Western Road
Glasgow G4 9HT
Phone: 0141 339 5070

#78
Cushion and Cake
Cuisines: Cafe, Desserts,
Patisserie/Cake Shop
Average price: Under £10
Area: West End
Address: 35 Old Dumbarton Road
Glasgow G3 8RD
Phone: 0141 339 4114

#79
Coia's Café
Cuisines: Cafe, Deli
Average price: £11-25
Area: Duke Street, Dennistoun
Address: 473 Duke Street
Glasgow G31 1RD
Phone: 0141 554 3822

#80
Cubatas Tapas Bar
Cuisines: Spanish, Tapas Bar
Average price: £11-25
Area: Charing Cross, West End
Address: 108 Elderslie Street
Glasgow G3 7AR
Phone: 0141 243 2227

#81
Cup Tea Lounge
Cuisines: Coffee & Tea,
Breakfast & Brunch, Sandwiches
Average price: £26-45
Area: City Centre
Address: 71 Renfield Street
Glasgow G2 1LP
Phone: 0141 353 2959

#82
Sisters Restaurant
Cuisines: British
Average price: £26-45
Area: West End
Address: 1a Ashwood Garden
Glasgow G13 1NU
Phone: 0141 434 1179

#83
The Hidden Lane Tearoom
Cuisines: Cafe
Average price: Under £10
Area: Finnieston, West End
Address: 1103 Argyle Street
Glasgow G3 8ND
Phone: 0141 237 4391

#84
The Hanoi Bike Shop
Cuisines: Vietnamese
Average price: £11-25
Area: West End
Address: 8 Ruthven Lane
Glasgow G12 9BG
Phone: 0141 334 7165

#85
Brian Maule at Chardon d'Or
Cuisines: French
Average price: Above £46
Area: City Centre
Address: 176 W Regent Street
Glasgow G2 4RL
Phone: 0141 248 3801

#86
Yo Sushi
Cuisines: Japanese
Average price: £11-25
Area: Buchanan Street, City Centre
Address: 45 Buchanan Street
Glasgow G1 3HL
Phone: 0141 413 2231

#87
Jack McPhee
Cuisines: British, Fish & Chips
Average price: Under £10
Area: City Centre
Address: 261 Hope Street
Glasgow G2 3PS
Phone: 0141 353 1240

#88
Sloans
Cuisines: Bar, American
Average price: £11-25
Area: City Centre
Address: 62 Argyll Arcade
Glasgow G2 8BG
Phone: 0141 221 8886

#89
Merchant Square
Cuisines: Restaurants, Bar,
Shopping Centre
Average price: £26-45
Area: City Centre, Merchant City
Address: Candleriggs
Glasgow G1 1LE
Phone: 0141 552 3452

#90
SoHo On Miller Street
Cuisines: Bar, Pizza
Average price: £11-25
Area: City Centre, Merchant City
Address: 84 Miller Street
Glasgow G1 1DT
Phone: 0141 221 1568

#91
Viva Brazil
Cuisines: Brazilian
Average price: £26-45
Area: City Centre
Address: 87-91 Bothwell Street
Glasgow G2 7AA
Phone: 0141 204 0240

#92
Naked Soup
Cuisines: Soup, Coffee & Tea
Average price: Under £10
Area: Great Western Road, Hillhead
Address: 6 Kersland Street
Glasgow G12 8BL
Phone: 0141 334 8999

#93
The Fish People Cafe
Cuisines: Cafe, Seafood
Average price: £26-45
Area: South Side
Address: 350 Scotland Street
Glasgow G5 8QB
Phone: 0141 429 8787

#94
Cafe Phoenix
Cuisines: Cafe
Average price: Under £10
Area: Woodlands, West End
Address: 262 Woodlands Road
Glasgow G3 6NE
Phone: 0141 339 3020

#95
Wudon
Cuisines: Japanese, Sushi Bar
Average price: £11-25
Area: Great Western Road, Hillhead
Address: 535 Great Western Road
Glasgow G12 8HN
Phone: 0141 357 3033

#96
Lychee Oriental
Cuisines: Chinese
Average price: £26-45
Area: City Centre
Address: 59 Mitchell Street
Glasgow G1 3LN
Phone: 0141 248 2240

#97
The Lansdowne Bar & Kitchen
Cuisines: Gastropub
Average price: £11-25
Area: Kelvinbridge, West End
Address: 7a Lansdowne Crescent
Glasgow G20 6NQ
Phone: 0141 334 4653

#98
Sapporo Teppanyaki
Cuisines: Japanese, Sushi Bar
Average price: £26-45
Area: City Centre, Merchant City
Address: 2-6 Ingram St
Glasgow G1 1HA
Phone: 0141 553 4060

#99
Tropeiro
Cuisines: Brazilian
Average price: £11-25
Area: City Centre
Address: 363 Argyle Street
Glasgow G2 8LT
Phone: 0141 222 2102

#100
Amber Restaurant
Cuisines: Chinese
Average price: Above £46
Area: Byres Road, West End
Address: 130 Byres Road
Glasgow G12 8TD
Phone: 0141 339 6121

#101
Ho Wong
Cuisines: Chinese
Average price: Above £46
Area: City Centre
Address: 82 York Street
Glasgow G2 8LE
Phone: 0141 221 3550

#102
Nando's
Cuisines: Flame-Grilled,
Fast Food & Takeaway
Average price: £11-25
Area: South Side, Kinning Park
Address: Springfield Quay
Glasgow G5 8NP
Phone: 0141 429 2540

#103
Sonny & Vito's
Cuisines: Cafe
Average price: £11-25
Area: Woodlands, Kelvinbridge
Address: 52 Park Road
Glasgow G4 9JG
Phone: 0141 357 0640

#104
**Mr India's West End Balti
and Dosa House**
Cuisines: Indian
Average price: £11-25
Area: Partick, West End
Address: 11-13 Hyndland Street
Glasgow G11 5QE
Phone: 0141 334 0084

#105
Jamie's Italian
Cuisines: Italian
Average price: £11-25
Area: City Centre, Merchant City
Address: 1 George Square
Glasgow G1 1HL
Phone: 0141 404 2690

#106
The Glad Cafe
Cuisines: Cafe
Average price: £11-25
Area: South Side, Queen's Park
Address: 1006a Pollokshaws Road
Glasgow G41 2HG
Phone: 0141 636 6119

#107
The Wee Guy's Café Deli
Cuisines: Cafe, Deli, Breakfast & Brunch
Average price: Under £10
Area: City Centre, Merchant City
Address: 51 Cochrane Street
Glasgow G1 1HL
Phone: 0141 552 5338

#108
The Living Room
Cuisines: American
Average price: Above £46
Area: City Centre
Address: 150 St Vincent Street
Glasgow G2 5NE
Phone: 0141 229 0607

#109
Nic's NYC Deli
Cuisines: Cafe
Average price: Under £10
Area: City Centre
Address: 50 St Enoch Square
Glasgow G1 4DH
Phone: 0141 226 3075

#110
Bacchus Cafe Bar
Cuisines: Pub, British, Lounge
Average price: Under £10
Area: City Centre, Merchant City
Address: 80 Glassford Street
Glasgow G1 1UR
Phone: 0141 572 0080

#111
Cafe Salma
Cuisines: Indian
Average price: £11-25
Area: Charing Cross, West End
Address: 523 SauchieHalls Street
Glasgow G3 7PQ
Phone: 0141 221 7636

#112
The Two Figs
Cuisines: Pub, Cafe
Average price: £11-25
Area: Partick, Byres Road, West End
Address: 5 and 9 Byres Road
Glasgow G11 5RD
Phone: 0141 334 7277

#113
Barbarossa Restaurant
Cuisines: Wine Bar, Italian
Average price: £26-45
Area: South Side
Address: 1/7 Clarkston Road
Glasgow G44 4EF
Phone: 0141 560 3898

#114
The Richmond Bar & Bistro
Cuisines: Cocktail Bar, British
Average price: £11-25
Area: Woodlands, West End
Address: 144 Park Road
Glasgow G4 9HB
Phone: 0141 334 3571

#115
Sapori D'Italia
Cuisines: Italian, Coffee & Tea
Average price: £11-25
Area: South Side, Mount Florida
Address: 1102 Cathcart Road
Glasgow G42 9EG
Phone: 0141 636 0444

#116
Siempre
Cuisines: Cafe
Average price: £11-25
Area: Partick, West End
Address: 162 Dumbarton Road
Glasgow G11 6XE
Phone: 0141 334 2385

#117
Asia Style
Cuisines: Chinese
Average price: £11-25
Area: Woodlands, West End
Address: 185 St Georges Road
Glasgow G3 6JD
Phone: 0141 332 8828

#118
Delizique
Cuisines: Deli
Average price: £26-45
Area: Partick, West End
Address: 66 Hyndland Street
Glasgow G11 5PT
Phone: 0141 339 2000

#119
NY Slice
Cuisines: Pizza, Fast Food & Takeaway
Average price: Under £10
Area: SauchieHalls Street, City Centre
Address: 369 SauchieHalls Street
Glasgow G2 3HU
Phone: 0141 353 1698

#120
Akbar's
Cuisines: Indian
Average price: £11-25
Area: Charing Cross, SauchieHalls Street
West, West End
Address: 573-581 SauchieHalls Street
Glasgow G3 7PQ
Phone: 0141 222 2258

#121
Lucky 7
Cuisines: British, American
Average price: £11-25
Area: City Centre
Address: 166 Bath Street
Glasgow G2 4TB
Phone: 0141 331 6227

#122
Piccolo Mondo
Cuisines: Italian
Average price: £11-25
Area: City Centre
Address: 344 Argyle Street
Glasgow G2 8LY
Phone: 0141 248 2481

#123
Bombay Blues
Cuisines: Indian
Average price: £11-25
Area: City Centre
Address: 41 Hope Street
Glasgow G2 6AE
Phone: 0141 221 1950

#124
The Shandon Belles
Cuisines: British
Average price: £11-25
Area: Finnieston, West End
Address: 652 Argyle Street
Glasgow G3 8UF
Phone: 0141 221 8188

#125
Little Urban Achievers Club
Cuisines: Bar, Hot Dogs, Pizza
Average price: £11-25
Area: Great Western Road, Kelvinbridge
Address: 508 Great Western Road
Glasgow G12 8EL
Phone: 0141 237 4040

#126
Ka Ka Lok
Cuisines: Chinese
Average price: £11-25
Area: Woodlands, West End
Address: 175 Saint Georges Road
Glasgow G3 6JD
Phone: 0141 353 6528

#127
Sarti
Cuisines: Italian
Average price: £11-25
Area: City Centre
Address: 42 Renfield Street
Glasgow G2 1NF
Phone: 0141 572 7000

#128
Cafe Antipasti
Cuisines: Italian, Coffee & Tea
Average price: £11-25
Area: SauchieHalls Street, City Centre
Address: 305 SauchieHalls Street
Glasgow G2 3HQ
Phone: 0141 332 9002

#129
Brutti Ma Buoni
Cuisines: Mediterranean, Tapas Bar
Average price: £11-25
Area: City Centre, Merchant City
Address: 106 Brunswick Street
Glasgow G1 1
Phone: 0141 552 0001

#130
Ichiban Noodle Cafe
Cuisines: Japanese
Average price: £11-25
Area: Partick, West End
Address: 184 Dumbarton Road
Glasgow G11 6UN
Phone: 0141 334 9222

#131
The Italian Caffè
Cuisines: Italian
Average price: £26-45
Area: City Centre, Merchant City
Address: 92 Albion Street
Glasgow G1 1NY
Phone: 0141 552 3186

#132
Hillhead Bookclub
Cuisines: Bar, Scottish
Average price: £11-25
Area: Hillhead, West End
Address: 17 Vinicombe Street
Glasgow G12 8
Phone: 0141 576 1700

#133
Kebabish Grill
Cuisines: Indian, Fast Food & Takeaway
Average price: £11-25
Area: South Side
Address: 323-325 Victoria Road
Glasgow G42 7SA
Phone: 0141 424 1879

#134
Curry Pot
Cuisines: British
Average price: £11-25
Area: Partick, West End
Address: 139 Dumbarton Road
Glasgow G11 6PR
Phone: 0141 334 1549

#135
Max's Bar & Grill
Cuisines: American
Average price: £11-25
Area: City Centre
Address: 73 Queen Street
Glasgow G1 3BZ
Phone: 0141 221 1379

#136
Shilla
Cuisines: Korean, Sushi Bar
Average price: £11-25
Area: Finnieston, West End
Address: 1138 Argyle Streete
Glasgow G3 8TD
Phone: 0141 334 5566

#137
Barca Tapas
Cuisines: Spanish, Basque
Average price: £11-25
Area: City Centre
Address: 48 Buchanan Street
Glasgow G1 3JX
Phone: 0141 248 6555

#138
Bo'Vine Meats & Wines
Cuisines: Steakhouse
Average price: £11-25
Area: Byres Road, Great Western Road
Address: 385 Byres Road
Glasgow G12 8AU
Phone: 0141 341 6540

#139
Bar 10
Cuisines: Pub, Mediterranean
Average price: £11-25
Area: City Centre
Address: 10 Mitchell Lane
Glasgow G1 3NU
Phone: 0141 572 1448

#140
Meat Bar
Cuisines: Bar, Burgers, Steakhouse
Average price: £11-25
Area: City Centre
Address: 142 West Regent Street
Glasgow G2 2RQ
Phone: 0141 204 3605

#141
Go Slow Cafe
Cuisines: Cafe
Average price: Above £46
Area: South Side
Address: 452 Victoria Road
Glasgow G42 8YU
Phone: 0141 423 9886

#142
Café Hula
Cuisines: Coffee & Tea, Mediterranean
Average price: £11-25
Area: City Centre
Address: 321 Hope Street
Glasgow G2 3PT
Phone: 0141 353 1660

#143
The Curler's Rest
Cuisines: Pub, Gastropub
Average price: £11-25
Area: Byres Road, Hillhead, West End
Address: 256-260 Byres Road
Glasgow G12 8SH
Phone: 0141 341 0737

#144
The Finnieston
Cuisines: Seafood, Bar
Average price: £11-25
Area: Finnieston, West End
Address: 1125 Argyle Street
Glasgow G3 8ND
Phone: 0141 222 2884

#145
Felix and Oscar
Cuisines: Cafe
Average price: £11-25
Area: Great Western Road, Kelvinbridge
Address: 459 Great Western Road
Glasgow G12 8HH
Phone: 0141 339 8585

#146
City Merchant Restaurant
Cuisines: Seafood
Average price: £26-45
Area: City Centre, Merchant City
Address: 97-99 Candleriggs
Glasgow G1 1NP
Phone: 0141 553 1577

#147
Joanna Goodbite
Cuisines: Fast Food & Takeaway
Average price: Under £10
Area: City Centre, Merchant City
Address: 92 George Street
Glasgow G1 1RF
Phone: 0141 552 4114

#148
Bella Napoli
Cuisines: Italian, Pizza
Average price: £11-25
Area: South Side, Shawlands
Address: 85 Kilmarnock Road
Glasgow G41 3YR
Phone: 0141 632 4222

#149
Kelvingrove Café
Cuisines: Cocktail Bar, Cafe
Average price: £11-25
Area: Finnieston, West End
Address: 1163 Argyle Street
Glasgow G3 8TB
Phone: 0141 221 8988

#150
Rishis Indian Aroma
Cuisines: Indian, Halal
Average price: £11-25
Area: City Centre
Address: 61 Bath Street
Glasgow G2 2DG
Phone: 0141 332 2522

#151
Prezzo
Cuisines: Italian
Average price: £11-25
Area: City Centre
Address: 35 St Vincent Place
Glasgow G1 2ER
Phone: 0141 248 9815

#152
Carluccio's
Cuisines: Italian
Average price: £11-25
Area: City Centre
Address: 7 W Nile Street
Glasgow G1 2PR
Phone: 0141 248 1166

#153
Bar Gumbo
Cuisines: Cajun/Creole, Bar, British
Average price: £11-25
Area: Partick, Byres Road, West End
Address: 71-77 Byres Road
Glasgow G11 5HN
Phone: 0141 334 7132

#154
Pesto
Cuisines: Italian
Average price: £11-25
Area: City Centre
Address: 57-61 St Vincent Street
Glasgow G2 5SH
Phone: 0141 204 0979

#155
Old Salty's
Cuisines: Fish & Chips,
Fast Food & Takeaway
Average price: Under £10
Area: Finnieston, West End
Address: 1126 Argyle Street
Glasgow G3 8TD
Phone: 0141 357 5677

#156
Nippon Kitchen
Cuisines: Japanese
Average price: £11-25
Area: City Centre
Address: 91 West George Street
Glasgow G2 1PB
Phone: 0141 328 3113

#157
Ad Lib
Cuisines: American, Fast Food, Takeaway, British
Average price: £11-25
Area: City Centre, Merchant City
Address: 33 Ingram Street
Glasgow G1 1HA
Phone: 0141 552 5736

#158
Big Slope
Cuisines: Pub, Sandwiches, Gastropub
Average price: £11-25
Area: SauchieHalls Street West
Address: 36a Kelvingrove Street
Glasgow G3 7SA
Phone: 0141 333 0869

#159
Ketchup
Cuisines: American, Burgers
Average price: £11-25
Area: Hillhead, West End
Address: 44 Ashton Lane
Glasgow G12 8SJ
Phone: 0845 166 6011

#160
The Local
Cuisines: British
Average price: Above £46
Area: SauchieHalls Street, City Centre
Address: 427 SauchieHalls Street
Glasgow G2 3LG
Phone: 0141 332 2528

#161
Mussel Inn Seafood Restaurant
Cuisines: Seafood
Average price: £11-25
Area: City Centre
Address: 157 Hope Street
Glasgow G2 5
Phone: 0141 572 1405

#162
Darcys
Cuisines: Brasserie, French
Average price: £11-25
Area: Buchanan Street, City Centre
Address: Princes Square
Glasgow G1 3JN
Phone: 0141 226 4309

#163
The Sir John Moore
Cuisines: Gastropub
Average price: Under £10
Area: City Centre
Address: 260-292 Argyle Street
Glasgow G2 8QW
Phone: 0141 222 1780

#164
Rumours Kopitiam
Cuisines: Malaysian
Average price: £11-25
Area: City Centre
Address: 21 Bath Street
Glasgow G2 1HT
Phone: 0141 353 0678

#165
Home Wok
Cuisines: Chinese, Fast Food & Takeaway
Average price: £26-45
Area: Partick, Byres Road, West End
Address: 101 Byres Road
Glasgow G11 5HW
Phone: 0141 334 8433

#166
Red Onion
Cuisines: Brasserie, Wine Bar
Average price: £11-25
Area: City Centre
Address: 257 W Campbell Street
Glasgow G2 4TT
Phone: 0141 221 6000

#167
Jacker De Viande
Cuisines: Steakhouse, Burgers
Average price: £11-25
Area: City Centre
Address: 111 W Regent Street
Glasgow G2 2RU
Phone: 0141 243 2405

#168
Khublai Khan
Cuisines: Mongolian
Average price: £11-25
Area: City Centre, Merchant City
Address: 26 Candleriggs
Glasgow G1 1LD
Phone: 0141 552 5646

#169
Urban Brasserie
Cuisines: Bar, Brasserie
Average price: £26-45
Area: City Centre
Address: 23-25 St Vincent Place
Glasgow G1 2DT
Phone: 0141 248 5636

#170
Brown's Bar and Brasserie
Cuisines: Brasserie
Average price: £26-45
Area: City Centre, Merchant City
Address: 1 George Square
Glasgow G2 1DY
Phone: 0141 221 7828

#171
Velvet Elvis
Cuisines: Bar, American
Average price: £11-25
Area: Partick, West End
Address: 566 Dumbarton Road
Glasgow G11 7
Phone: 0141 334 6677

#172
Chillies West End
Cuisines: Indian, Fast Food & Takeaway
Average price: £11-25
Area: Woodlands, West End
Address: 176-182 Woodlands Road
Glasgow G3 6LL
Phone: 0141 331 0494

#173
Chow
Cuisines: Chinese
Average price: £26-45
Area: Partick, Byres Road, West End
Address: 98 Byres Road
Glasgow G12 8TB
Phone: 0141 334 9818

#174
Banana Leaf
Cuisines: Indian
Average price: Under £10
Area: West End
Address: 76 Old Dumbarton Road
Glasgow G3 8RE
Phone: 0141 334 4445

#175
Cafe Andaluz
Cuisines: Spanish
Average price: £11-25
Area: Hillhead, West End
Address: 2 Cresswell Lane
Glasgow G12 8AA
Phone: 0141 339 1111

#176
Don Costanzo
Cuisines: Italian
Average price: £11-25
Area: Charing Cross, Woodlands
Address: 13 Woodside Crescent
Glasgow G3 7UL
Phone: 0141 332 3070

#177
The Wee Curry Shop
Cuisines: Indian, Pakistani
Average price: £11-25
Area: City Centre
Address: 7 Buccleuch Street
Glasgow G3 6SJ
Phone: 0141 353 0777

#178
The Plum Tree
Cuisines: Cafe, Bistro
Average price: £11-25
Area: City Centre, Merchant City
Address: 6 Wilson Street
Glasgow G1 1SS
Phone: 0141 552 6980

#179
Cottier's
Cuisines: Pub, American
Average price: £11-25
Area: Partick, West End
Address: 93-95 Hyndland Street
Glasgow G11 5PX
Phone: 0141 357 5825

#180
Tribeca
Cuisines: Breakfast & Brunch,
American, American
Average price: £11-25
Area: Partick, West End
Address: 102 Dumbarton Road
Glasgow G11 6NX
Phone: 0844 357 7777

#181
Tinto Tapas Bar
Cuisines: Tapas Bar, Spanish
Average price: £11-25
Area: South Side, Mount Florida
Address: 138 Battlefield Road
Glasgow G42 9JT
Phone: 0141 636 6838

#182
Brutti Compadres
Cuisines: Bar, Tapas Bar, Mediterranean
Average price: £11-25
Area: City Centre, Merchant City
Address: 3 Virginia Court
Glasgow G1 1TS
Phone: 0141 552 1777

#183
Lovestruck Cheesecakes
Cuisines: Desserts, Cafe
Average price: £11-25
Area: South Side
Address: 751-753 Pollokshaws Road
Glasgow G41 2AX
Phone: 0141 387 8664

#184
Nakodar Grill
Cuisines: Indian
Average price: £11-25
Area: Duke Street, Dennistoun
Address: 13 Annfield Place
Glasgow G31 2NF
Phone: 0141 556 4430

#185
Biscuit
Cuisines: Cafe
Average price: £11-25
Area: South Side, Shawlands
Address: 17 Skirving Street
Glasgow G41 3AB
Phone: 0141 632 3466

#186
Nick's Italian Kitchen & Bar
Cuisines: Italian
Average price: £11-25
Area: West End
Address: 168 Hyndland Road
Glasgow G12 9HZ
Phone: 0141 357 6336

#187
Restauracja U Jarka
Cuisines: Polish
Average price: Under £10
Area: West End
Address: 5 Parkgrove Terrace
Glasgow G3 7SD
Phone: 0141 339 1368

#188
Qua Restaurant
Cuisines: Italian
Average price: £11-25
Area: City Centre, Merchant City
Address: 68 Ingram Street
Glasgow G1 1EX
Phone: 0141 552 6233

#189
Roast
Cuisines: Sandwiches
Average price: Under £10
Area: West End
Address: 1299 Argyle Street
Glasgow G3 8TL
Phone: 0141 334 1413

#190
Morello's
Cuisines: Turkish, Fast Food & Takeaway
Average price: £26-45
Area: Woodlands, Great Western Road
Address: 253 Great Western Road
Glasgow G4 9EG
Phone: 0141 332 3119

#191
The Corinthian Club
Cuisines: British, Lounge, Gastropub
Average price: £26-45
Area: City Centre, Merchant City
Address: 191 Ingram St
Glasgow G1 1DA
Phone: 0141 552 1101

#192
The Bay Tree Cafe Bistro
Cuisines: Breakfast & Brunch,
Mediterranean
Average price: Under £10
Area: Great Western Road, Kelvinbridge
Address: 403 Great Western Road
Glasgow G4 9HY
Phone: 0141 334 5898

#193
Booly Mardy's
Cuisines: Gastropub, Cocktail Bar
Average price: £11-25
Area: Byres Road, Hillhead, West End
Address: 28 Vinicombe Street
Glasgow G12 8BE
Phone: 0141 560 8004

#194
Lettuce Eat
Cuisines: Sandwiches
Average price: Under £10
Area: City Centre
Address: 361 Argyle Street
Glasgow G2 8LT
Phone: 0141 221 3233

#195
Ketchup
Cuisines: Burgers
Average price: £11-25
Area: South Side, Shawlands
Address: 1179 Pollokshaws Road
Glasgow G41 3NH
Phone: 0845 659 5902

#196
Alston Bar & Beef
Cuisines: Steakhouse, Cocktail Bar
Average price: £11-25
Area: City Centre
Address: 79 Gordon Street
Glasgow G1 3PE
Phone: 0141 221 7627

#197
Crepe á Croissant
Cuisines: Creperie, Desserts
Average price: £11-25
Area: Byres Road, Hillhead, West End
Address: 396 Byres Road
Glasgow G12 8AR
Phone: 0141 339 7003

#198
Singl-end
Cuisines: Italian, Delicatessen
Average price: £26-45
Area: Charing Cross, City Centre
Address: 265 Renfrew Street
Glasgow G3 6TT
Phone: 0141 611 7270

#199
Fanny Trollopes Bistro
Cuisines: Coffee & Tea, British, Seafood
Average price: £26-45
Area: Finnieston, West End
Address: 1066 Argyle Street
Glasgow G3 8LY
Phone: 0141 564 6464

#200
Pulcinella Restaurant
Cuisines: Italian
Average price: Under £10
Area: City Centre
Address: 167 Hope Street
Glasgow G2 2UQ
Phone: 0141 572 0575

#201
Ecco 808 il Cafe
Cuisines: Italian, Butcher
Average price: Under £10
Area: Great Western Road, Anniesland
Address: 808 Crow Road
Glasgow G13 1LY
Phone: 0141 950 2067

#202
Kings Cafe
Cuisines: Cafe
Average price: Under £10
Area: Charing Cross, City Centre
Address: 71 Elmbank Street
Glasgow G2 4PQ
Phone: 0141 332 3247

#203
Paperino's
Cuisines: Italian
Average price: £11-25
Area: City Centre
Address: 78 St Vincent Street
Glasgow G2 5UB
Phone: 0141 248 7878

#204
Crystal Palace
Cuisines: Pub, Gastropub
Average price: Under £10
Area: City Centre
Address: 36 Jamaica St
Glasgow G1 4QD
Phone: 0141 221 2624

#205
Anarkali Indian
Cuisines: Indian, Pakistani
Average price: £11-25
Area: South Side
Address: 531 Victoria Road
Glasgow G42 8BH
Phone: 0141 423 8266

#206
Bothy Restaurant
Cuisines: British, Scottish
Average price: £11-25
Area: Byres Road, West End
Address: 11 Ruthven Lane
Glasgow G12 9BG
Phone: 0845 166 6032

#207
Bella Fresca
Cuisines: Deli, Italian
Average price: £11-25
Area: South Side
Address: 2093 Paisley Road W
Glasgow G52 3JH
Phone: 0141 882 6995

#208
O' Sole Mio
Cuisines: Italian, Pizza
Average price: £11-25
Area: City Centre
Address: 32 Bath Street
Glasgow G2 1HG
Phone: 0141 331 1397

#209
Bread + Butter
Cuisines: Diner
Average price: Under £10
Area: City Centre
Address: 23 Royal Exchange Sq
Glasgow G1 3AJ
Phone: 0141 221 4383

#210
The Social
Cuisines: Bar, Gastropub
Average price: £11-25
Area: City Centre
Address: 27 Royal Exchange Square
Glasgow G1 3AJ
Phone: 0845 166 6016

#211
Da Vinci Takeaway
Cuisines: Fast Food & Takeaway
Average price: £11-25
Area: South Side, Mount Florida
Address: 126 Holmlea Road
Glasgow G44 4
Phone: 0141 649 6725

#212
Kimble's
Cuisines: Cafe
Average price: £11-25
Area: City Centre
Address: Upper Mall
Glasgow G1 4BW
Phone: 0141 249 9955

#213
Moskito
Cuisines: Pub, Gastropub
Average price: £11-25
Area: City Centre
Address: 198-200 Bath Street
Glasgow G2 4HG
Phone: 0141 331 1777

#214
Ichiban
Cuisines: Japanese, Sushi Bar
Average price: £11-25
Area: City Centre, Merchant City
Address: 50 Queen Street
Glasgow G1 3DS
Phone: 0141 204 4200

#215
Dakhin Indian Restaurant
Cuisines: Indian
Average price: £11-25
Area: City Centre, Merchant City
Address: 89 Candleriggs
Glasgow G1 1NP
Phone: 0141 553 2585

#216
Taco Mazama
Cuisines: Mexican
Average price: Under £10
Area: Byres Road, West End
Address: 263 Byres Rd
Glasgow G12 8TL
Phone: 0141 337 3399

#217
Wok to Walk
Cuisines: Asian Fusion
Average price: Under £10
Area: SauchieHalls Street, City Centre
Address: 306 SaucieHalls Street
Glasgow G2 3
Phone: 0141 332 1168

#218
The Koh-I-Noor
Cuisines: Indian, Pakistani
Average price: Above £46
Area: Charing Cross, West End,
SauchieHalls Street West
Address: 235 North Street
Glasgow G3 7DL
Phone: 0141 221 1555

#219
Torres
Cuisines: Spanish, Tapas Bar
Average price: £11-25
Area: SauchieHalls Street, City Centre
Address: 327 SauchieHalls Street
Glasgow G2 3HW
Phone: 0141 332 6789

#220
The Arches Cafe Bar
Cuisines: French, Bar
Average price: £11-25
Area: City Centre
Address: 253 Argyle Street
Glasgow G2 8DL
Phone: 0141 565 1035

#221
Il Pavone
Cuisines: Italian
Average price: £11-25
Area: City Centre
Address: 48 Buchanan Street
Glasgow G1 3JN
Phone: 0141 221 0543

#222
Harry Ramsden's
Cuisines: Fish & Chips
Average price: £26-45
Area: South Side, Kinning Park
Address: 251 Paisley Road
Glasgow G5 8RA
Phone: 0141 429 3700

#223
Elia
Cuisines: Greek
Average price: £26-45
Area: City Centre
Address: 24 George Sq
Glasgow G2 1EG
Phone: 0141 221 9988

#224
Amber Regent
Cuisines: Chinese
Average price: £26-45
Area: City Centre
Address: 50 West Regent Street
Glasgow G2 2RA
Phone: 0141 331 1655

#225
Le Bistro Beaumartin
Cuisines: French
Average price: £11-25
Area: City Centre
Address: 161 Hope Street
Glasgow G2 2UQ
Phone: 0141 226 4442

#226
The Butterfly and Pig West End
Cuisines: Bar, British, Music Venues
Average price: £11-25
Area: Partick, West End
Address: 2 Partickbridge Street
Glasgow G11 6PL
Phone: 0141 337 1200

#227
Coffee Etc
Cuisines: Coffee & Tea, British
Average price: £26-45
Area: West End
Address: 150 Queen Margaret Drive
Glasgow G20 8NY
Phone: 0141 945 4120

#228
Fratelli Sarti
Cuisines: Italian
Average price: £11-25
Area: City Centre
Address: 121 Bath Street
Glasgow G2 2SZ
Phone: 0141 572 3344

#229
Cafe Andaluz
Cuisines: Spanish, Basque
Average price: £11-25
Area: City Centre
Address: 15 St Vincent Pl
Glasgow G1 2DW
Phone: 0141 222 2255

#230
The Hyndland Fox
Cuisines: Cafe, Scottish, Bar
Average price: £11-25
Area: West End
Address: 43 Clarence Drive
Glasgow G12 9QN
Phone: 0141 357 2909

#231
Anatolia
Cuisines: Turkish
Average price: Under £10
Area: City Centre
Address: 140 St Vincent St
Glasgow G2 5LA
Phone: 0141 221 8777

#232
Pelican
Cuisines: Seafood
Average price: £11-25
Area: West End
Address: 1377 Argyle Street
Glasgow G3 8AF
Phone: 0844 573 0670

#233
The Hyndland Cafe
Cuisines: Coffee & Tea,
Breakfast & Brunch, British
Average price: Under £10
Area: Hyndland, West End
Address: 96 Clarence Drive
Glasgow G12 9RN
Phone: 0141 334 2719

#234
The Bungo
Cuisines: Gastropub,
Breakfast & Brunch
Average price: £11-25
Area: South Side
Address: 17-21 Nithsdale Road
Glasgow G41 2AL
Phone: 0141 423 0023

#235
Rose & Grants
Cuisines: Breakfast & Brunch
Average price: Under £10
Area: City Centre, Merchant City
Address: 27 Trongate
Glasgow G1 5EZ
Phone: 0141 553 0501

#236
Nur
Cuisines: African, Middle Eastern
Average price: £11-25
Area: South Side, Tradeston
Address: 22 Bridge Street
Glasgow G5 9HR
Phone: 0141 258 2326

#237
Wee Lochan
Cuisines: Scottish
Average price: £26-45
Area: Partick, West End
Address: 340 Crow Road
Glasgow G11 7HT
Phone: 0141 338 6606

#238
Calabash
Cuisines: African
Average price: £11-25
Area: City Centre
Address: 57 Union St
Glasgow G1 3RB
Phone: 0141 221 2711

#239
Avant Garde
Cuisines: Pub, Mediterranean
Average price: £11-25
Area: City Centre, Merchant City
Address: 34-44 King Street
Glasgow G1 5QT
Phone: 0141 552 7123

#240
Esca
Cuisines: Italian
Average price: £26-45
Area: City Centre, Merchant City
Address: 27 Chisholm St
Glasgow G1 5HA
Phone: 0141 553 0880

#241
Masala Twist
Cuisines: Indian
Average price: £11-25
Area: Byres Road, Hillhead, West End
Address: 192 -194 Byres Road
Glasgow G12 8SN
Phone: 0141 339 3777

#242
Arisaig
Cuisines: Seafood, British
Average price: £11-25
Area: City Centre, Merchant City
Address: 1 Merchant Square
Glasgow G1 1NY
Phone: 0141 553 1010

#243
Lamora
Cuisines: Italian, Mediterranean
Average price: £11-25
Area: Finnieston, West End
Address: 1166 - 1170 Argyle St
Glasgow G3 8TE
Phone: 0141 560 2070

#244
Tony Macaroni
Cuisines: Italian
Average price: £11-25
Area: City Centre, Merchant City
Address: 17 John Street
Glasgow G1 1HP
Phone: 0141 552 6009

#245
The Gannet
Cuisines: Scottish, Bistro
Average price: £11-25
Area: Finnieston, West End
Address: 1155 Argyle Street
Glasgow G3 8TB
Phone: 0141 204 2081

#246
Cafe Cherubini
Cuisines: Coffee & Tea, Italian
Average price: £11-25
Area: Great Western Road, West End
Address: 360 Great Western Road
Glasgow G4 9HT
Phone: 0141 334 8894

#247
Choco-Latte
Cuisines: Coffee & Tea,
Breakfast & Brunch
Average price: £11-25
Area: Great Western Road, West End
Address: 536 Great Western Road
Glasgow G12 8EL
Phone: 0141 337 3736

#248
Arta
Cuisines: Mediterranean,
Spanish, Basque
Average price: £11-25
Area: City Centre, Merchant City
Address: 62 Albion Street
Glasgow G1 1PA
Phone: 0845 166 6018

#249
Citation Taverne and Restaurant
Cuisines: Pub, Gastropub
Average price: £26-45
Area: City Centre, Merchant City
Address: 40 Wilson Street
Glasgow G1 1HD
Phone: 0141 559 6799

#250
Ashoka Southside
Cuisines: Indian, Fast Food & Takeaway
Average price: £11-25
Area: South Side
Address: 268 Clarkston Road
Glasgow G44 3EA
Phone: 0141 637 0711

#251
Buddy's Bar Diner Grill
Cuisines: American, Barbeque, Bar
Average price: Under £10
Area: South Side
Address: 677-681 Pollokshaws Road
Glasgow G41 2AB
Phone: 0141 423 9988

#252
Grosvenor Cafe
Cuisines: Cafe
Average price: £11-25
Area: Hillhead, West End
Address: 24 Ashton Lane
Glasgow G12 8SJ
Phone: 0845 166 6028

#253
Crazy Wok
Cuisines: Chinese, Fast Food & Takeaway
Average price: £11-25
Area: Partick, West End
Address: 173 Dumbarton Rd
Glasgow G11 6AA
Phone: 0141 334 1888

#254
Al Dente
Cuisines: Italian
Average price: £11-25
Area: City Centre, Merchant City
Address: 120 Stockwell Street
Glasgow G1 4LW
Phone: 0141 237 7689

#255
Di'Maggios Pizzeria
Cuisines: Pizza
Average price: £11-25
Area: South Side, Shawlands
Address: 1038 Pollokshaws Road
Glasgow G41 3EB
Phone: 0141 632 4194

#256
West End Festival Glasgow
Cuisines: Local Flavour
Average price: Under £10
Area: Partick, West End
Address: 50 Havelock Street
Glasgow G11 5JE
Phone: 0141 341 0844

#257
Bruti Ma Buoni
Cuisines: Italian, Mediterranean
Average price: £11-25
Area: City Centre, Merchant City
Address: 106 - 108 Brunswick St
Glasgow G1 1TF
Phone: 0141 552 0001

#258
Paperinos
Cuisines: Italian, Pizza,
Fast Food & Takeaway
Average price: £11-25
Area: Byres Road, West End
Address: 227 Byres Rd
Glasgow G12 8UD
Phone: 0141 334 3811

#259
Hong Kong Express
Cuisines: Chinese, Fast Food & Takeaway
Average price: Under £10
Area: City Centre
Address: 437 SauchieHalls Street
Glasgow G2 3LG
Phone: 0141 332 2008

#260
The Burrell
Cuisines: Pub, British
Average price: £11-25
Area: South Side
Address: 1534 Pollokshaws Road
Glasgow G43 1RF
Phone: 0141 632 0161

#261
The Fifteen
Cuisines: Chinese, Fast Food & Takeaway
Average price: Under £10
Area: South Side
Address: Clarkston Road Glasgow
Phone: 0141 637 3336

#262
Roastit Bubbly Jocks
Cuisines: British
Average price: £11-25
Area: Partick, West End
Address: 450 Dumbarton Rd
Glasgow G11 6SE
Phone: 0141 339 3355

#263
Epicures of Hyndland
Cuisines: International
Average price: £11-25
Area: West End
Address: 159 Hyndland Rd
Glasgow G12 9JA
Phone: 0141 334 3599

#264
La Vita Spuntini
Cuisines: Italian, Tapas Bar
Average price: £26-45
Area: Byres Road, West End
Address: 199 Byres Road
Glasgow G12 8TN
Phone: 0141 339 4222

#265
Poa San Restaurant
Cuisines: Chinese
Average price: Under £10
Area: Dennistoun
Address: 402 Cumbernauld Road
Glasgow G31 3NN
Phone: 0141 554 1063

#266
Una Storia
Cuisines: Italian
Average price: £11-25
Area: Hillhead, West End
Address: 31 Ashton Lane
Glasgow G12 8SJ
Phone: 0141 339 1848

#267
Boteco Do Brasil
Cuisines: Bar, Brazilian, Tapas Bar
Average price: £11-25
Area: City Centre, Merchant City
Address: 62 Trongate
Glasgow G1 5EP
Phone: 0141 548 1330

#268
Hummingbird
Cuisines: Bar, British
Average price: £11-25
Area: City Centre
Address: 186 Bath St
Glasgow G2 4HG
Phone: 0141 332 8513

#269
Bar Soba
Cuisines: Bar, Asian Fusion
Average price: £11-25
Area: Byres Road, West End
Address: 116-122 Byres Road
Glasgow G12 8TB
Phone: 0141 357 5482

#270
Thai Orchid
Cuisines: Thai
Average price: £26-45
Area: City Centre
Address: 336 Argyle Street
Glasgow G2 8LY
Phone: 0141 847 0315

#271
Skinny's
Cuisines: Pub, Burgers
Average price: £11-25
Area: West End
Address: 61 Otago Street
Glasgow G12 8PQ
Phone: 0141 339 8455

#272
Assam's
Cuisines: Pakistani, Indian
Average price: £11-25
Area: City Centre
Address: 51 W Regent Street
Glasgow G2 2
Phone: 0141 331 1980

#273
Soups U
Cuisines: Coffee & Tea, Juice Bar
Average price: Under £10
Area: City Centre
Address: 146 Wellington Street
Glasgow G2 2XW
Phone: 0141 332 0500

#274
Chinatown Restaurant Glasgow
Cuisines: Chinese
Average price: £11-25
Area: City Centre
Address: 42-66 New City Rd
Glasgow G4 9JT
Phone: 0141 332 5867

#275
Panevino
Cuisines: Italian
Average price: £11-25
Area: Finnieston, West End
Address: 1075 Argyle Street
Glasgow G3 8LZ
Phone: 0141 221 1136

#276
Village Curry House
Cuisines: Indian, Pakistani
Average price: £11-25
Area: South Side, Tradeston
Address: 119 W Street
Glasgow G5 8BA
Phone: 0141 429 4610

#277
Trader Joe's
Cuisines: Gastropub
Average price: £11-25
Area: City Centre
Address: 325 Hope Street
Glasgow G2 3PT
Phone: 0141 332 4017

#278
Radisson S A S Hotel
Cuisines: Hotel, Mediterranean
Average price: £26-45
Area: City Centre
Address: Argyle Street
Glasgow G2 8DL
Phone: 0141 204 3333

#279
Bella Italia
Cuisines: Italian
Average price: £11-25
Area: City Centre
Address: 96-98 Hope Street
Glasgow G2 6PH
Phone: 0141 221 5321

#280
Fratelli Sarti
Cuisines: Italian
Average price: £11-25
Area: City Centre
Address: 133 Wellington Street
Glasgow G2 2XD
Phone: 0141 248 2228

#281
The 'Crepe A Croissant' Van
Cuisines: Coffee & Tea, Creperie
Average price: £26-45
Area: Woodlands, West End
Address: 1 Ashley St
Glasgow G3 6DR
Phone: 0141 353 2170

#282
Oriental West
Cuisines: Chinese, Fast Food & Takeaway
Average price: £11-25
Area: Great Western Road, Hillhead
Address: 609 Great Western Road
Glasgow G12 8HX
Phone: 0141 337 2370

#283
Neighbourhood Bar &Kitchen
Cuisines: Gastropub
Average price: Under £10
Area: Finnieston, West End
Address: 1046 Argyle Street
Glasgow G3 8LY
Phone: 0141 237 7931

#284
Di Maggio's Pizzeria
Cuisines: Pizza
Average price: £11-25
Area: West End
Address: 61 Ruthven Ln
Glasgow G12 9BG
Phone: 0141 334 8560

#285
Cullis Cafe Diner
Cuisines: Coffee & Tea,
Breakfast & Brunch
Average price: £11-25
Area: Partick, West End
Address: 200 Dumbarton Road
Glasgow G11 6UN
Phone: 0141 339 9788

#286
Scherezade
Cuisines: Deli
Average price: Under £10
Area: West End
Address: 47 Bank St
Glasgow G12 8NE
Phone: 0141 334 2121

#287
Alberto's
Cuisines: Fast Food & Takeaway
Average price: Under £10
Area: Dennistoun
Address: 506 Alexandra Parade
Glasgow G31 3BQ
Phone: 0141 554 2707

#288
The Libertine
Cuisines: Bar, Diner
Average price: £11-25
Area: City Centre, Merchant City
Address: 45-47 Bell Street
Glasgow G1 1NX
Phone: 0141 552 3539

#289
The Rock
Cuisines: Pub, Gastropub
Average price: Under £10
Area: Partick, West End
Address: 205 Hyndland Rd
Glasgow G12 9HE
Phone: 0141 334 6977

#290
New York Jacks
Cuisines: Fast Food & Takeaway
Average price: £11-25
Area: South Side, Mount Florida
Address: 1009 Cathcart Road
Glasgow G42 9XJ
Phone: 0141 632 8815

#291
Alla Turca
Cuisines: Turkish
Average price: £11-25
Area: City Centre
Address: 192 Pitt Street
Glasgow G2 4DY
Phone: 0141 332 5300

#292
The Waverley Tea Room
Cuisines: Bar, Italian, British
Average price: £11-25
Area: South Side
Address: 18 Moss Side Road
Glasgow G41 3TN
Phone: 0845 659 5903

#293
Tony Macaroni
Cuisines: Italian
Average price: Under £10
Area: Partick, Byres Road, West End
Address: 4 Byres Rd
Glasgow G11 5JY
Phone: 0141 334 5959

#294
Social Bite
Cuisines: Delicatessen, Cafe
Average price: Under £10
Area: City Centre
Address: 103 St Vincent Street
Glasgow G2 5EA
Phone: 0141 220 8206

#295
Las Iguanas
Cuisines: Mexican, Latin American
Average price: £11-25
Area: City Centre
Address: 16-20 West Nile Street
Glasgow G1 2PW
Phone: 0141 248 5705

#296
Blue Lagoon
Cuisines: Fast Food & Takeaway,
Fish & Chips
Average price: £11-25
Area: SauchieHalls Street, City Centre
Address: 299 SauchieHalls Street
Glasgow G2 4
Phone: 0141 332 3279

#297
Cafe Asia
Cuisines: Indian
Average price: £11-25
Area: South Side, Nitshill
Address: 1357 Barrhead Road
Glasgow G53 7DA
Phone: 0141 880 9555

#298
Lloyds No.1
Cuisines: Pub, Gastropub
Average price: £11-25
Area: City Centre
Address: 151 West George Street
Glasgow G2 2JJ
Phone: 0141 229 7560

#299
Pommes Frites
Cuisines: Fast Food & Takeaway
Average price: Under £10
Area: Charing Cross, City Centre
Address: 476 SauchieHalls Street
Glasgow G2 3JU
Phone: 0141 332 0860

#300
The Cabin
Cuisines: Irish, Karaoke
Average price: £26-45
Area: Partick
Address: 998 Dumbarton Road
Glasgow G14 9UJ
Phone: 0141 569 1036

#301
Grillicious
Cuisines: Italian
Average price: Under £10
Area: Partick, West End
Address: 643 Dumbarton Road
Glasgow G11 6HZ
Phone: 0141 337 7077

#302
The Granary
Cuisines: Pub, Gastropub
Average price: £11-25
Area: South Side, Shawlands
Address: 10 Kilmarnock Rd
Glasgow G41 3NH
Phone: 0141 649 0594

#303
Buddy's BBQ & Burgers
Cuisines: Fast Food & Takeaway
Average price: Under £10
Area: South Side, Shawlands
Address: 44 Skirving Street
Glasgow G41 3AJ
Phone: 0141 632 5417

#304
King's Lodge
Cuisines: Chinese
Average price: Under £10
Area: City Centre
Address: 91 Union Street
Glasgow G1 3TA
Phone: 0141 229 1833

#305
Shenaz Restaurant
Cuisines: Indian, Pakistani
Average price: £26-45
Area: Charing Cross, West End
Address: 17 Granville Street
Glasgow G3 7EE
Phone: 0141 564 5555

#306
Artisan Roast
Cuisines: Cafe
Average price: £11-25
Area: West End
Address: 15-17 Gibson Street
Glasgow G12 8NU
Phone: 07864 984253

#307
Italian Kitchen
Cuisines: Italian
Average price: £26-45
Area: City Centre, Merchant City
Address: 64 Ingram Street
Glasgow G1 1EX
Phone: 0141 572 1472

#308
Merchant Chippie
Cuisines: Fish & Chips
Average price: Under £10
Area: City Centre, Merchant City
Address: 155 High Street
Glasgow G1 1PH
Phone: 0141 552 5789

#309
Frankie & Benny's
Cuisines: American
Average price: £11-25
Area: South Side, Kinning Park
Address: Springfield Quay
Glasgow G5 8NP
Phone: 0141 429 0055

#310
La Tasca
Cuisines: Spanish
Average price: £26-45
Area: South Side, Nitshill
Address: Silverburn Shopping Centre
Glasgow G53 6QR
Phone: 0845 126 2964

#311
Loon Fung Restaurant
Cuisines: Chinese
Average price: Under £10
Area: Charing Cross, SauchieHalls
Street, City Centre
Address: 417-419 SauchieHalls Street
Glasgow G2 3LG
Phone: 0141 332 1240

#312
Grove Chip Shop
Cuisines: Fish & Chips
Average price: Under £10
Area: Finnieston, West End
Address: 1092 Argyle Street
Glasgow G3 8LY
Phone: 0141 221 4147

#313
Malaga Tapas
Cuisines: Tapas, Spanish
Average price: £11-25
Area: South Side
Address: 215 St Andrews Road
Glasgow G41 1PD
Phone: 0141 429 4604

#314
Pancho Villa's
Cuisines: Mexican, Tex-Mex
Average price: £11-25
Area: City Centre, Merchant City
Address: 26 Bell St
Glasgow G1 1LG
Phone: 0141 552 7737

#315
Spice Garden
Cuisines: Indian
Average price: £11-25
Area: South Side, Tradeston
Address: Clyde Place
Glasgow G5 8AQ
Phone: 0141 429 4455

#316
Malmaison Brasserie
Cuisines: Brasserie
Average price: £26-45
Area: City Centre
Address: 278 West George Street
Glasgow G2 4LL
Phone: 0141 572 1000

#317
Yiamas Greek Taverna
Cuisines: Greek
Average price: £11-25
Area: City Centre
Address: 16-20 Bath Street
Glasgow G2 1HB
Phone: 0141 353 1386

#318
Chilli Grill
Cuisines: Indian
Average price: Under £10
Area: Charing Cross, SauchieHalls Street
West, West End
Address: 515 SauchieHalls St
Glasgow G3 7PQ
Phone: 0141 221 6327

#319
Tandoori Plus
Cuisines: Fast Food & Takeaway
Average price: Under £10
Area: City Centre, Cowcaddens
Address: 21 Kennedy Path
Glasgow G4 0PP
Phone: 0141 552 5758

#320
Mings
Cuisines: Chinese
Average price: £11-25
Area: City Centre
Address: 48 Buchanan Street
Glasgow G1 3JX
Phone: 0141 248 2255

#321
McDonald's Restaurant
Cuisines: American
Average price: £26-45
Area: Finnieston, West End
Address: 47 Finnieston Street
Glasgow G3 8HB
Phone: 0141 221 9582

#322
Moyra Janes
Cuisines: Coffee & Tea,
Breakfast & Brunch
Average price: £11-25
Area: South Side
Address: 20 Kildrostan Street
Glasgow G41 4LU
Phone: 0141 423 5628

#323
Hyde Bar & Dining
Cuisines: Lounge, Steakhouse,
Cocktail Bar
Average price: £11-25
Area: Partick, West End
Address: 9-17 Partick Bridge Street
Glasgow G11 6PN
Phone: 0141 334 9568

#324
Dennistoun Bar-B-Que
Cuisines: Barbeque, Burgers,
Fast Food & Takeaway
Average price: £11-25
Area: Duke Street, Dennistoun
Address: 585 Duke Street
Glasgow G31 1PY
Phone: 0141 237 7200

#325
The Hill
Cuisines: Bar, British
Average price: £11-25
Area: Partick, Byres Road, West End
Address: 94 Byres Road
Glasgow G12 8TB
Phone: 0141 339 8558

#326
Tony's
Cuisines: Fish & Chips,
Fast Food & Takeaway
Average price: Under £10
Area: South Side
Address: Allison Street
Glasgow G42 7RX
Phone: 0141 423 4450

#327
The LUV Café
Cuisines: Coffee & Tea, Deli
Average price: Under £10
Area: South Side, Govan
Address: 1121 Govan Rd
Glasgow G51 4RX
Phone: 0141 445 0200

#328
Taco Mazama
Cuisines: Mexican
Average price: Under £10
Area: City Centre
Address: 6 Renfield Street
Glasgow G2 5AL
Phone: 0141 248 8940

#329
McDonald's Restaurant
Cuisines: American
Average price: Under £10
Area: South Side
Address: Helen Street
Glasgow G51 3HR
Phone: 0141 445 3474

#330
Michael's Superchippy
Cuisines: Fast Food & Takeaway,
Fish & Chips
Average price: £26-45
Area: South Side
Address: 891 Aikenhead Rd
Glasgow G42 0NT
Phone: 0141 632 5585

#331
Di Maggio's
Cuisines: Italian
Average price: £11-25
Area: City Centre
Address: 163 West Nile Street
Glasgow G1 2RL
Phone: 0141 333 4999

#332
Brooklyn Café
Cuisines: Cafe
Average price: £11-25
Area: South Side, Shawlands
Address: 21-23 Minard Road
Glasgow G41 2HR
Phone: 0141 632 3427

#333
Ho Wah
Cuisines: Chinese
Average price: £11-25
Area: South Side, Shawlands
Address: 95 Kilmarnock Road
Glasgow G41 3YR
Phone: 0141 632 6303

#334
Vespbar
Cuisines: Bar, Italian, Comedy Club
Average price: £11-25
Area: City Centre
Address: 14 Drury Street
Glasgow G2 5AA
Phone: 0141 204 0060

#335
Panda House
Cuisines: Chinese
Average price: £11-25
Area: South Side
Address: 665-667 Pollokshaws Rd
Glasgow G41 2AB
Phone: 0141 424 3200

#336
Walkabout
Cuisines: Pub, Sports Bar, Australian
Average price: £11-25
Area: City Centre
Address: 128 Renfield Street
Glasgow G2 3AL
Phone: 0141 332 8209

#337
Barbeque Kings
Cuisines: Fast Food & Takeaway
Average price: Under £10
Area: Great Western Road, Kelvinbridge
Address: 488 Great Western Road
Glasgow G12 8EW
Phone: 0141 357 1020

#338
Noodle Bar
Cuisines: Japanese
Average price: Under £10
Area: Charing Cross, City Centre
Address: 482 SauchieHalls Street
Glasgow G2 3LW
Phone: 0141 333 1883

#339
Clockwork Beer
Cuisines: Pub, Gastropub
Average price: £26-45
Area: South Side, Mount Florida
Address: 1153-1155 Cathcart Road
Glasgow G42 9HB
Phone: 0141 649 0184

#340
iCafe
Cuisines: Tea Room, Cafe
Average price: £11-25
Area: SauchieHalls Street, City Centre
Address: 315 SauchieHalls Street
Glasgow G2 3HW
Phone: 0141 353 1553

#341
The Bank
Cuisines: Pub, Gastropub
Average price: £11-25
Area: South Side
Address: 443 Clarkston Rd
Glasgow G44 3LL
Phone: 0141 637 8461

#342
Cafe Lapadella
Cuisines: Mediterranean
Average price: Under £10
Area: Woodlands, West End
Address: 112-124 Woodlands Road
Glasgow G3 6HB
Phone: 0141 332 6104

#343
La Parmigiana
Cuisines: Italian
Average price: Above £46
Area: Great Western Road, Kelvinbridge
Address: 447 Great Western Road
Glasgow G12 8HH
Phone: 0141 334 0686

#344
The Manchurian
Cuisines: Chinese
Average price: £11-25
Area: Partick, West End
Address: 494 Dumbarton Road
Glasgow G11 6SL
Phone: 0141 357 5858

#345
Casa Blanca
Cuisines: Italian, Fast Food & Takeaway
Average price: £11-25
Area: West End
Address: 35 Clarence Dr
Glasgow G12 9QN
Phone: 0141 339 9190

#346
Massimo Restaurant
Cuisines: Italian
Average price: £11-25
Area: Charing Cross, City Centre
Address: 57 Elmbank Street
Glasgow G2 4PQ
Phone: 0141 332 3227

#347
Juan Chihuahua
Cuisines: Mexican
Average price: £11-25
Area: SauchieHalls Street, City Centre
Address: 375 SauchieHalls Street
Glasgow G2 3HU
Phone: 0141 333 3940

#348
OKO Express
Cuisines: Sushi Bar
Average price: £11-25
Area: SauchieHalls Street, City Centre
Address: 302 SauchieHalls Street
Glasgow G2
Phone: 0141 332 5200

#349
Mr V's Fast Food
Cuisines: Fish & Chips
Average price: Under £10
Area: South Side, Mount Florida
Address: 118 Battlefield Road
Glasgow G42 9JT
Phone: 0141 649 5200

#350
Cafe India
Cuisines: Indian, Pakistani
Average price: £11-25
Area: City Centre, Merchant City
Address: 29 Albion Street
Glasgow G1 1LH
Phone: 0141 552 5115

#351
Millenium Platter
Cuisines: Buffet, Asian Fusion, Bar
Average price: £11-25
Area: Partick, West End
Address: 120 Dumbarton Rd
Glasgow G11 6NY
Phone: 0141 339 2068

#352
Italian Job Express
Cuisines: Italian
Average price: Under £10
Area: West End
Address: 607 Mayhill Road
Glasgow G20 7TY
Phone: 0141 946 6710

#353
Papa Gills Restaurant
Cuisines: British, Indian
Average price: £11-25
Area: Partick, West End
Address: 339 Dumbarton Road
Glasgow G11 6AL
Phone: 0141 337 3777

#354
Enzos Fish & Chips
Cuisines: Fish & Chips,
Fast Food & Takeaway
Average price: £11-25
Area: Shettleston
Address: 1200 Shettleston Road
Glasgow G32 7PG
Phone: 0141 778 4053

#355
Cafe Royale
Cuisines: Fast Food & Takeaway
Average price: Under £10
Area: South Side
Address: 172 Holmlea Road
Glasgow G44 4BA
Phone: 0141 637 0578

#356
Gambrino
Cuisines: Pizza, Italian
Average price: £11-25
Area: Woodlands, Great Western Road
Address: 331-333 Great Western Road
Glasgow G4 9HS
Phone: 0141 339 4111

#357
The Lee
Cuisines: Pub, Gastropub
Average price: Under £10
Area: City Centre
Address: 100 ST James Road
Glasgow G4 0PS
Phone: 0141 564 1973

#358
Pizza Magic
Cuisines: Pizza
Average price: Under £10
Area: Hyndland, West End
Address: 72 Hyndland Road
Glasgow G12 9UT
Phone: 0141 339 8544

#359
Rock Lobster
Cuisines: British, Seafood, Wine Bar
Average price: £11-25
Area: City Centre, Merchant City
Address: Unit 1/4 43 Virginia Ct
Glasgow G1
Phone: 0141 553 2326

#360
Marco Polo
Cuisines: Brasserie, Italian, French
Average price: £11-25
Area: SauchieHalls Street, City Centre
Address: 148 West Nile Street
Glasgow G1 2RQ
Phone: 0141 332 2944

#361
Arcaffe Restaurant
Cuisines: Italian
Average price: £11-25
Area: West End
Address: 11 North Claremont Street
Glasgow G3 7NR
Phone: 0141 333 1333

#362
The Project Cafe
Cuisines: Cafe
Average price: Under £10
Area: City Centre
Address: 134 Renfrew Street
Glasgow G3 6ST
Phone: 0141 332 9520

#363
Fifi & Ally
Cuisines: Tea Room, European
Average price: £26-45
Area: City Centre
Address: 80 Wellington Street
Glasgow G2 6UA
Phone: 0141 229 0386

#364
The Bistro
Cuisines: Fast Food & Takeaway
Average price: Under £10
Area: Charing Cross
Address: 488 SauchieHalls Street
Glasgow G2 3LW
Phone: 0141 332 3334

#365
Manhattans Bar Diner
Cuisines: American, Bar
Average price: £11-25
Area: South Side
Address: 235 St Andrews Road
Glasgow G41 1PD
Phone: 0141 429 4657

#366
Aubergine
Cuisines: Deli, Coffee & Tea
Average price: Above £46
Area: South Side
Address: 356 Victoria Road
Glasgow G42 8YW
Phone: 0141 423 0022

#367
Far East
Cuisines: Fast Food & Takeaway
Average price: Above £46
Area: South Side
Address: 26 Allison Street
Glasgow G42 8NN
Phone: 0141 424 1114

#368
No Way Back
Cuisines: Cafe
Average price: Under £10
Area: South Side
Address: 38 Nithsdale Road
Glasgow G41 2AN
Phone: 0141 423 6506

#369
Rasoi Indian Kitchen
Cuisines: Indian
Average price: £11-25
Area: Partick, West End
Address: 120 Dumbarton Road
Glasgow G11 6NY
Phone: 0141 339 2068

#370
Cafe Sejuiced
Cuisines: Cafe
Average price: £11-25
Area: Dennistoun
Address: 77 Hanson Street
Glasgow G31 2HF
Phone: 0141 556 6733

#371
Operetta
Cuisines: Italian
Average price: £11-25
Area: City Centre
Address: 58 Waterloo Street
Glasgow G2 7DA
Phone: 0141 204 3444

#372
China Sea Restaurant
Cuisines: Chinese
Average price: Under £10
Area: City Centre
Address: 12 Renfield Street
Glasgow G2 5AL
Phone: 0141 221 2719

#373
The Pacific
Cuisines: Bar, Thai, Mexican
Average price: £11-25
Area: Partick, West End
Address: 562 Dumbarton Road
Glasgow G11 6RH
Phone: 0141 334 9000

#374
Bombay Leaf
Cuisines: Indian
Average price: £11-25
Area: Rutherglen
Address: 209 Main Street
Glasgow G73 2HH
Phone: 0141 643 0444

#375
Ceqwa
Cuisines: Cafe
Average price: £11-25
Area: Partick, West End
Address: 692 Dumbarton Road
Glasgow G11 6RB
Phone: 0141 334 0291

#376
Cafecart
Cuisines: Cafe
Average price: Under £10
Area: South Side, Mount Florida
Address: 1036 Cathcart road
Glasgow G42
Phone: 07939 179105

#377
All Star Brunch Bar
Cuisines: Breakfast & Brunch
Average price: Under £10
Area: Charing Cross, SauchieHalls Street
West, Woodlands, West End
Address: 531 SauchieHalls Street
Glasgow G3 7PQ
Phone: 0141 222 2848

#378
Frosoulla's
Cuisines: Greek
Average price: £26-45
Area: South Side
Address: 33 Sinclair Drive
Glasgow G42 9AX
Phone: 07887 528490

#379
Stazione
Cuisines: Specialty Food, British, Italian
Average price: £26-45
Area: Great Western Road, West End
Address: 1051 Great Western Road
Glasgow G12 0XP
Phone: 0141 576 7576

#380
Missoula
Cuisines: Gastropub
Average price: £11-25
Area: City Centre
Address: 110-114 West George Street
Glasgow G2 1NF
Phone: 0141 332 9724

#381
Shimla Pinks
Cuisines: Indian, Pakistani,
Fast Food & Takeaway
Average price: £11-25
Area: South Side
Address: 777 Pollokshaws Rd
Glasgow G41 2AX
Phone: 0141 423 4488

#382
Yates
Cuisines: Pub, Gastropub
Average price: Under £10
Area: City Centre
Address: 134-136 W George Street
Glasgow G2 2HG
Phone: 0141 353 3926

#383
The Mini Bar
Cuisines: Pub, Scottish, British
Average price: £11-25
Area: City Centre
Address: 244a Bath Street
Glasgow G2 4JW
Phone: 0141 332 2732

#384
Baby Grand
Cuisines: Bar, Brasserie
Average price: £11-25
Area: Charing Cross, City Centre
Address: 3 - 7 Elmbank Garden
Glasgow G2 4NQ
Phone: 0141 248 4942

#385
Boulevard Fish Bar
Cuisines: Fast Food & Takeaway
Average price: Under £10
Area: South Side
Address: 595 Mosspark Boulevard
Glasgow G52 1SB
Phone: 0141 810 1595

#386
La Sandwicherie
Cuisines: Sandwiches, Coffee & Tea
Average price: £26-45
Area: City Centre, Cowcaddens
Address: 59 Port Dundas Road
Glasgow G4 0HF
Phone: 0141 353 3853

#387
Guido's Coronation Restaurant
Cuisines: Fish & Chips
Average price: Under £10
Area: Dennistoun, Gallowgate
Address: 55 Gallowgate
Glasgow G1 5AP
Phone: 0141 552 3994

#388
Bennys Fish & Chicken Bar
Cuisines: Fish & Chips
Average price: £11-25
Area: Dennistoun
Address: 693 Alexandra Parade
Glasgow G31 3LN
Phone: 0141 554 2915

#389
Rogano
Cuisines: Seafood, Champagne Bar
Average price: Above £46
Area: City Centre
Address: 11 Exchange Place
Glasgow G1 3AN
Phone: 0141 248 4055

#390
Gordon St Coffee
Cuisines: Cafe
Average price: Under £10
Area: City Centre
Address: 79 Gordon Street
Glasgow G1 3PE
Phone: 04414 1221 1367

#391
Himalaya
Cuisines: Indian
Average price: £11-25
Area: South Side
Address: 1878b Paisley Road W
Glasgow G52 3TN
Phone: 0141 882 3099

#392
Muse
Cuisines: Pub, Gastropub
Average price: Under £10
Area: City Centre
Address: 35 - 41 Queen Street
Glasgow G1 3EF
Phone: 0141 221 1779

#393
Panda Chinese Restaurant
Cuisines: Chinese
Average price: £11-25
Area: South Side, Kinning Park
Address: Unit D3 Springfield Quay
Glasgow G5 8NP
Phone: 0141 429 0988

#394
Pinto
Cuisines: Mexican
Average price: Under £10
Area: Buchanan Street, City Centre
Address: 5 Gordon Street
Glasgow G1 3PL
Phone: 0141 221 9330

#395
Bollywood Spice
Cuisines: Indian
Average price: Under £10
Area: Partick, West End
Address: 477 Dumbarton Road
Glasgow G11 6EJ
Phone: 0141 334 9888

#396
Mario & Sons Fast Foods
Cuisines: Fast Food & Takeaway
Average price: Under £10
Area: South Side
Address: 5 Croftfoot Road
Glasgow G44 5JR
Phone: 0141 634 3814

#397
Koh-I-Noor
Cuisines: Indian, Fast Food & Takeaway
Average price: Under £10
Area: West End
Address: 12 Gibson Street
Glasgow G12 8NX
Phone: 0141 339 1597

#398
Bella Vita
Cuisines: Italian, Pizza
Average price: £11-25
Area: South Side
Address: 597 Mosspark Boulevard
Glasgow G52 1SB
Phone: 0141 882 1144

#399
Giffnock Ivy
Cuisines: British
Average price: £26-45
Area: Giffnock, South Side
Address: 219 Fenwick Road
Glasgow G46 6JD
Phone: 0141 620 1003

#400
Simply Foods
Cuisines: Deli
Average price: Under £10
Area: Giffnock, South Side
Address: 146 Fenwick Road
Glasgow G46 6XW
Phone: 0141 621 1617

#401
The Olive Pip
Cuisines: Coffee & Tea,
Breakfast & Brunch
Average price: £11-25
Area: Partick, West End
Address: 231 Crow Rd
Glasgow G11 7PZ
Phone: 0141 334 7753

#402
Cookies Takeaway
Cuisines: Fast Food & Takeaway
Average price: Under £10
Area: City Centre
Address: 31 Hope Street
Glasgow G2 6AE
Phone: 0141 248 2458

#403
Tivoli Fish & Chips
Cuisines: Fish & Chips,
Fast Food & Takeaway
Average price: £11-25
Area: City Centre, Merchant City
Address: 39 Stockwell St
Glasgow G1 4RZ
Phone: 0141 552 1690

#404
Sutherlands
Cuisines: Fast Food & Takeaway
Average price: £11-25
Area: SauchieHalls Street West
Address: 973 SauchieHalls Street
Glasgow G3 7TQ
Phone: 0141 375 4711

#405
Crepe A Croissant
Cuisines: Fast Food & Takeaway
Average price: £11-25
Area: Woodlands, West End
Address: Ashley St
Glasgow G3 6DR
Phone: 0141 353 2170

#406
Veldt Deli
Cuisines: African, Delicatessen
Average price: Under £10
Area: Great Western Road, Kelvinbridge
Address: 407 Great Western Road
Glasgow G4 9JA
Phone: 0141 237 3352

#407
Bier Hallse
Cuisines: Pub, Gastropub, Pizza
Average price: £11-25
Area: City Centre
Address: 7-9 Gordon Street
Glasgow G1 3PL
Phone: 0141 204 0706

#408
Station Wok
Cuisines: Fast Food & Takeaway
Average price: Under £10
Area: Partick, West End
Address: 34 Merkland St
Glasgow G11 6DB
Phone: 0141 339 9988

#409
San Siro
Cuisines: Italian, Fast Food & Takeaway
Average price: Under £10
Area: Charing Cross, SauchieHalls Street West, West End
Address: 563 SauchieHalls Street
Glasgow G3 7PQ
Phone: 0141 248 4632

#410
The Sandwich Concept
Cuisines: Coffee & Tea, Sandwiches
Average price: £11-25
Area: West End
Address: 11 N Claremont St
Glasgow G3 7NR
Phone: 0141 332 3330

#411
Cailin's Sushi
Cuisines: Japanese
Average price: Under £10
Area: Finnieston, West End
Address: 1136 Argyle Street
Glasgow G3 8TD
Phone: 0141 334 8637

#412
O'Briens Sandwich Bar
Cuisines: Sandwiches
Average price: Under £10
Area: City Centre, Merchant City
Address: 241 Ingram Street
Glasgow G1 1DA
Phone: 0141 204 3552

#413
Bank Street Bar Kitchen
Cuisines: Bar, British
Average price: £11-25
Area: Hillhead, West End
Address: 52 Bank Street
Glasgow G12
Phone: 0141 334 4343

#414
Cafe Source Too
Cuisines: Gastropub
Average price: £11-25
Area: Hyndland, West End
Address: 32 Hughenden Road
Glasgow G12 9XP
Phone: 0141 357 6437

#415
Rawalpindi
Cuisines: Indian, Pakistani
Average price: £11-25
Area: SauchieHalls Street, City Centre
Address: 321 SauchieHalls Street
Glasgow G2 3HW
Phone: 0141 332 4180

#416
Wongs Restaurant
Cuisines: Chinese, Fast Food & Takeaway
Average price: £11-25
Area: West End
Address: 920 Maryhill Rd
Glasgow G20 7TA
Phone: 0141 945 4164

#417
Andiamo
Cuisines: Italian
Average price: £11-25
Area: Giffnock, South Side
Address: 223 Fenwick Road
Glasgow G46 6JG
Phone: 0141 620 3587

#418
Subway
Cuisines: Sandwiches
Average price: Under £10
Area: City Centre, Merchant City
Address: 35 Glassford Street
Glasgow G1 1UG
Phone: 0141 552 3399

#419
Eats 1 Pizza Parlour
Cuisines: Fast Food & Takeaway
Average price: Under £10
Area: City Centre
Address: 58 Howard Street
Glasgow G1 4EE
Phone: 0141 248 4260

#420
Barbushka
Cuisines: Bar, Gastropub, Pizza
Average price: Under £10
Area: SauchieHalls Street, City Centre
Address: 426-430 SauchieHalls Street
Glasgow G2 3JD
Phone: 0141 353 6715

#421
Emilia Cafe
Cuisines: Cafe, Breakfast & Brunch
Average price: Under £10
Area: Charing Cross, West End
Address: 86 Elderslie Street
Glasgow G3 7AL
Phone: 0141 204 5045

#422
Panda Hut
Cuisines: Fast Food & Takeaway
Average price: Under £10
Area: South Side, Kinning Park
Address: 61-63 Paisley Road West
Glasgow G51 1LG
Phone: 0141 429 1970

#423
Etain
Cuisines: French
Average price: £26-45
Area: City Centre
Address: Springfield Court
Glasgow G1 3DQ
Phone: 0141 225 5630

#424
China Blue
Cuisines: Chinese
Average price: £11-25
Area: SauchieHalls Street, City Centre
Address: 96 Renfield Street
Glasgow G2 1NH
Phone: 0141 333 1881

#425
Marks & Spencer Cafe
Cuisines: Coffee & Tea
Average price: Under £10
Area: City Centre, Merchant City
Address: 2-12 Argyle Street
Glasgow G2 8AA
Phone: 0141 552 4546

#426
Master Sun's Hotpot
Cuisines: Chinese
Average price: £11-25
Area: City Centre
Address: 87 Cambridge Street
Glasgow G3 6RU
Phone: 0141 258 4179

#427
Enzo's
Cuisines: Fast Food & Takeaway,
Coffee & Tea, Cafe
Average price: Under £10
Area: City Centre
Address: 138 Renfield Street
Glasgow G2 3AU
Phone: 0141 331 2272

#428
Delice of Paradise
Cuisines: Cafe
Average price: £11-25
Area: City Centre, Merchant City
Address: 7 King Street
Glasgow G1 5QZ
Phone: 0141 375 7322

#429
Roma Mia
Cuisines: Italian
Average price: £26-45
Area: South Side
Address: 164 Darnley Street
Glasgow G41 2LL
Phone: 0141 423 6694

#430
Byblos Cafe
Cuisines: Cafe, Middle Eastern
Average price: Under £10
Area: Great Western Road, Kelvinbridge
Address: 6 Park Road
Glasgow G4 9JG
Phone: 0141 339 7980

#431
Cafe Crepe
Cuisines: Coffee & Tea, Creperie
Average price: Under £10
Area: Merchant City
Address: 155 High Street
Glasgow G1 1PH
Phone: 0141 552 3256

#432
Café Source
Cuisines: Pub, Gastropub
Average price: £11-25
Area: Gallowgate
Address: 1 St Andrews Square
Glasgow G1 5PP
Phone: 0141 548 6020

#433
Tina's Quality Fries
Cuisines: Fish & Chips
Average price: £11-25
Area: South Side
Address: 329 Calder Street
Glasgow G42 7NQ
Phone: 0141 424 0585

#434
The Balcony Cafe
Cuisines: Cafe, Coffee & Tea
Average price: Under £10
Area: South Side
Address: 534 Paisley Road W
Glasgow G51 1RN
Phone: 0141 427 9550

#435
Punjabi
Cuisines: Indian
Average price: Under £10
Area: South Side
Address: 560 Paisley Rd W
Glasgow G51 1RF
Phone: 0141 427 0521

#436
Cook and Indi's World Buffet
Cuisines: Buffet
Average price: Under £10
Area: SauchieHalls Street, City Centre
Address: 410 SauchieHalls Street
Glasgow G2 3JD
Phone: 0141 333 9933

#437
KFC
Cuisines: Chicken Wings
Average price: £11-25
Area: SauchieHalls Street, City Centre
Address: 104-106 Renfield Street
Glasgow G2 1NH
Phone: 0141 332 6469

#438
Buongiorno Restaurant
Cuisines: Italian
Average price: Under £10
Area: South Side, Queen's Park
Address: 1012 Pollokshaws Road
Glasgow G41 2HG
Phone: 0141 649 1029

#439
Da Vinci
Cuisines: Indian, Food Delivery Services
Average price: Under £10
Area: South Side, Shawlands
Address: 1133 Pollokshaws Road
Glasgow G41 3YH
Phone: 0141 632 0866

#440
Steampunk Café
Cuisines: Cafe
Average price: £11-25
Area: City Centre
Address: 8 Drury Street
Glasgow G2 5AP
Phone: 0141 221 3929

#441
Fairfield Dairy
Cuisines: Deli, Sandwiches
Average price: Under £10
Area: South Side, Govan
Address: 13 Elder Street
Glasgow G51 3DY
Phone: 0141 440 2006

#442
Philpotts
Cuisines: Sandwiches, Coffee & Tea
Average price: Under £10
Area: City Centre
Address: 81 Bothwell Street
Glasgow G2 6
Phone: 0845 206 8800

#443
Roscoe's Deli Bar
Cuisines: Delicatessen, Gluten-Free
Average price: Under £10
Area: Hyndland, West End
Address: 23 Clarence Drive
Glasgow G12 9QN
Phone: 0141 334 2263

#444
Madisons
Cuisines: Fast Food & Takeaway
Average price: Under £10
Area: City Centre, Merchant City
Address: 90 George St
Glasgow G1 1RF
Phone: 0141 552 1094

#445
Blue Lagoon
Cuisines: Fast Food & Takeaway
Average price: Under £10
Area: City Centre
Address: 50 Howard Street
Glasgow G1 4EE
Phone: 0141 248 4770

#446
Balbirs Tiffin Room
Cuisines: Indian
Average price: £11-25
Area: Charing Cross, SauchieHalls Street
West, West End
Address: 573-581 SauchieHalls St
Glasgow G3 7PQ
Phone: 0141 222 2258

#447
Four Seasons
Cuisines: Chinese
Average price: £11-25
Area: City Centre
Address: 87 Cambridge St
Glasgow G3 6RU
Phone: 0141 332 2666

#448
The City Cafe
Cuisines: British
Average price: £26-45
Area: Finnieston, West End
Address: Finnieston Quay
Glasgow G3 8HN
Phone: 0141 227 1010

#449
Yen
Cuisines: Japanese, Thai
Average price: £26-45
Area: Finnieston, West End
Address: 28 Tunnel Street
Glasgow G3 8HL
Phone: 0141 847 0220

#450
Oko Express
Cuisines: Japanese, Sushi Bar
Average price: £11-25
Area: City Centre, Merchant City
Address: 80 Queen Street
Glasgow G1 3DN
Phone: 0141 248 9666

#451
La Riviera
Cuisines: Italian
Average price: £11-25
Area: Partick, West End
Address: 147 Dumbarton Road
Glasgow G11 6PT
Phone: 0141 334 8494

#452
Happy Garden
Cuisines: Chinese, Fast Food & Takeaway
Average price: £11-25
Area: South Side
Address: 186 Riverford Road
Glasgow G43 2DE
Phone: 0141 636 1421

#453
Natural Spice
Cuisines: Fast Food & Takeaway
Average price: £11-25
Area: South Side
Address: 184 Riverford Road
Glasgow G43 2DE
Phone: 0141 636 6969

#454
Kai Xin Cuisine
Cuisines: Chinese, Fast Food & Takeaway
Average price: £11-25
Area: Rutherglen
Address: 173 Main Street
Glasgow G73 2HF
Phone: 0141 647 2111

#455
New Sky Dragon
Cuisines: Cantonese,
Fast Food & Takeaway
Average price: £11-25
Area: Anniesland, West End
Address: 944 Crow Road N
Glasgow G13 1JD
Phone: 0141 950 6611

#456
The Laurels
Cuisines: Coffee & Tea,
Breakfast & Brunch
Average price: £11-25
Area: South Side
Address: 421 Clarkston Road
Glasgow G44 3LL
Phone: 0141 637 9222

#457
McDonald's Restaurant
Cuisines: Fast Food & Takeaway
Average price: Under £10
Area: City Centre
Address: 209 Argyle Street
Glasgow G2 8DL
Phone: 0141 248 7324

#458
Piazza Italia Restaurant
Cuisines: Italian
Average price: £26-45
Area: City Centre, Merchant City
Address: 15 John Street
Glasgow G1 1HP
Phone: 0141 552 4433

#459
The Lebanese
Cuisines: Middle Eastern
Average price: Under £10
Area: West End
Address: 27 Gibson Street
Glasgow G12 8NU
Phone: 0141 334 1414

#460
Happy Chippy
Cuisines: Fish & Chips
Average price: £11-25
Area: Tollcross
Address: 794 Shettleston Road
Glasgow G32 7DP
Phone: 0141 763 1118

#461
Cafe Avanti
Cuisines: Cafe
Average price: Under £10
Area: Partick, West End
Address: 24-26 Merkland Street
Glasgow G11 6DB
Phone: 0141 576 5120

#462
3 in 1 Xtra
Cuisines: Fast Food & Takeaway
Average price: Under £10
Area: Charing Cross, SauchieHalls Street
Address: 67-69 Elmbank Street
Glasgow G2 4PQ
Phone: 0141 332 4501

#463
Viva
Cuisines: Italian
Average price: £11-25
Area: City Centre
Address: 77 Bothwell Street
Glasgow G2 6TS
Phone: 0141 243 2162

#464
Burger King
Cuisines: American,
Fast Food & Takeaway
Average price: Under £10
Area: City Centre
Address: Queen Street Railway Station
Glasgow G1 2AF
Phone: 0141 332 1354

#465
Mercado Bar Espagnol
Cuisines: Spanish
Average price: £11-25
Area: City Centre, Merchant City
Address: 17 Bell St
Glasgow G1 1NU
Phone: 0141 552 3400

#466
Azzimo
Cuisines: Italian, Fast Food & Takeaway
Average price: Under £10
Area: City Centre, Merchant City
Address: 6a John Street
Glasgow G1 1
Phone: 0141 552 5151

#467
Lupe Pintos Deli
Cuisines: Deli
Average price: £11-25
Area: Woodlands, Great Western Road
Address: 313 Great Western Road
Glasgow G4 9HR
Phone: 0141 334 5444

#468
McDonalds Restaurant
Cuisines: Burgers, American
Average price: Under £10
Area: City Centre
Address: St Enoch Ctr
Glasgow G1 4BW
Phone: 0141 221 2053

#469
Baby Grand City Centre
Cuisines: Greek, Seafood, Mediterranean
Average price: Under £10
Area: City Centre, Merchant City
Address: 17 John Street
Glasgow G1 1HP
Phone: 0141 552 4017

#470
Ruby Palace
Cuisines: Chinese, Fast Food & Takeaway
Average price: £11-25
Area: South Side, Clarkston
Address: 562 Clarkston Road
Glasgow G44 3RT
Phone: 0141 637 5467

#471
Amore
Cuisines: Italian
Average price: £11-25
Area: City Centre, Merchant City
Address: 30 Ingram Street
Glasgow G1 1EZ
Phone: 0141 553 0810

#472
Chapati 3
Cuisines: Fast Food & Takeaway
Average price: Under £10
Area: Partick, West End
Address: 339 Dumbarton Road
Glasgow G11 6AL
Phone: 0141 337 1059

#473
Buongiorno
Cuisines: Brasserie
Average price: £11-25
Area: South Side, Queen's Park
Address: 1012 Pollokshaws Rd
Glasgow G41 2
Phone: 0141 649 1029

#474
Toni Restaurant
Cuisines: Italian
Average price: £26-45
Area: City Centre
Address: 64 Renfield Street
Glasgow G2 1NQ
Phone: 0141 332 5063

#475
Fino
Cuisines: Tapas Bar
Average price: £11-25
Area: Finnieston, West End
Address: North Rotunda 28 Tunnel Street,
Glasgow G3 8HL
Phone: 0141 375 1111

#476
Annie's Independent Cafe
Cuisines: British, Coffee & Tea
Average price: Under £10
Area: South Side, Shawlands
Address: 5 Abbot Street
Glasgow G41 3XE
Phone: 0141 632 3551

#477
Clansman Retail
Cuisines: Cafe, Newsagent
Average price: £11-25
Area: City Centre, Cowcaddens
Address: Killermont Street
Glasgow G2 3NW
Phone: 0141 331 1391

#478
Elbow's Cafe
Cuisines: Cafe
Average price: Under £10
Area: City Centre, Merchant City
Address: 85 High St
Glasgow G1 1NB
Phone: 0141 552 7905

#479
Smooth Boys Deli
Cuisines: Fast Food & Takeaway,
Delicatessen, Deli
Average price: £11-25
Area: South Side
Address: 26 Maxwell Road
Glasgow G41 1QE
Phone: 0141 429 1007

#480
Henleys Byre
Cuisines: Coffee & Tea, Sandwiches
Average price: Under £10
Area: Partick, Byres Road, West End
Address: 43 Byres Road
Glasgow G11 5RG
Phone: 0141 334 5270

#481
Fratelli's Restaurant
Cuisines: Italian
Average price: Above £46
Area: Cambuslang
Address: 85
Glasgow Road
Glasgow G72 7DW
Phone: 0141 642 0642

#482
Morrison's Cafe
Cuisines: Cafe
Average price: Under £10
Area: Partick, West End
Address: 1-2 Merkland Court
Glasgow G11 6BZ
Phone: 0141 399 8446

#483
KFC
Cuisines: Fried Chicken,
Fast Food & Takeaway
Average price: Under £10
Area: South Side, Nitshill
Address: 5 Darnley Mains Road
Glasgow G53 7RH
Phone: 0141 638 5474

#484
Dario Pizzaria
Cuisines: Italian, Pizza
Average price: Under £10
Area: South Side, Shawlands
Address: 20 Kilmarnock Road
Glasgow G41 3NH
Phone: 0141 636 6658

#485
Bellini
Cuisines: Italian
Average price: £11-25
Area: South Side, Shawlands
Address: 67 Kilmarnock Road
Glasgow G41 3YR
Phone: 0141 649 6096

#486
JAYZ Bar & Restaurant
Cuisines: Bar, British
Average price: £11-25
Area: South Side, Shawlands
Address: 87 Kilmarnock Road
Glasgow G41 3YR
Phone: 0141 387 9046

#487
Blue Lagoon
Cuisines: Fish & Chips,
Fast Food & Takeaway
Average price: £11-25
Area: City Centre
Address: 208 Argyle St
Glasgow G2 8HA
Phone: 0141 221 4154

#488
Wagamama
Cuisines: Japanese
Average price: £11-25
Area: South Side, Nitshill
Address: Barrhead Rd
Glasgow G53 6QR
Phone: 0141 880 5877

#489
Cafe Ludovic
Cuisines: Coffee & Tea,
Breakfast & Brunch, Sandwiches
Average price: Under £10
Area: South Side, Mount Florida
Address: 9 Lochleven Road
Glasgow G42 9JU
Phone: 0141 632 2725

#490
Brunch Cafe
Cuisines: Coffee & Tea, Sandwiches,
Fast Food & Takeaway
Average price: £11-25
Area: South Side
Address: 134 Newlands Road
Glasgow G44 4ER
Phone: 0141 633 1420

#491
AMPM
Cuisines: Fast Food & Takeaway
Average price: Under £10
Area: City Centre, Cowcaddens
Address: Buchanan Bus Station
Glasgow G2 3NW
Phone: 0141 353 2141

#492
Dragons Way
Cuisines: Fast Food & Takeaway
Average price: £11-25
Area: Rutherglen
Address: 43 Stonelaw Road
Glasgow G73 3TN
Phone: 0141 647 7676

#493
O'Neill's Irish Bar
Cuisines: Pub, Irish
Average price: Under £10
Area: City Centre
Address: 155 Queen Street
Glasgow G1 3BJ
Phone: 0141 229 5871

#494
D'nisi
Cuisines: Coffee & Tea, Cafe
Average price: £11-25
Area: South Side, Shawlands
Address: 256 Kilmarnock Road
Glasgow G41 3JF
Phone: 0141 649 2551

#495
Alishan Tandoori
Cuisines: Indian, Pakistani,
Fast Food & Takeaway
Average price: £11-25
Area: South Side, Mount Florida
Address: 250 Battlefield Road
Glasgow G42 9HU
Phone: 0141 636 1811

#496
Shezan Tandoori
Cuisines: Indian, Pakistani
Average price: £11-25
Area: South Side, Mount Florida
Address: 1096 Cathcart Road
Glasgow G42 9XW
Phone: 0141 649 4776

#497
Place to Eat
Cuisines: Brasserie
Average price: Under £10
Area: Buchanan Street, City Centre
Address: 220 Buchanan Street
Glasgow G1 2GF
Phone: 0141 353 6677

#498
Chicken Cottage
Cuisines: Fast Food & Takeaway
Average price: Under £10
Area: Gallowgate
Address: 18 High Street
Glasgow G1
Phone: 0141 552 2511

#499
Pret A Manger
Cuisines: Coffee & Tea, Sandwiches
Average price: £26-45
Area: City Centre
Address: 102-104 St Vincent Street
Glasgow G2 5UB
Phone: 020 7932 5315

#500
Wau Cafe
Cuisines: Malaysian
Average price: Under £10
Area: West End
Address: 27 Old Dumbarton Road
Glasgow G3 8RD
Phone: 07733 391447

TOP 500 ATTRACTIONS

The Most Recommended by Locals & Trevelers

(From #1 to #500)

#1
City Chambers
Category: Landmark, Historical Building
Area: City Centre, Merchant City
Address: 80 George Square
Glasgow G2 2DU United Kingdom
Phone: 0141 287 2000

#2
Glasgow Film Theatre
Category: Cinema
Area: City Centre
Address: 12 Rose Street
Glasgow G3 6RB
Phone: 0141 332 6535

#3
House For An Art Lover
Category: Landmark, Historical Building
Area: South Side
Address: 10 Dumbreck Road
Glasgow G41 5BW United Kingdom
Phone: 0141 353 4770

#4
Barrowland Ballroom
Category: Arcade, Music Venues
Area: Gallowgate
Address: 244 Gallowgate
Glasgow G4 0TT
Phone: 0141 552 4601

#5
Imax
Category: Cinema
Area: South Side, Kinning Park
Address: 50 Pacific Quay
Glasgow G51 1EA
Phone: 0141 420 5000

#6
Mitchell Library
Category: Library
Area: Charing Cross, Finnieston
Address: North Street
Glasgow G3 7DN United Kingdom
Phone: 0141 287 2872

#7
The Burrell Collection
Category: Museum
Area: South Side
Address: 2060 Pollokshaws Road
Glasgow G43 1AT
Phone: 0141 287 2550

#8
13th Note
Category: Music Venues
Area: City Centre, Merchant City
Address: 50-60 King Street
Glasgow G1 5QT
Phone: 0141 553 1638

#9
Clyde Arc Bridge
Category: Landmark, Historical Building
Area: Finnieston, West End
Address: Finnieston Glasgow
United Kingdom

#10
Grosvenor Cinema
Category: Cinema
Area: Hillhead, West End
Address: 31 Ashton Lane
Glasgow G12 8SJ
Phone: 0845 166 6002

#11
Hillhead Library
Category: Library
Area: Byres Road, Hillhead, West End
Address: 348 Byres Road
Glasgow G12 8AP United Kingdom
Phone: 0141 339 7223

#12
The Old Fruitmarket
Category: Music Venues, Theatre
Area: City Centre, Merchant City
Address: Candleriggs
Glasgow G1 1NQ
Phone: 0141 353 8000

#13
Duke of Wellington Statue
Category: Landmark, Historical Building
Area: City Centre
Address: Queen Street
Glasgow G1 3 United Kingdom
Phone:

#14
Wild Cabaret
Category: Cabaret
Area: City Centre, Merchant City
Address: 18 Candleriggs
Glasgow G1 1LD
Phone: 0141 552 6165

#15
The Kelvin Bridge
Category: Landmark, Historical Building
Area: Great Western Road, Hillhead
Address: Great Western Road
Glasgow G12 United Kingdom

#16
St Mungo Museum
of Religious Life & Art
Category: Museum
Area: Dennistoun
Address: 2 Castle St
Glasgow G4 0RH
Phone: 0141 276 1625

#17
Scotland Street School Museum
Category: Museum
Area: South Side
Address: 225 Scotland Street
Glasgow G5 8QB
Phone: 0141 287 0500

#18
Langside Library
Category: Library
Area: South Side
Address: 2 Sinclair Drive
Glasgow G42 9QE United Kingdom
Phone: 0141 276 0777

#19
Gallery Of Modern Art
Category: Art Gallery
Area: City Centre
Address: Royal Exchange Square
Glasgow G1 3AH
Phone: 0141 229 1996

#20
Tramway
Category: Theatre
Area: South Side
Address: 25 Albert Drive
Glasgow G41 2PE
Phone: 0845 330 3501

#21
Stewart Memorial Fountain
Category: Park, Landmark,
Historical Building
Area: Kelvingrove, West End
Address: Kelvingrove Park
Glasgow G12 8NR United Kingdom

#22
Theatre Royal
Category: Theatre
Area: City Centre
Address: 282 Hope Street
Glasgow G2 3QA
Phone: 0844 871 7647

#23
The Lighthouse
Category: Art Gallery
Area: City Centre
Address: 11 Mitchell Lane
Glasgow G1 3NU
Phone: 0141 276 5365

#24
Dennistoun Library
Category: Library
Area: Dennistoun
Address: 2a Craigpark
Glasgow G31 2NA United Kingdom
Phone: 0141 554 0055

#25
The Classic Grand
Category: Music Venues
Area: City Centre
Address: 18 Jamaica St
Glasgow G1 4QD
Phone: 0141 847 0820

#26
02 ABC
Category: Music Venues
Area: City Centre
Address: 300 SauchieHalls St
Glasgow G2 3JA
Phone: 0141 332 2232

#27
University of Glasgow Library
Category: Library
Area: Hillhead, West End
Address: Hillhead St
Glasgow G12 8 United Kingdom
Phone: 0141 330 6704

#28
The Shop of Interest
Category: Arts & Crafts, Art Gallery
Area: Finnieston, West End
Address: 1058 Argyle Street
Glasgow G3 8LY
Phone: 0141 221 7316

#29
Donald Dewar Statue
Category: Landmark, Historical Building
Area: Buchanan Street, City Centre
Address: Buchanan St
Glasgow G1 2FF United Kingdom

#30
Clyde Auditorium
The Armadillo
Category: Music Venues, Theatre
Area: Finnieston, West End
Address: Finnieston St
Glasgow G3 8YW
Phone: 0870 040 4000

#31
Business @ The Mitchell
Category: Library
Area: Charing Cross, West End
Address: North Street
Glasgow G3 7DN United Kingdom
Phone: 0141 287 2872

#32
King's Theatre
Category: Theatre
Area: Charing Cross, City Centre
Address: 335 Bath Street
Glasgow G2 4JN
Phone: 0844 871 7648

#33
Distill
Category: Music Venues
Area: Finnieston, West End
Address: 1102-1106 Argyle Street
Glasgow G3 7RX
Phone: 0141 337 3006

#34
The Saltire Centre
Category: Library
Area: City Centre, Cowcaddens
Address: 70 Cowcaddens Road
Glasgow G4 0BA United Kingdom
Phone: 0141 273 1000

#35
The Tenement House
Category: Local Flavour
Area: Charing Cross, City Centre
Address: 145 Buccleuch Street
Glasgow G3 6QN
Phone: 0141 333 0183

#36
Library at GOMA
Category: Library
Area: City Centre
Address: Royal Exchange Square
Glasgow G1 3AH United Kingdom

#37
O2 Academy Glasgow
Category: Music Venues
Area: South Side, Gorbals
Address: 121 Eglinton Street
Glasgow G5 9NT
Phone: 0870 0771 2000

#38
Ferry
Category: British, Music Venues
Area: Finnieston, West End
Address: 25 Anderston Quay
Glasgow G3 8BX
Phone: 0141 553 0606

#39
Giffnock Library
Category: Library
Area: Giffnock, South Side
Address: Station Road
Glasgow G46 6JF United Kingdom
Phone: 0141 577 4976

#40
Sharmanka Kinetic Theatre
Category: Cinema
Area: City Centre, Merchant City
Address: 103 Trongate
Glasgow G1 5HD
Phone: 0141 552 7080

#41
Scottish Youth Theatre
Category: Theatre
Area: City Centre, Merchant City
Address: 105 Brunswick Street
Glasgow G1 1TF
Phone: 0141 552 3988

#42
The Briggait
Category: Landmark, Historical Building
Area: City Centre, Merchant City
Address: 141 Bridgegate
Glasgow G1 5HZ United Kingdom
Phone: 0141 553 5890

#43
Maggie May's
Category: Music Venues
Area: City Centre, Merchant City
Address: 60 Trongate
Glasgow G1 5EP
Phone: 0141 548 1350

#44
Finnieston Crane
Category: Landmark, Historical Building
Area: Finnieston, West End
Address: Congress Road
Glasgow G3 8QT United Kingdom

#45
The Queen Margaret Union
Category: Music Venues
Area: Hillhead, West End
Address: University Garden
Glasgow G12 8QN
Phone: 0141 339 9784

#46
The Anatomy Museum
Category: Museum
Area: West End
Address: University of Glasgow
Glasgow G12 8QQ
Phone: 0141 330 4221

#47
Govanhill Library
Category: Library
Area: South Side
Address: 170 Langside Road
Glasgow G42 7JU United Kingdom
Phone: 0141 423 0335

#48
Citizens Theatre
Category: Theatre
Area: South Side, Gorbals
Address: 119 Gorbals Street
Glasgow G5 9DS
Phone: 0141 429 0022

#49
Cardonald Library
Category: Library
Area: South Side
Address: 1113 Mosspark Drive
Glasgow G52 3BU United Kingdom
Phone: 0141 276 0880

#50
**The Scottish Exhibition
and Conference Centre**
Category: Music Venues
Area: Finnieston, West End
Address: Finnieston Quay
Glasgow G3 8HN
Phone: 0870 040 4000

#51
Pollokshaws Library
Category: Library
Area: South Side
Address: 50 Shawbridge Street
Glasgow G43 1RW United Kingdom
Phone: 0141 632 3544

#52
Glasgow Street Feastival
Category: Festival
Area: Gallowgate
Address: 54 Carlton Entry
Glasgow G40 2SB

#53
Couper Institute Library
Category: Library
Area: South Side
Address: 84 Clarkston Road
Glasgow G44 3DA United Kingdom
Phone: 0141 637 1544

#54
University of Strathclyde Library
Category: Library
Area: City Centre, Merchant City
Address: Cathedral St
Glasgow G1 1HX United Kingdom
Phone: 0141 548 4752

#55
Kibble Palace
Category: Botanical Garden
Area: Great Western Road, Botanics
Address: 730 Great Western Road
Glasgow G12 0UE
Phone: 0141 276 1614

#56
The SSE Hydro
Category: Music Venues
Area: Finnieston, West End
Address: Exhibition Way
Glasgow G3 8WY
Phone: 0141 248 3000

#57
Alea Casino
Category: Casino
Area: South Side, Kinning Park
Address: Springfield Quay
Glasgow G5 8NP
Phone: 0141 530 1263

#58
Bell's Bridge
Category: Landmark, Historical Building
Area: Finnieston, West End
Address: Congress Road
Glasgow G3 8 United Kingdom

#59
The Ramshorn Theatre
Category: Theatre
Area: City Centre, Merchant City
Address: 98 Ingram Street
Glasgow G1 1EX
Phone: 0141 552 3489

#60
La Pasionaria
Category: Landmark, Historical Building
Area: City Centre
Address: Clyde Street
Glasgow G1 United Kingdom

#61
Glasgow Grand Ole Opry Club
Category: Social Club
Area: South Side, Kinning Park
Address: 2-4 Govan Rd
Glasgow G51 1HS
Phone: 0141 429 5396

#62
The Lighthouse Trust
Category: Museum
Area: City Centre
Address: 11 Mitchell Lane
Glasgow G1 3NU
Phone: 0141 221 6362

#63
Tolbooth Steeple
Category: Landmark, Historical Building
Area: City Centre, Merchant City
Address: Merchant City
Glasgow G13 4 United Kingdom

#64
The Cathouse
Category: Club, Music Venues
Area: City Centre
Address: 15 Union St
Glasgow G1 3RB
Phone: 0141 248 6606

#65
Centre For Contemporary Arts
Category: Theatre, Art Gallery, Museum
Area: City Centre
Address: 350 SauchieHalls Street
Glasgow G2 3JD
Phone: 0141 352 4900

#66
Tron Steeple
Category: Landmark, Historical Building
Area: City Centre, Merchant City
Address: 63 Trongate
Glasgow G1 5HB United Kingdom

#67
Riverside Museum
Category: Museum
Area: Finnieston, West End
Address: 100 Pointhouse Place
Glasgow G3 8RS
Phone: 0141 287 2720

#68
Charing Cross
Category: Landmark, Historical Building
Area: Charing Cross, SauchieHalls Street
West, Woodlands, West End
Address: 537 SauchieHalls St
Glasgow G3 7PQ United Kingdom
Phone: 07974 732371

#69
Tron Theatre
Category: Theatre
Area: City Centre, Merchant City
Address: 63 Trongate
Glasgow G1 5HB
Phone: 0141 552 3748

#70
The Mercat Building
Category: Landmark, Historical Building
Area: Gallowgate
Address: 26 Gallowgate
Glasgow G1 5AB United Kingdom

#71
Annan Gallery
Category: Art Gallery
Area: Woodlands, West End
Address: 164 Woodlands Road
Glasgow G3 6LL
Phone: 0141 332 0028

#72
3D Map Sculpture
Category: Landmark, Historical Building
Area: City Centre
Address: Buchanan Street
Glasgow United Kingdom

#73
The Butterfly and Pig West End
Category: Bar, British, Music Venues
Area: Partick, West End
Address: 2 Partickbridge Street
Glasgow G11 6PL
Phone: 0141 337 1200

#74
Odeon Cinema
Category: Cinema
Area: South Side, Kinning Park
Address: 3 Springfield Quay
Glasgow G5 8NP
Phone: 0871 224 4007

#75
The Psalmist
Category: Landmark, Historical Building
Area: Kelvingrove, West End
Address: Kelvingrove Park
Glasgow G3 8AG United Kingdom

#76
Hard Rock Café
Category: Music Venues
Area: Buchanan Street, City Centre
Address: 179 Buchanan Street
Glasgow G2 1BT

#77
Tom John Seating Area
Category: Landmark, Historical Building
Area: Kelvingrove, West End
Address: Kelvingrove Park
Glasgow G3 8AG United Kingdom

#78
Hampden Park
Category: Stadium
Area: South Side, Mount Florida
Address: Letherby Drive
Glasgow G42 9
Phone: 0141 620 4000

#79
Pollokshields Burgh Halls
Category: Landmark, Historical Building
Area: South Side
Address: 70 Glencairn Drive
Glasgow G41 4LL United Kingdom
Phone: 0141 423 8858

#80
Scottish Music Centre
Category: Music Venues
Area: City Centre, Merchant City
Address: City Halls
Glasgow G1 1NQ
Phone: 0141 552 5222

#81
Gregory Building Statue
Category: Landmark, Historical Building
Area: Hillhead, West End
Address: Lilybank Garden
Glasgow G12 8QQ United Kingdom
Phone: 0141 330 2000

#82
The Old Hairdressers
Category: Music Venues
Area: City Centre
Address: 20-28 Renfield Lane
Glasgow G2 5AR
Phone: 0141 222 2254

#83
King's Theatre
Category: Theatre, Cinema
Area: City Centre
Address: 297 Bath Street
Glasgow G2 4JN
Phone: 0141 248 5153

#84
Whiteinch Library
Category: Library
Area: Partick
Address: 14 Victoria Park Drive South
Glasgow G14 9RL United Kingdom
Phone: 0141 276 0695

#85
Mind The Gap
Category: Art Gallery
Area: Hillhead, West End
Address: 5 Cresswell Ln
Glasgow G12 8AA
Phone: 0141 334 2144

#86
West End Festival Glasgow
Category: Music Venues
Area: Partick, West End
Address: 50 Havelock Street
Glasgow G11 5JE
Phone: 0141 341 0844

#87
Partick Library
Category: Library
Area: Partick, West End
Address: 305 Dumbarton Rd
Glasgow G11 6AB United Kingdom
Phone: 0141 276 1560

#88
**Glasgow Museum
Resource Centre**
Category: Museum
Area: South Side, Nitshill
Address: 200 Woodhead Road
Glasgow G53 7NN
Phone: 0141 276 9300

#89
Cineworld Cinema
Category: Cinema
Area: Parkhead
Address: 1221 Gallowgate
Glasgow G31 4EB
Phone: 0871 200 2000

#90
Springfield Quay
Category: Landmark, Historical Building
Area: South Side, Kinning Park
Address: Paisley Road
Glasgow G5 8NP United Kingdom
Phone: 0141 418 0810

#91
Pollok House
Category: Museum
Area: South Side
Address: 2060 Pollokshaws Road
Glasgow G43 1AT
Phone: 0844 493 2202

#92
Cyril Gerber Fine Art
Category: Art Gallery
Area: City Centre
Address: 148 West Regent Street
Glasgow G2 2RQ
Phone: 0141 221 3095

#93
Winterfest George Square
Category: Music Venues
Area: City Centre, Merchant City
Address: George Sq
Glasgow G1 1DU
Phone: 0141 302 2845

#94
Andersonian Library
Category: Library
Area: City Centre
Address: 101 St James Road
Glasgow G4 0NS United Kingdom
Phone: 0141 548 3701

#95
Gilmorehill G12 Theatre
Category: Theatre
Area: Kelvingrove, West End
Address: 9-11 University Ave
Glasgow G12 8QQ
Phone: 0141 330 5522

#96
**Charles Rennie Mackintosh
Sculptures**
Category: Landmark, Historical Building
Area: City Centre
Address: Parson Street
Glasgow G4 0RX United Kingdom

#97
Glasgow Police Museum
Category: Museum
Area: City Centre, Merchant City
Address: 30 Bell Street
Glasgow G1 1LQ
Phone: 0141 552 1818

#98
**Kelvin Halls International
Sports Arena**
Category: Leisure Centre, Arena
Area: West End
Address: 1445 Argyle St
Glasgow G3 8AW
Phone: 0141 276 1450

#99
Kelvingrove Art Gallery & Museum
Category: Museum
Area: Kelvingrove, West End
Address: Argyle Street
Glasgow G3 8AG
Phone: 0141 276 9599

#100
Broadcast
Category: Music Venues
Area: Charing Cross
Address: 427 SauchieHalls Street
Glasgow G2 3LG
Phone: 0141 332 7304

#101
Medieval Garden
Category: Landmark, Historical Building
Area: City Centre, Merchant City
Address: Nicholas Street
Glasgow G1 1QB United Kingdom

#102
Roger Billcliffe Gallery
Category: Art Gallery
Area: SauchieHalls Street, City Centre
Address: 134 Blythswood Street
Glasgow G2 4EL
Phone: 0141 332 4027

#103
Spirit of Glasgow Horror Walk
Category: Walking Tour
Area: City Centre, Merchant City
Address: George Square
Glasgow G2 1DY
Phone: 0141 586 5378

#104
Ibrox Library
Category: Library
Area: South Side, Kinning Park
Address: 1-7 Midlock St
Glasgow G51 1SL United Kingdom
Phone: 0141 427 5831

#105
Aye Write!
Category: Festival
Area: Charing Cross, West End
Address: North Street
Glasgow G3 7DN
Phone: 0844 847 1683

#106
The Cameronians Scottish Rifles War Memorial
Category: Landmark, Historical Building
Area: Kelvingrove, West End
Address: Kelvingrove Park
Glasgow G3 8AG United Kingdom

#107
Glasgay
Category: Festival
Area: City Centre, Merchant City
Address: 87-91 Saltmarket
Glasgow G1 5LE
Phone: 0141 552 7578

#108
The Normandy Veterans Association Monument
Category: Landmark, Historical Building
Area: Kelvingrove, West End
Address: Kelvingrove Park
Glasgow G3 8AG United Kingdom

#109
Otis B Driftwood
Category: Music Venues
Area: SauchieHalls Street, City Centre
Address: 201 Hope Street
Glasgow G2 2UW
Phone: 0141 332 1469

#110
Quaker Burial Ground
Category: Landmark, Historical Building
Area: Partick, West End
Address: Keith Street
Glasgow G11 6QQ United Kingdom

#111
Trongate 103
Category: Art Gallery
Area: City Centre, Merchant City
Address: 103 Trongate
Glasgow G1 5HD
Phone: 0141 276 8380

#112
Scottish Ballet
Category: Theatre
Area: South Side
Address: 25 Albert Drive
Glasgow G41 2PE
Phone: 0141 331 2931

#113
Rolls Royce Social Club
Category: Social Club
Area: South Side
Address: 1 Beech Avenue
Glasgow G41 5DF
Phone: 0141 427 7708

#114
**Elder Park Library
and Learning Centre**
Category: Library
Area: South Side, Govan
Address: 228A Langlands Road
Glasgow G51 3TZ United Kingdom
Phone: 0141 276 1540

#115
Gatekeeper's Building
Category: Landmark, Historical Building
Area: South Side
Address: 2060 Pollokshaws Rd
Glasgow G43 1AT United Kingdom

#116
Southside Art
Category: Art Gallery
Area: South Side
Address: 26-28 Battlefield Road
Glasgow G42 9QH
Phone: 0141 649 8888

#117
Pollokshields Library
Category: Library
Area: South Side
Address: 30 Leslie Street
Glasgow G41 2LB United Kingdom
Phone: 0141 423 1460

#118
Thornliebank Library
Category: Library
Area: Thornliebank, South Side
Address: 1 Spiersbridge Road
Glasgow G46 7SJ United Kingdom
Phone: 0141 577 4983

#119
Celtic Park
Category: Stadium
Area: Parkhead
Address: Kerrydale St
Glasgow G40 3
Phone: 0845 671 1888

#120
The Howlin' Wolf
Category: Music Venues
Area: City Centre
Address: 100 Bath St
Glasgow G2 2EN
Phone: 0141 333 3333

#121
Ivory Blacks
Category: Music Venues
Area: City Centre
Address: 56 Oswald St
Glasgow G1 4PL
Phone: 0141 248 4114

#122
Braehead Arena
Category: Theatre, Arena,
Music Venues
Area: City Centre
Address: Unit 25 Braehead Shopping
Centre, Glasgow G51 4BN
Phone: 0141 885 4600

#123
Arteries Gallery
Category: Art Gallery
Area: SauchieHalls Street, City Centre
Address: 127 Douglas Street
Glasgow G2 4JX
Phone: 0141 333 0999

#124
Creation Studio
Category: Music Venues
Area: City Centre, Merchant City
Address: 16 Trongate
Glasgow G1 5EU
Phone: 0141 237 7653

#125
**Glasgow International
Jazz Festival**
Category: Festival
Area: City Centre, Merchant City
Address: 81 High St
Glasgow G1 1NB
Phone: 0141 552 3552

#126
**Castlemilk Library
and Learning Centre**
Category: Library
Area: South Side
Address: 100 Castlemilk Drive
Glasgow G45 9TN United Kingdom
Phone: 0141 276 0731

#127
The Box
Category: Music Venues
Area: City Centre
Address: 431 SauchieHalls Street
Glasgow G2 3LG
Phone: 0141 332 5059

#128
**Royal Highland Fusiliers
Regimental Museum**
Category: Museum
Area: Charing Cross, City Centre
Address: 518 SauchieHalls Street
Glasgow G2 3LW
Phone: 0141 332 5639

#129
The Stitchery
Category: Creative Sewing Classes
Area: Charing Cross, West End
Address: 2/2 50 Kent Road
Glasgow G3 7EF
Phone: 07969 044462

#130
Mitchell Theatre
Category: Theatre
Area: Charing Cross, West End
Address: 6 Granville Street
Glasgow G3 7EE
Phone: 0141 287 4855

#131
Ceroc Scotland Glasgow
Category: Music Venues,
Dance Studio, Jazz & Blues
Area: City Centre
Address: 292 SauchieHalls Street
Glasgow G2 3JA
Phone: 07528 694901

#132
Welcome Home
Category: Art Gallery
Area: City Centre
Address: 350 SauchieHalls Street
Glasgow G2 3JD
Phone: 0141 334 9598

#133
Scottish Ensemble
Category: Musician/Band
Area: City Centre
Address: 350 SauchieHalls Street
Glasgow G2 3JD
Phone: 0141 332 4747

#134
Art In The City
Category: Art Gallery
Area: City Centre, Merchant City
Address: 157 Howard Street
Glasgow G1 4HF
Phone: 0141 552 5017

#135
Glasgow Bridge
Category: Landmark, Historical Building
Area: City Centre
Address: 80 Jamaica Street
Glasgow G1 4QG United Kingdom

#136
**Scottish Food
and Drink Fortnight**
Category: Festival
Area: West End
Address: 11 Fitzroy Place
Glasgow G3 7RW
Phone: 0141 221 0707

#137
Friends of Sharmanka
Category: Theatre
Area: City Centre, Merchant City
Address: 64 Osborne St
Glasgow G1 5QH
Phone: 0141 552 7080

#138
**Dr Sketchy's Burlesque
Art WorkShop**
Category: Theatre
Area: City Centre
Address: 253 Argyle St
Glasgow G2 8
Phone: 0141 565 1000

#139
Wincher's Stance
Category: Sculpture
Area: City Centre, Cowcaddens
Address: Killermont Street
Glasgow G2 3NW

#140
Gala Casinos
Category: Casino
Area: Charing Cross, City Centre
Address: 528 SauchieHalls Street
Glasgow G2 3LW
Phone: 0141 332 8171

#141
Glasgow Print Studio
Category: Theatre
Area: City Centre, Merchant City
Address: Trongate 103
Glasgow G1 5HD
Phone: 0141 552 0704

#142
Rutherglen Library
Category: Library
Area: Rutherglen
Address: 163 Main Street
Glasgow G73 2HB United Kingdom
Phone: 0141 647 6453

#143
Indepen Dance
Category: Theatre
Area: City Centre, Merchant City
Address: 141 Bridgegate
Glasgow G1 5HZ
Phone: 0141 559 4930

#144
Scotfairs Antique &
Collectors Fair
Category: Antiques
Area: West End
Address: Argyle St
Glasgow G3 8AW
Phone: 01764 654555

#145
The Coach House Trust Gallery
Category: Art Gallery
Area: Great Western Road, West End
Address: 518 Great Western Rd
Glasgow G12 8EL
Phone: 0141 341 0993

#146
Carlton Bingo Club
Category: Bingo
Area: Partick, West End
Address: 201-203 Dumbarton Road
Glasgow G11 6AA
Phone: 0141 339 8812

#147
Dance Factory
Category: Dance School, Theatre
Area: South Side
Address: 142 Calder Street
Glasgow G42 7QP
Phone: 0141 423 9430

#148
Hunterian Art Gallery
and The Mackintosh House
Category: Art Gallery, Museum
Area: Hillhead, West End
Address: 82 Hillhead Street
Glasgow G12 8QQ
Phone: 0141 330 5431

#149
By Distinction Art
Category: Art Gallery
Area: Partick, Byres Road, West End
Address: 100 Byres Road
Glasgow G12 8TB
Phone: 07973 315460

#150
Shawfield Greyhound
Racing & Leisure
Category: Stadium
Area: Rutherglen
Address: Rutherglen Road
Glasgow G73 1SZ
Phone: 0141 647 4121

#151
Glasgow Summer Sessions
Category: Music Venues
Area: South Side
Address: Bellahouston Park
Glasgow GB41

#152
The Gallery
Category: Art Gallery
Area: City Centre, Merchant City
Address: Virginia Ct
Glasgow G1 1TS

#153
Flat Rate Theatre Company
Category: Theatre
Area: Dennistoun
Address: 224 Meadowpark Street
Glasgow G31 3DJ

#154
The Old Barn
Category: Yoga, Cultural Center
Area: South Side
Address: 82 Dumbreck Rd
Glasgow G41 4SN
Phone: 07712 674802

#155
The Scottish Football Museum
Category: Football, Museum
Area: South Side, Mount Florida
Address: Hampden Park
Glasgow G42 9BA
Phone: 0141 616 6139

#156
Cambuslang Library
Category: Library
Area: Cambuslang
Address: 6 Glasgow Road
Glasgow G72 7BW United Kingdom
Phone: 0141 641 3909

#157
Zebra Bar & Cafe
Category: Music Venues
Area: City Centre, Merchant City
Address: 32-34 Queen Street
Glasgow G1 3DX
Phone: 0141 221 8954

#158
**The Glasgow Royal
Concert Halls**
Category: Music Venues
Area: Buchanan Street, City Centre
Address: 2 SauchieHalls Street
Glasgow G2 3NY
Phone: 0141 353 8000

#159
Gala Casino
Category: Casino
Area: City Centre, Merchant City
Address: 16-18 Glassford Street
Glasgow G1 1UL
Phone: 0141 553 5410

#160
Linen 1906
Category: Music Venues
Area: South Side, Shawlands
Address: 1110 Pollokshaws Road
Glasgow G41 2HG
Phone: 0141 649 3815

#161
Tall Ship At Glasgow Harbour
Category: Museum
Area: Finnieston, West End
Address: 100 Stobcross Road
Glasgow G3 8QQ
Phone: 0141 222 2513

#162
The Arches Theatre
Category: Art Gallery
Area: City Centre
Address: 253 Argyle Street
Glasgow G2 8DL
Phone: 0141 585 1000

#163
Fireman Gates
Category: Theatre
Area: Maryhill
Address: Maryhill Glasgow G20

#164
Visible Fictions
Category: Theatre
Area: City Centre
Address: 11 Bothwell Street
Glasgow G2 6LY
Phone: 0141 221 8727

#165
Arc Studio
Category: Theatre, Music Venues
Area: South Side, Tradeston
Address: 65 Commerce Street
Glasgow G5 8AD
Phone: 0141 418 0818

#166
Mecca Bingo
Category: Bingo
Area: South Side, Kinning Park
Address: Springfield Quay
Glasgow G5 8NP
Phone: 0141 418 0106

#167
Highlight
Category: Comedy Club
Area: City Centre
Address: 11 Renfrew St
Glasgow G2 3AB
Phone: 0844 844 0044

#168
Carlton Studio
Category: Music Venues, Theatre
Area: South Side, Gorbals
Address: 54 Carlton Pl
Glasgow G5 9TW
Phone: 0141 429 5723

#169
Art Exposure Gallery
Category: Art Gallery
Area: City Centre, Merchant City
Address: 19 Parnie Street
Glasgow G1 5
Phone: 0141 552 7779

#170
Hope Street Studio
Category: Creative Workspace
Area: City Centre
Address: 15 Hope St
Glasgow G2 8
Phone: 0141 221 5888

#171
National Theatre Of Scotland
Category: Theatre
Area: City Centre
Address: 45 Hope Street
Glasgow G2 6AE
Phone: 0141 221 8181

#172
Berkeley 2
Category: Music Venues,
Recording Studio
Area: Finnieston, West End
Address: 93 Lancefield Street
Glasgow G3 8HZ
Phone: 0141 248 1822

#173
Audio
Category: Music Venues
Area: City Centre
Address: 14 Midland Street
Glasgow G1 4PP

#174
B A F T A Scotland
Category: Social Club
Area: City Centre
Address: 249 West George Street
Glasgow G2 4QE
Phone: 0141 302 1770

#175
Scottish Opera
Category: Theatre
Area: Charing Cross, City Centre
Address: 39 Elmbank Crescent
Glasgow G2 4PT
Phone: 0141 332 9000

#176
Royal Faculty Of Procurators
Category: Library
Area: Buchanan Street, City Centre
Address: 12 Nelson Mandela Place
Glasgow G2 1BT United Kingdom
Phone: 0141 331 0533

#177
Compass Gallery
Category: Art Gallery
Area: City Centre
Address: 178 West Regent Street
Glasgow G2 4RL
Phone: 0141 221 6370

#178
Apollo Players
Category: Theatre
Area: South Side, Gorbals
Address: 71 Oxford Street
Glasgow G5 9EP
Phone: 0141 420 3636

#179
Merchant City Public Art Trail
Category: Landmark, Historical Building
Area: City Centre
Address: Royal Exchange Square
Glasgow G1 United Kingdom

#180
Vanishing Point Theatre
Category: Theatre
Area: City Centre
Address: 350 SauchieHalls Street
Glasgow G2 3JD
Phone: 0141 353 1315

#181
Cryptic
Category: Theatre
Area: City Centre
Address: 350 SauchieHalls St
Glasgow G2 3JD
Phone: 0141 354 0544

#182
Suspect Culture
Category: Theatre
Area: City Centre
Address: 350 SauchieHalls Street
Glasgow G2 3JD
Phone: 0141 332 9775

#183
Art
Category: Art Supplies, Art Gallery
Area: Buchanan Street, City Centre
Address: 220 Buchanan Street
Glasgow G2 3GF

#184
Theatre Babel
Category: Theatre
Area: Charing Cross, SauchieHalls Street
West, West End
Address: 11 Sandyford Place
Glasgow G3 7NB
Phone: 0141 226 8806

#185
Playwrights Studio Scotland
Category: Theatre
Area: SauchieHalls Street, City Centre
Address: SauchieHalls Street
Glasgow G2 3JD
Phone: 0141 332 6352

#186
Mischief La Bas
Category: Theatre
Area: City Centre, Merchant City
Address: 141 Bridgegate
Glasgow G1 5HZ
Phone: 0141 559 4920

#187
**The Royal Scottish
National Orchestra**
Category: Symphony Orchestra
Area: Charing Cross, West End
Address: 73 Claremont Street
Glasgow G3 7JB
Phone: 0141 226 3868

#188
Street Level Photo Works
Category: Photographers, Art Gallery
Area: City Centre, Merchant City
Address: 26 King St
Glasgow G1 5QP
Phone: 0141 552 2323

#189
Glasgow Print Studio
Category: Theatre, Art Gallery
Area: City Centre, Merchant City
Address: 48 King Street
Glasgow G1 5QT
Phone: 0141 552 0704

#190
Anderston Library
Category: Library
Area: Charing Cross, West End
Address: Berkeley Street
Glasgow G3 7DX United Kingdom
Phone: 0141 287 2872

#191
Transmission Gallery
Category: Art Gallery
Area: City Centre, Merchant City
Address: 28 King St
Glasgow G1 5QP
Phone: 0141 552 7141

#192
Sounds Of Progress
Category: Theatre
Area: City Centre, Merchant City
Address: 73-77 Trongate
Glasgow G1 5HB
Phone: 0141 548 8929

#193
Irn Bru Carnival
Category: Festival, Amusement Park
Area: Finnieston, West End
Address: Exhibition Way
Glasgow G3 8YW
Phone: 0141 248 3000

#194
Tracey McNee Fine Art
Category: Art Gallery
Area: City Centre, Merchant City
Address: 45 Parnie St
Glasgow G1 5LU

#195
R A F A Club
Category: Social Club
Area: Woodlands, West End
Address: 27 Ashley Street
Glasgow G3 6DR
Phone: 0141 332 4465

#196
Gallery 23
Category: Art Gallery
Area: City Centre, Merchant City
Address: 23 Parnie Street
Glasgow G1 5RJ
Phone: 0141 552 6325

#197
Glasgow International
Festival of Visual Art
Category: Festival
Area: City Centre, Merchant City
Address: 20 Trongate
Glasgow G1 5

#198
Cherub Statue
Category: Statue
Area: City Centre, Merchant City
Address: Trongate
Glasgow G1 5HB

#199
Vertigo
Category: Music Venues
Area: City Centre, Merchant City
Address: 90 John Street
Glasgow G1 1JH

#200
The Barony Halls
Category: Music Venues
Area: City Centre, Merchant City
Address: 16 Rottenrow East
Glasgow G4 0

#201
The Italian Garden
Category: Botanical Garden
Area: Kelvingrove, West End
Address: Argyle Street
Glasgow G3 8AG

#202
Bard in the Botanics
Category: Botanical Garden
Area: Hillhead, West End
Address: Byres Rd
Glasgow G12 8

#203
Otago Studio
Category: Art Gallery
Area: Great Western Road, Kelvinbridge
Address: 39b Otago St
Glasgow G12 8JJ
Phone: 0141 334 1159

#204
Junction 25
Category: Theatre
Area: South Side
Address: 25 Albert Dr
Glasgow G41 2PE

#205
The Mackintosh Church
at Queens Cross
Category: Museum, Church
Area: West End
Address: 870 Garscube Road
Glasgow G20 7EL
Phone: 0141 946 6600

#206
Sweeney's on the Park
Category: Music Venues
Area: South Side, Queen's Park
Address: 958 Pollokshaws Road
Glasgow G41 2ET
Phone: 0141 632 6741

#207
Cottier Theatre
Category: Theatre
Area: Partick, West End
Address: Hyndland Street
Glasgow G11 5PS
Phone: 0141 357 4000

#208
Urban Central
Category: Theatre, Comedy Club
Area: City Centre
Address: 5 Dixon Street
Glasgow G1 4AL
Phone: 0141 248 1223

#209
**National Trust for Scotland
Pollok House**
Category: Museum
Area: City Centre
Address: Pollok Country Park
Glasgow G43 1AT
Phone: 0141 616 6410

#210
Yarrow Recreation Club
Category: Social Club
Area: Anniesland
Address: 223 Anniesland Road
Glasgow G13 1RP
Phone: 0141 959 5298

#211
Manor Park Hotel
Category: Art Gallery
Area: Partick, West End
Address: 28 Balshagray Drive
Glasgow G11 7DD
Phone: 0141 339 2143

#212
Mansfield Park Gallery
Category: Art Gallery
Area: Partick, West End
Address: 5 Hyndland Street
Glasgow G11 5QE
Phone: 0141 342 4124

#213
Pollok Garden
Category: Botanical Garden
Area: South Side
Address: 2060 Pollokshaws Road
Glasgow G43 1AT

#214
William Hill Bookmakers
Category: Bookmakers
Area: Partick, West End
Address: 395 Dumbarton Rd
Glasgow G11 6BE
Phone: 0870 518 1715

#215
Linn Park Adventure Playground
Category: Playground
Area: South Side, Clarkston
Address: 145 Netherlee Road
Glasgow G44 3ST
Phone: 0141 633 1493

#216
Scout Association
Category: Youth Organisation,
Social Club
Area: South Side
Address: 147 Mossgiel Road
Glasgow G43 2BY
Phone: 0141 637 4683

#217
William Hill
Category: Gambling
Area: South Side
Address: 279 Clarkston Road
Glasgow G44 3

#218
Gala Riverboat
Category: Gambling
Area: City Centre
Address: 61 Broomielaw
Glasgow G1 4RJ
Phone: 0141 226 6000

#219
ScotlandArt
Category: Art Gallery
Area: City Centre
Address: 193 Bath St
Glasgow G2 4HU
Phone: 0141 221 4502

#220
McMillan Reading Room
Category: Library
Area: West End
Address: University Avenue
Glasgow G12 United Kingdom
Phone: 0141 330 6705

#221
The Forbidden Gentlemen's Club
Category: Social Club
Area: City Centre, Merchant City
Address: 96 Maxwell Street
Glasgow G1 4EQ
Phone: 0141 221 6511

#222
McLellan Gallery
Category: Art Gallery
Area: City Centre
Address: 270 SauchieHalls Street
Glasgow G2 3EH
Phone: 0141 353 4500

#223
2Canvas Gallery
Category: Art Gallery, Framing
Area: City Centre, Merchant City
Address: 155 Stockwell St
Glasgow G1 4LR
Phone: 0141 552 0005

#224
Bean Sculptures
Category: Sculptures
Area: City Centre
Address: 15 York Street
Glasgow G2 8JQ

#225
Jongleurs Comedy Club
Category: Social Club
Area: City Centre, Merchant City
Address: 20 Glassford Street
Glasgow G1 1UL
Phone: 0870 011 1960

#226
The Hidden Lane Gallery
Category: Art Gallery
Area: Finnieston, West End
Address: 1081 Argyle Street
Glasgow G3 8LZ
Phone: 0141 204 3139

#227
Starving Artist Studio
Category: Art Gallery
Area: City Centre
Address: SauchieHalls Street
Glasgow G2 3DH
Phone: 0141 332 4287

#228
Ladywell Crystals and Healing
Category: Psychic, Astrologer
Area: Dennistoun
Address: 270 High Street
Glasgow G4 0QT
Phone: 0141 552 7810

#229
One World Shop
Category: Fair Trade
Area: Partick, Byres Road, West End
Address: 100 Byres Road
Glasgow G12 8TB
Phone: 0141 337 6117

#230
Upfront Originals
Category: Library
Area: South Side, Queen's Park
Address: 5 Maybank Street
Glasgow G42 8QP United Kingdom
Phone: 0141 423 3168

#231
Fablevision
Category: Theatre
Area: South Side, Govan
Address: 7 Water Row
Glasgow G51 3UW
Phone: 0141 425 2020

#232
Mishka
Category: Psychic, Astrologer
Area: Partick, West End
Address: 7 Hayburn Street
Glasgow G11 6DE
Phone: 0141 334 7414

#233
Shawfield Stadium
Category: Stadium
Area: Rutherglen
Address: 137 Rutherglen Road
Glasgow G73 1SZ
Phone: 0141 647 4121

#234
Mecca Bingo
Category: Bingo
Area: Parkhead
Address: 1221 Gallowgate
Glasgow G31 4EB
Phone: 0141 550 3774

#235
Glencairn Football Social Club
Category: Social Club
Area: Rutherglen
Address: Glasgow Road
Glasgow G73 1ST
Phone: 0141 647 4831

#236
Coral
Category: Gambling
Area: South Side
Address: 216 Newlands Road
Glasgow G44 4EU

#237
Snookascene
Category: Social Club,
Snooker & Pool Halls
Area: Parkhead
Address: 22-24 Tollcross Road
Glasgow G31 5EH

#238
Christo's
Category: Art Gallery
Area: Great Western Road, Hillhead
Address: 595 Great Western Road
Glasgow G12 8HX
Phone: 0141 579 0004

#239
Noble Leisure
Category: Gambling
Area: City Centre
Address: 14-16 Renfield Street
Glasgow G2 5AL
Phone: 0141 248 5099

#240
Red Leaf Restaurant
Category: Gambling, British
Area: South Side, Kinning Park
Address: Springfield Quay
Glasgow G5 8NP
Phone: 0141 555 6100

#241
Genting Casino
Category: Casino
Area: Charing Cross, SauchieHalls Street
West, Woodlands, West End
Address: 506 - 516 SauchieHalls Street
Glasgow G2 3LW
Phone: 0141 332 0992

#242
James Walter Gallery
Category: Art Gallery
Area: City Centre, Merchant City
Address: 47 Parnie St
Glasgow G1 5LU
Phone: 0141 552 8207

#243
Glasgow Art Centre
Category: Contemporary Arts
Area: City Centre, Merchant City
Address: 7 Trongate
Glasgow G1 5
Phone: 0141 552 1311

#244
William Hill Bookmakers
Category: Gambling
Area: Great Western Road, Hillhead
Address: 532 Great Western Road
Glasgow G12 8EL
Phone: 0870 518 1715

#245
Ladbrokes
Category: Gambling
Area: Partick, West End
Address: 326 Dumbarton Road
Glasgow G11 6

#246
Gymboree Play
Category: Play & Music,
Children's Classes
Area: Partick, West End
Address: 117 Crow Road
Glasgow G11 7SJ
Phone: 0141 357 3597

#247
Cineworld Cinema
Category: Cinema
Area: City Centre
Address: 7 Renfrew Street
Glasgow G2 3AB
Phone: 0871 200 2000

#248
**Wine UnearthedGlasgow
Wine Tasting**
Category: Wineries
Area: City Centre
Address: 301 Argyle Street
Glasgow G2 8DL
Phone: 0845 680 8367

#249
Maryhill Burgh Halls
Category: Cultural Center,
Music Venues
Area: West End
Address: 10-24 Gairbraid Avenue
Glasgow G20 8YE
Phone: 0845 860 1891

#250
Hands On Production Services
Category: Event Planning & Services
Area: South Side, Govan
Address: 79 Loanbank Quadrant
Glasgow G51 3HZ
Phone: 0141 440 2005

#251
Castle Gallery
Category: Art Gallery
Area: City Centre
Address: Princes Square 48 Buchanan
Street, Glasgow G1 2GF
Phone: 0141 221 6867

#252
Headhunter Records
Category: Independent Record Label
Area: South Side, Kinning Park
Address: Stanley Street Lane
Glasgow G41
Phone: 0141 429 7111

#253
G12
Category: Theatre, Dance Studio, Dance
School, Kids Activities
Area: City Centre
Address: With studio's all over Glasgow
Glasgow G2 3PN
Phone: 0845 299 0842

#254
Love Drawing!
Category: Painting & Sculpture
Area: Buchanan Street, City Centre
Address: Unit 6932 PO Box 26965
Glasgow G1 2NG
Phone: 07758 561050

#255
Shadow Sound
Category: Theatre
Area: City Centre
Address: Andrew Ct
Glasgow G1 5
Phone: 0141 941 2654

#256
Toby's Bar
Category: Social Club
Area: Anniesland
Address: 76 Southbrae Drive
Glasgow G13 1PP
Phone: 0141 950 3253

#257
JMD Entertainments
Category: Wedding Dj Hire
Area: South Side, Kinning Park
Address: Middlesex Garden
Glasgow G41 1
Phone: 07907 201735

#258
**Glasgow International
Comedy Festival**
Category: Festival
Area: Dennistoun
Address: 278 High Street
Glasgow G4 0QT
Phone: 0141 552 2070

#259
Mosque Al-Khizra
Category: Muslim Mosque
Area: South Side
Address: 7 Langside Road
Glasgow G42 7

#260
The Dawn Patrol
Category: Theatre
Area: Kelvinbridge, West End
Address: 32 Lansdowne Crescent
Glasgow G20 6NH
Phone: 07580 423813

#261
Welcome Home
Category: Art Gallery
Area: Partick, West End
Address: 19 Keith Street
Glasgow G11 6QQ
Phone: 0141 334 9598

#262
Vivace Theatre School
Category: Specialty School,
Theatre, Kids Activities
Area: City Centre
Address: 5 Dixon House
Glasgow G1 4AL
Phone: 07740 585506

#263
Mary Mary
Category: Art Gallery
Area: City Centre
Address: Suite 2/1 6 Dixon Street
Glasgow G1 4AX
Phone: 0141 226 2257

#264
Mandors Fabric Store
Mandor Textile Centre
Category: Haberdashery & Fabrics
Area: City Centre
Address: Fleming House 134 Renfrew
Street, Glasgow G3 6ST
Phone: 0141 332 4435

#265
K J M Management
Category: Arts & Entertainment
Area: Charing Cross, Woodlands
Address: 4 Woodside Place
Glasgow, Glasgow G3 7QF
Phone: 0141 353 5000

#266
DNA hub
Category: Art Gallery
Area: City Centre, Merchant City
Address: 12-16 S Frederick St
Glasgow G1 1HJ

#267
The Hidden Lane
Category: Art Gallery
Area: Finnieston, West End
Address: 1103 Argyle St
Glasgow G3 8ND

#268
Tracey Mcmee
Category: Art Gallery
Area: City Centre, Merchant City
Address: 47-51 Parnie Street
Glasgow G1 5LU
Phone: 0141 552 5627

#269
Limelight Studio
Category: Cultural Center
Area: City Centre, Merchant City
Address: 73 Trongate
Glasgow G1

#270
Clyde Marine Recruitment
Category: Theatre
Area: South Side, Kinning Park
Address: 209 Govan Road
Glasgow G51
Phone: 0141 427 5100

#271
High Street Gallery
Category: Art Gallery
Area: Dennistoun, Gallowgate
Address: 40a High Street
Glasgow G1 1NL
Phone: 0141 552 4100

#272
Caveroom
Category: Art Gallery
Area: Dennistoun, Gallowgate
Address: 203 Bell Street
Glasgow G4

#273
Ivan Coghill
Category: School of Art
Area: West End
Address: Otago Street
Glasgow G12 8PB
Phone: 07946 860949

#274
Barras Art & Design Centre
Category: Art & Design
Area: Gallowgate
Address: 54 Calton Entry
Glasgow G40 2SB

#275
Whoyalookinit Tours
Category: Tour
Area: Dennistoun
Address: 23 Appin Crescent
Glasgow G31 3RL
Phone: 0141 550 4607

#276
Gestalt Glass
Category: Glass Studio
Area: Dennistoun, Parkhead
Address: 23 Fleming Street
Glasgow G31
Phone: 07963 028550

#277
The West End Wedding Show
Category: Festival, Wedding Planning
Area: Byres Road, West End
Address: Oran Mor 731 - 735 Great
Western Road Glasgow
Phone: 0845 269 2189

#278
Lime Blew Gallery
Category: Art Gallery, Eyelash Service
Area: West End
Address: 18 Ruthven Lane
Glasgow G12 9BG
Phone: 0141 339 4886

#279
Pollok Ex Servicemens Club
Category: Social Club
Area: South Side
Address: 111 Titwood Road
Glasgow G41 2DG
Phone: 0141 632 9182

#280
Westbourne Music
Category: Arcade
Area: Partick, West End
Address: 50 Havelock Street
Glasgow G11 5JE
Phone: 0141 337 3262

#281
Joe Hendry Original Art
Category: Paintings, Art Prints
Area: Dennistoun
Address: 77 Hanson Street
Glasgow G31 2HF
Phone: 07869 117769

#282
McTear's Fine Art
Auctioneers & Valuers
Category: Antiques, Auction House
Area: South Side
Address: 31 Meiklewood Road
Glasgow G51
Phone: 0141 810 2880

#283
Southside Beer Festival
Category: Festival
Area: South Side, Queen's Park
Address: 5 Langside Avenue
Glasgow G41 2QR
Phone: 0141 649 9460

#284
Paddy Power
Category: Arcade
Area: Duke Street, Dennistoun
Address: 581 Duke Street
Glasgow G31 1PY

#285
Fairfield Working Men's
Club & Institute
Category: Social Club
Area: South Side, Govan
Address: 211 Crossloan Road
Glasgow G51 3QD
Phone: 0141 445 1791

#286
Mother's Day Pampering
at Hampden
Category: Entertainment
Area: South Side
Address: Hampden Park
Glasgow G42
Phone: 0845 269 2189

#287
The Southside Wedding
Show at Hampden
Category: Festival, Wedding Planning
Area: South Side, Mount Florida
Address: Hampden Park
Glasgow G42 9BA
Phone: 0845 269 2189

#288
Karla Kinsella Fortune Teller
Category: Psychic, Astrologer
Area: Parkhead
Address: 1221 Gallowgate
Glasgow G31 4EB
Phone: 0141 556 4690

#289
Bigdaddy Productions
Category: Event Planning & Services
Area: Tollcross
Address: 52 Maukinfauld Road
Glasgow G32 8TH
Phone: 07742 261709

#290
Lourdes Theatre Group
Category: Theatre
Area: South Side
Address: Lourdes Avenue
Glasgow G52 3

#291
Mega Amusements
Category: Arcade
Area: Parkhead
Address: 1199 Duke St
Glasgow G31 5NZ

#292
Richard Self Contained Caberet At It's Best.
Category: Theatre, Wedding Planning
Area: Partick
Address: 1/1 162 Curle Steet whiteinch
Glasgow, G14 0TT
Phone: 0141 959 9269

#293
Theatre Guild Glasgow
Category: Theatre
Area: South Side, Rutherglen
Address: Croftpark Avenue
Glasgow G44 5NR
Phone: 0141 573 7485

#294
Royal Scottish Pipe Band Association
Category: Social Club
Area: City Centre
Address: 45 Washington Street
Glasgow G3 8AZ
Phone: 0141 221 5414

#295
Gravity Studio
Category: Recording Studio
Area: City Centre
Address: 54 Washington Street
Glasgow G3 8AZ
Phone: 0141 204 5394

#296
The Modern Institute
Category: Art Gallery
Area: City Centre
Address: 73 Robertson Street
Glasgow G2 8QD
Phone: 0141 248 3711

#297
Bti UK Hogg Robinson
Category: Entertainment
Area: City Centre
Address: 55 Blythswood Street
Glasgow G2 7AT
Phone: 0141 222 8700

#298
Secret Music
Category: Entertainment
Area: Finnieston, West End
Address: 752 Argyle Street
Glasgow G3 8UJ
Phone: 0141 847 0002

#299
Paw Paw Productions
Category: Recording Studio
Area: Finnieston, West End
Address: 752-756 Argyle Street
Glasgow G3 8UJ
Phone: 0141 847 0006

#300
The Art House
Category: Art Gallery
Area: Finnieston, West End
Address: 752-756 Argyle Street
Glasgow G3 8UJ

#301
West End Mangement
Category: Theatre
Area: City Centre
Address: 188 ST. Vincent Street
Glasgow G2 5SG
Phone: 0141 226 8941

#302
Royal British Legion
Category: Social Club
Area: City Centre
Address: 36 Washington Street
Glasgow G3 8AZ
Phone: 0141 221 7485

#303
The Scottish National Arena
Category: Arena
Area: City Centre
Address: Exhibition Way
Glasgow G3 8WY
Phone: 0141 248 3000

#304
Paddy Power
Category: Gambling
Area: City Centre
Address: 109 Union St
Glasgow G1 3

#305
Ewan Mundy
Category: Art Gallery
Area: City Centre
Address: 211 West George Street
Glasgow G2 2LW
Phone: 0141 248 9755

#306
Cincinnati
Category: Social Club
Area: South Side, Gorbals
Address: 67 Bridge Street
Glasgow G5 9JB
Phone: 0141 418 2399

#307
Supreme Grand Chapter
Of Scotland
Category: Social Club
Area: City Centre
Address: 143 West Regent Street
Glasgow G2 2SG
Phone: 0141 221 4716

#308
The Mixing Room Studio
Category: Recording Studio
Area: City Centre
Address: 220-226 West Regent Street
Glasgow G2 4DQ
Phone: 0141 221 7795

#309
Pacific Audio
Category: Recording Studio
Area: City Centre
Address: 226 West Regent Street
Glasgow G2 4DQ
Phone: 0141 248 2002

#310
Morris Amusements
Category: Theatre
Area: City Centre
Address: 180 West Regent Street
Glasgow G2 4RW
Phone: 0141 847 0402

#311
Riverside Club
Category: Social Club
Area: City Centre
Address: 33 Fox Street
Glasgow G1 4AU
Phone: 0141 248 3144

#312
Robert C Kelly
Category: Theatre
Area: City Centre
Address: 82 Mitchell Street
Glasgow G1 3NA
Phone: 0141 229 1444

#313
R G I Kelley
Category: Art Gallery
Area: City Centre
Address: 118 Douglas Street
Glasgow G2 4ET
Phone: 0141 248 6386

#314
City Of Glasgow Municipal Club
Category: Social Club
Area: South Side, Kinning Park
Address: 2 Govan Road
Glasgow G51 1HS
Phone: 0141 429 4578

#315
J Crowe
Category: Visual Art, Spanish
Area: City Centre
Address: Robertson Street
Glasgow G2 8QD
Phone: 0141 204 3323

#316
Da Da Events
Category: Marketing Consultants
Area: Buchanan Street, City Centre
Address: 30 Buchanan Street
Glasgow G1 3LB
Phone: 0141 222 2266

#317
Carlton Digital Recording
Category: Recording Studio
Area: South Side, Gorbals
Address: 54 Carlton Place
Glasgow G5 9TW
Phone: 0141 429 5723

#318
The Railway Staff
Category: Social Club
Area: City Centre
Address: 151 Bath Street
Glasgow G2 4SQ
Phone: 07885 283406

#319
Hallsion Club
Category: Social Club
Area: City Centre
Address: 186 Bath Street
Glasgow G2 4HG
Phone: 0141 331 1972

#320
Teegenius
Category: Social Club
Area: SauchieHalls Street, City Centre
Address: 180 SauchieHalls Lane
Glasgow G2 4JD
Phone: 0141 644 1001

#321
Scottish Cultural Enterprise
Category: Contemporary Arts
Area: City Centre
Address: 53 Bothwell Street
Glasgow G2 6TS
Phone: 0141 248 5862

#322
Pantheon Club Glasgow
Category: Theatre
Area: Charing Cross, City Centre
Address: 268 Bath Street
Glasgow G2 4JR
Phone: 0141 332 3507

#323
Acting Coach Scotland
Category: Theatre
Area: City Centre
Address: 19 Queen St
Glasgow G2 8
Phone: 0800 756 9535

#324
Arches Theatre
Category: Music Venues
Area: City Centre
Address: Midland St
Glasgow G1 4PR
Phone: 09010 220300

#325
Central Studio
Category: Recording Studio
Area: Charing Cross, West End
Address: 61 Berkeley Street
Glasgow G3 7DX
Phone: 0141 248 8665

#326
Ladbrokes
Category: Gambling
Area: Charing Cross
Address: 455 SauchieHalls St
Glasgow G2 3LG
Phone: 0800 731 4171

#327
Stanley Glasgow Casino
Category: Gambling
Area: Charing Cross, City Centre
Address: 506-516 SauchieHalls Street
Glasgow G2 3LW
Phone: 0141 332 0992

#328
Rotunda Casino
Category: Gambling
Area: Finnieston, West End
Address: 28a Tunnel Street
Glasgow G3 8HL
Phone: 0141 243 2430

#329
Princes Casino
Category: Gambling, Arcade
Area: Charing Cross
Address: 535 SauchieHalls Street
Glasgow G2 3LX

#330
Global Gaming Corp
Category: Social Club
Area: SauchieHalls Street, City Centre
Address: 3 Savoy Centre
Glasgow G2 3DH
Phone: 0141 331 0677

#331
Secret Music
Category: Entertainment
Area: Charing Cross, West End
Address: 5 Newton Terrace Lane
Glasgow G3 7PB
Phone: 0141 564 1161

#332
Ankur Productions
Category: Theatre
Area: Charing Cross, SauchieHalls Street
West, Woodlands, West End
Address: 537 SauchieHalls Street
Glasgow G3 7PQ
Phone: 0141 248 8889

#333
Maura
Category: Psychic, Astrologer
Area: City Centre
Address: 116 SauchieHalls Street
Glasgow G2 3DH
Phone: 0141 332 7375

#334
Taylor Made Events
Category: Entertainment
Area: City Centre
Address: 34 ST. Enoch Square
Glasgow G1 4DF
Phone: 0141 221 7744

#335
Raeburn Supper Club
Yvonne Carvel & Diane Goudie
Category: Social Club
Area: Charing Cross, City Centre
Address: 3/1 351 Renfrew Street
Glasgow G3 6UW
Phone: 0141 333 1321

#336
Zap Entertainment
Category: Summer Music Festivals
Area: Buchanan Street, City Centre
Address: 166 Buchanan Street
Glasgow G1 2LW
Phone: 0845 009 1290

#337
Coral
Category: Gambling
Area: SauchieHalls Street, City Centre
Address: 127 West Nile Street
Glasgow G1 2RX
Phone: 0800 328 4273

#338
C P L Entertainment Group
Category: Entertainment
Area: Charing Cross, SauchieHalls Street
West, West End
Address: 21 Sandyford Place
Glasgow G3 7NG
Phone: 0141 221 5020

#339
The Glasgow Room
Category: Art Gallery
Area: Buchanan Street, City Centre
Address: 48 Buchanan Street
Glasgow G1 3JN
Phone: 0141 221 8162

#340
Lyon & Turnbull
Category: Art Gallery
Area: Charing Cross, Woodlands
Address: 4 Woodside Place
Glasgow G3 7QF
Phone: 0141 353 5070

#341
Wasps Artists' Studio
Category: Art Gallery
Area: City Centre, Merchant City
Address: 141 Bridgegate
Glasgow G1 5HZ
Phone: 0141 553 5890

#342
Tag Theatre Co.
Category: Theatre
Area: South Side, Gorbals
Address: 119 Gorbals Street
Glasgow G5 9DS
Phone: 0141 429 5561

#343
St Andrew Bridge Club
Category: Social Club
Area: Charing Cross, West End
Address: 13 Somerset Place
Glasgow G3 7JT
Phone: 0141 332 4583

#344
Buchanan Bridge Club
Category: Social Club
Area: Charing Cross, West End
Address: 4 Clairmont Garden
Glasgow G3 7LW
Phone: 0141 332 5131

#345
Hentertainment
Category: Wedding Entertainment, Cabarets,
Singers and Dancers
Area: City Centre, Merchant City
Address: 4/3 53 Hutcheson Street
Glasgow G1 1SJ
Phone: 07917 118947

#346
Spring Radio Cars
Category: Taxis & Minicabs,
Music Venues
Area: Buchanan Street, City Centre
Address: 2 SauchieHalls Street
Glasgow G2 3NY
Phone: 0141 332 8308

#347
Apple Basement
Category: Theatre
Area: Finnieston, West End
Address: 1103 Argyle Street
Glasgow G3 8ND
Phone: 0141 248 7377

#348
Numb Music
Category: Theatre
Area: Finnieston, West End
Address: 1103 Argyle Street
Glasgow G3 8ND
Phone: 0141 221 7111

#349
Banchory Music
Category: Arcade
Area: Finnieston, West End
Address: 1103 Argyle Street
Glasgow G3 8ND
Phone: 0141 227 2751

#350
National Trust
Category: Art Gallery
Area: City Centre, Merchant City
Address: 158 Ingram Street
Glasgow G1 1EJ
Phone: 0141 552 8391

#351
Alexander Gibson Opera Studio
Category: Theatre
Area: City Centre
Address: RSAMD 100 Renfrew Street
Glasgow G2 3DB
Phone: 0141 332 5057

#352
P B Events
Category: Event Management
Area: South Side, Kinning Park
Address: 542 Scotland St West
Glasgow G41 1BZ
Phone: 0141 429 3066

#353
The Old Sheriff Court
Category: Theatre
Area: City Centre, Merchant City
Address: 105 Brunswick Street
Glasgow G1 1TF
Phone: 0141 552 3988

#354
Tag Theatre Co.
Category: Theatre
Area: City Centre, Merchant City
Address: 20 King Street
Glasgow G1 5QP
Phone: 0141 552 4949

#355
Grandslam Events
Category: Event Management
Area: SauchieHalls Street, City Centre
Address: 141 West Nile Street
Glasgow G1 2RN
Phone: 0141 572 8880

#356
Sorche Dallas
Category: Art Gallery
Area: City Centre
Address: 5 St.Margarets Place
Glasgow G1 5JY
Phone: 0141 553 2662

#357
Classical Pets
Category: Art Gallery
Area: Partick
Address: 5-9 St Margarets Place
Glasgow G1 5JY
Phone: 0141 5521132

#358
John Strange Management
Category: Theatre
Area: Woodlands, West End
Address: 11 Ashley Street
Glasgow G3 6DR
Phone: 07859 820445

#359
Blue Star Social Club
Category: Social Club
Area: South Side, Kinning Park
Address: 26 Lorne Street
Glasgow G51 1DP
Phone: 0141 427 2574

#360
Quizmedia
Category: Event Management
Area: City Centre
Address: 36 North Hanover Street
Glasgow G1 2AD
Phone: 0141 572 8462

#361
Project Ability
Category: Art Gallery
Area: City Centre, Merchant City
Address: 18 Albion Street
Glasgow G1 1LH
Phone: 0141 552 2822

#362
Cava Sound WorkShop
Category: Recording Studio
Area: West End
Address: 49 Derby Street
Glasgow G3 7TU
Phone: 0141 334 5099

#363
The Third Step
Category: Art Gallery
Area: City Centre, Merchant City
Address: 7 Trongate
Glasgow G1 5EZ
Phone: 0141 552 2220

#364
City Inn Hotel
Category: Hotel, Music Venues
Area: Finnieston, West End
Address: Finnieston Quay
Glasgow G3 8HN
Phone: 0141 240 1002

#365
Impel Music Group
Category: Theatre
Area: Kelvingrove, Park Circus
Address: 1 Park Terrace
Glasgow G3 6BY
Phone: 0141 305 0011

#366
Britannia Theatre
Category: Theatre, Music Venues
Area: City Centre, Merchant City
Address: Trongate
Glasgow G1 5

#367
Bell Booke And Candle Psychics
Category: Psychic, Astrologer
Area: Gallowgate
Address: 18 London Rd
Glasgow G1 5
Phone: 0844 888 4098

#368
Rave Music
Category: Event Management
Area: Kelvingrove, Park Circus
Address: Woodlands Terrace
Glasgow G3 6DF
Phone: 0141 572 0245

#369
Roots In The Community
Category: Event Management
Area: South Side, Kinning Park
Address: Cornwall Street
Glasgow G41 1AH
Phone: 0141 419 9299

#370
Maybank Studio
Category: Recording Studio
Area: South Side
Address: 652-654 Eglinton Street
Glasgow G5 9RP
Phone: 0141 429 8822

#371
Chimes International
Category: Theatre
Area: South Side
Address: 2 Bruce Road
Glasgow G41 5EJ
Phone: 0141 420 3084

#372
Robin Anderson Theatre
Category: Theatre
Area: Woodlands, West End
Address: 261 West Princes Street
Glasgow G4 9EE
Phone: 0141 331 2931

#373
Basement Jazz
Category: Theatre
Area: West End
Address: 7 Old Dumbarton Road
Glasgow G3 8QY
Phone: 0141 576 5035

#374
Coulter Management Agency
Category: Theatre
Area: Woodlands, West End
Address: 333 Woodlands Road
Glasgow G3 6NG
Phone: 0141 357 6666

#375
Ferda
Category: Psychic, Astrologer
Area: South Side, Kinning Park
Address: 54-56 Clifford Lane
Glasgow G51 1NR
Phone: 0141 427 0486

#376
Clyde Maritime Centre
Category: Museum
Area: Finnieston, West End
Address: 100 Stobcross Road
Glasgow G3 8QQ
Phone: 0141 222 2513

#377
Quizmaster
Category: Event Management
Area: West End
Address: 28 Burnbank Garden
Glasgow G20 6HD
Phone: 0141 579 2496

#378
Pitch Perfect
Category: Event Management
Area: South Side
Address: 5 Aytoun Road
Glasgow G41 5RL
Phone: 0141 423 5577

#379
Clydebank Masonic Social Club
Category: Social Club
Area: City Centre, Cowcaddens
Address: 31 Canal Street
Glasgow G4 0QU
Phone: 0141 952 3869

#380
Psychic & Healing
Centre In Scotland
Category: Psychic, Astrologer
Area: South Side
Address: 82 Victoria Road
Glasgow G42 7AA
Phone: 0141 575 1205

#381
Gallowgate Studio
Category: Arts Organisation
Area: Dennistoun, Gallowgate
Address: 15-17 East Campbell Street
Glasgow G1 5DT
Phone: 0141 552 7250

#382
Kelvin
Category: Pub, Arena
Area: West End
Address: 1377 Argyle Street
Glasgow G3 8AF
Phone: 0141 576 5026

#383
Cameronian Scottish Rifles
Memorial Club
Category: Social Club
Area: West End
Address: 9 Holyrood Cresent
Glasgow G20 6HJ
Phone: 07779 610319

#384
U C Entertainment
Category: Event Management
Area: South Side
Address: 110 Victoria Road
Glasgow G42 7JD
Phone: 0141 424 3701

#385
Barrowland Rehearsal Room
Category: Music Venues
Area: Gallowgate
Address: 244 Gallowgate
Glasgow G4 0TT
Phone: 0141 553 2515

#386
Margaret Mciver
Category: Theatre
Area: Gallowgate
Address: 244 Gallowgate
Glasgow G4 0TT
Phone: 0141 552 4601

#387
Studio Sixty
Category: Art Gallery
Area: Woodlands, Great Western Road,
Kelvinbridge, West End
Address: 22-24 Park Rd
Glasgow G4 9JG
Phone: 0141 334 6600

#388
Capital Sound Hire
Category: Sound Equipment Hire
Area: West End
Address: Office 1, Yorkhill Quay
Glasgow G3 8QE
Phone: 0141 357 4035

#389
Cottiers Kelvinbridge Theatre
Category: Theatre
Area: Great Western Road, Kelvinbridge
Address: 416 Great Western Road
Glasgow G4 9HZ

#390
St Mungo's Old Folks Day Centre
Category: Social Club
Area: City Centre
Address: Mcaslin Court
Glasgow G4 0PQ
Phone: 0141 552 8999

#391
Woodside Social Club
Category: Social Club
Area: West End
Address: 329 North Woodside Road
Glasgow G20 6ND
Phone: 0141 337 1643

#392
The Pan African Arts
Category: Theatre
Area: West End
Address: 39 NapiersHalls Street
Glasgow G20 6EZ
Phone: 0141 334 3706

#393
The Poetry Club
Category: Club, Music Venues
Area: West End
Address: 100 Eastvale Place
Glasgow G3 8QG
Phone: 0141 357 7246

#394
Survivors' Poetry Scotland
Category: Theatre
Area: Kelvingrove, West End
Address: 2/R 5 Westbank Quad
Glasgow G12 8NT
Phone: 0141 357 6838

#395
SSK Conferences & Events
Category: Arcade
Area: South Side, Ibrox
Address: 161 Woodville Street
Glasgow G51 2RQ
Phone: 0141 445 1800

#396
Glasgow Science Festival
Category: Festival
Area: West End
Address: The University of Glasgow
Glasgow G12 8QQ
Phone: 0141 330 5370

#397
Immediate Arts
Category: Theatre
Area: West End
Address: 33 Kirkland St
Glasgow G20 6SY
Phone: 0141 589 1384

#398
Lipton Club
Category: Social Club
Area: South Side
Address: 97 Pollokshaws Road
Glasgow G41 1PU
Phone: 0141 429 0505

#399
Events Co.
Category: Event Management
Area: South Side
Address: 16 Moray Place
Glasgow G41 2BA
Phone: 0141 423 3242

#400
Neptune Social Club
Category: Social Club
Area: South Side
Address: 101 Clifford Street
Glasgow G51 1QP
Phone: 0141 427 5878

#401
Govanhill Neighbourhood Centre
Category: Social Club
Area: South Side
Address: 6 Daisy Street
Glasgow G42 8JL
Phone: 0141 423 6492

#402
Top Hat Casino
Category: Casino Hire
Area: Hillhead, West End
Address: 64 Ashton Lane
Glasgow G12 8SJ
Phone: 0141 579 5070

#403
Gyct Theatre Ecole
Category: Theatre
Area: South Side
Address: 170 Queens Drive
Glasgow G42 8QZ
Phone: 0141 423 6037

#404
**British Association
Of Teachers Of Dancing**
Category: Social Club
Area: South Side
Address: 23 Marywood Square
Glasgow G41 2BP
Phone: 0141 423 4029

#405
88 Events Co.
Category: Luxury Wedding Planner
Area: South Side, Ibrox
Address: 143 Woodville Street
Glasgow G51 2RQ
Phone: 0141 445 2288

#406
Tradeston Ex Servicemens Club
Category: Social Club
Area: South Side
Address: 6 Beech Ave
Glasgow G41 5BY
Phone: 0141 427 0332

#407
Scottish Academy Of Asian Arts
Category: Event Management
Area: South Side
Address: Daisy Street
Glasgow G42 8JL
Phone: 0141 423 2210

#408
Comhairle Nan Leabhraichean
Category: Theatre
Area: Partick, West End
Address: 22 Mansfield Street
Glasgow G11 5QP
Phone: 0141 337 6211

#409
Take Note Music
Category: Arcade
Area: Cambuslang
Address: 47 Stewarton Drive
Glasgow G72 8DQ
Phone: 0141 641 3365

#410
New Scottish Choir & Orchestra
Category: Musical Artist
Area: Partick, West End
Address: 19 Havelock Street
Glasgow G11 5JF
Phone: 0141 579 0013

#411
Andre & Ossie
Category: Art Gallery
Area: West End
Address: 37 Ruthven Lane
Glasgow G12 9BG
Phone: 0141 357 4158

#412
Unlimited Studio
Category: Art Gallery
Area: Partick, West End
Address: 25 Hyndland Street
Glasgow G11 5QE
Phone: 0141 338 6052

#413
Pavla's Entertainers
Category: EventManagement
Area: West End
Address: 8 Victoria Crescent Road
Glasgow G12 9DB
Phone: 0141 339 3816

#414
**Painting & Restoration
Studio Acr**
Category: Theatre
Area: Dennistoun
Address: 77 Hanson Street
Glasgow G31 2HF
Phone: 0141 551 8401

#415
G R Management
Category: Theatre
Area: South Side, Queen's Park
Address: 974 Pollokshaws Road
Glasgow G41 2HA
Phone: 0141 632 1111

#416
Cma Actors Agency
Category: Theatre
Area: West End
Address: 74 Victoria CR Road
Glasgow G12 9JN
Phone: 0141 579 1400

#417
Non Sono Computer Graphics
Category: Sound Recording
Area: West End
Address: 74 Victoria Crescent Road
Glasgow G12 9JN
Phone: 0141 576 9300

#418
**Scottish Music
Information Centre**
Category: National Music Resource
Area: West End
Address: 1 Bowmont Garden
Glasgow G12 9LR
Phone: 0141 334 6393

#419
Wild Horses Productions
Category: Arcade
Area: West End
Address: 7 Crown Terrace
Glasgow G12 9EZ
Phone: 0141 357 0547

#420
Giant Productions
Category: Theatre
Area: Partick, West End
Address: 96-100 Beith Street
Glasgow G11 6DQ
Phone: 0141 334 2000

#421
Hyndland After School Club
Category: Out-Of-School Services
Area: Partick, West End
Address: 44 Fortrose Street
Glasgow G11 5LP
Phone: 0141 339 9526

#422
Glasgow Bridge Centre
Category: Social Club
Area: South Side, Shawlands
Address: 1055 Pollokshaws Road
Glasgow G41 3YF
Phone: 0141 632 3773

#423
Karla Kinsella
Category: Psychic, Astrologer
Area: Partick, West End
Address: 1 Hayburn Street
Glasgow G11 6DE
Phone: 0141 586 9003

#424
Childrens Classic Concerts
Category: Theatre
Area: Partick, West End
Address: 46 Fortrose Street
Glasgow G11 5LP
Phone: 0141 334 8500

#425
Mega Amusements
Category: Arcade
Area: Duke Street, Dennistoun
Address: 435 Duke St
Glasgow G31 1RY
Phone: 0141 554 5396

#426
Mega Amusements
Category: Arcade, Adult Entertainment
Area: Duke Street, Dennistoun
Address: 527 Duke St
Glasgow G31 1DL
Phone: 0141 554 5396

#427
Performance Plus
Category: Event Management
Area: Dennistoun
Address: 39 Garthland Drive
Glasgow G31 2RE
Phone: 0141 551 8789

#428
Ceilidh Bands
Category: Ceilidh and Function Band
Area: South Side, Shawlands
Address: 4 Moss Side Road
Glasgow G41 3TL
Phone: 0141 632 4580

#429
Flicker Magazine
Category: Mass Media
Area: West End
Address: 1/2 61 Avenuepark Street
Glasgow G20 8LN
Phone: 0141 563 0459

#430
Psychic Sanctuary
Category: Psychic, Astrologer
Area: Springburn
Address: 3 3 52 Keppochhill Road
Glasgow G21 1ST
Phone: 0141 558 7014

#431
Glasgow Indoor Bowling
Category: Theatre
Area: South Side, Mount Florida
Address: 177 Prospecthill Road
Glasgow G42 9LQ
Phone: 0141 632 3302

#432
Ardery Street Masonic Halls
Category: Social Club
Area: Partick, West End
Address: 9 Ardery Street
Glasgow G11 7SX
Phone: 0141 334 7710

#433
Orange Halls Springburn
Category: Social Club
Area: Springburn
Address: 63 Millarbank Street
Glasgow G21 1BT
Phone: 0141 558 6225

#434
Azteck Indoor Play
Category: Arcade
Area: South Side, Shawlands
Address: 1273 Pollokshaws Road
Glasgow G41 3RR
Phone: 0141 649 5455

#435
Kenburn Social Club
Category: Social Club
Area: Springburn
Address: 43 Vulcan Street
Glasgow G21 4BP
Phone: 0141 558 0746

#436
Quiz Inquisitor
Category: Pub Quizzes
Area: South Side, Mount Florida
Address: 37 Stanmore Road
Glasgow G42 9AJ
Phone: 0141 587 8827

#437
Lodge Alexandra 1282
Category: Social Club
Area: Dennistoun
Address: 15 Wood Street
Glasgow G31 3BZ
Phone: 0141 554 1498

#438
**Sporty Race Nights
& Casino Evenings**
Category: Gambling
Area: South Side, Mount Florida
Address: 37 Clincart Road
Glasgow G42 9DZ
Phone: 0131 225 3067

#439
King Tut's Wah Wah Hut
Category: Music Venues
Area: City Centre
Address: 272 St Vincent Street
Glasgow G2 5RL
Phone: 0141 221 5279

#440
Phipps
Category: Event Management
Area: Partick, West End
Address: Thornwood Avenue
Glasgow G11 7QY
Phone: 0141 357 3562

#441
Baldy Bane Theatre
Category: Theatre
Area: South Side, Shawlands
Address: 13 Carment Drive
Glasgow G41 3PP
Phone: 0141 632 0193

#442
Scotlands National Stadium
Category: Stadium
Area: South Side, Mount Florida
Address: Letherby Drive
Glasgow G42 9BA
Phone: 0141 620 4000

#443
Demus Productions
Category: Event Management
Area: Great Western Road, Hyndland
Address: 6 Devonshire Terrace
Glasgow G12 0XF
Phone: 0141 342 4959

#444
David John Associates
Category: Event Management
Area: West End
Address: 16a Winton Drive
Glasgow G12 0QA
Phone: 0141 357 0532

#445
Bands Of Gold
Category: Event Management
Area: Partick, West End
Address: 2 Broomhill Avenue
Glasgow G11 7AE
Phone: 0141 337 2358

#446
Reform Club
Category: Social Club
Area: South Side
Address: 1-4 Cressy Street
Glasgow G51 4RB
Phone: 0141 440 0771

#447
Criznikalis Nikilas
Category: Psychic, Astrologer
Area: Dennistoun
Address: Aberfoyle Street
Glasgow G31 3RW
Phone: 0141 550 8317

#448
R A O B Caledonia Institute
Category: Social Club
Area: Partick, West End
Address: 937 Dumbarton Road
Glasgow G14 9UF
Phone: 0141 341 0807

#449
Glasgow Veteran Seafarers Association
Category: Social Club
Area: Partick, West End
Address: 937 Dumbarton Road
Glasgow G14 9UF
Phone: 0141 337 2632

#450
Glasgow Central Railway Club
Category: Social Club
Area: South Side
Address: 108 Carmunnock Road
Glasgow G44 4UN
Phone: 0141 632 0766

#451
South Western Social & Recreation Club
Category: Social Club
Area: South Side
Address: 20 Corkerhill Garden
Glasgow G52 1SE
Phone: 0141 810 3422

#452
E L S Discos
Category: Wedding Dj's
Area: Springburn
Address: 68 Boghead Road
Glasgow G21 4XU
Phone: 0141 557 3955

#453
Karla Kinsella
Category: Psychic, Astrologer
Area: Parkhead
Address: Unit 45
Glasgow G31 4EB
Phone: 0141 556 4690

#454
Shaws-Bank Social Club
Category: Social Club
Area: South Side
Address: 183 Shawbridge Street
Glasgow G43 1QQ
Phone: 0141 632 6081

#455
Neil Drover Agency
Category: Event Management
Area: Partick, West End
Address: 437 Crow Road
Glasgow G11 7DZ
Phone: 0141 357 3377

#456
Twenty Social Club
Category: Social Club
Area: Rutherglen
Address: 52 Cathcart Road
Glasgow G73 2QZ
Phone: 0141 647 3687

#457
Kirsty Duncan
Category: Theatre
Area: Partick
Address: 63 Curle Street
Glasgow G14 0
Phone: 07912 360704

#458
Moira Colvan
Category: Event Management
Area: South Side
Address: 24 Kingsland Drive
Glasgow G52 2NE
Phone: 0141 810 3543

#459
Margaret E Maclean
Category: Event Management
Area: South Side
Address: 131 Muirdrum Avenue
Glasgow G52 3AW
Phone: 0141 882 6983

#460
Ledgowan Tennants Halls
Category: Social Club
Area: Maryhill
Address: Ledgowan Place
Glasgow G20 0JZ
Phone: 0141 946 8999

#461
Maryhill Bowling Club
Category: Social Club
Area: Maryhill
Address: 29 Duart Street
Glasgow G20 0EG
Phone: 0141 576 0170

#462
Animal Man
Category: Mini Zoo Parties
Area: South Side
Address: 120 Pentland Road
Glasgow G43 2AR
Phone: 0141 649 7181

#463
Skykirk
Category: Arcade
Area: Maryhill
Address: Unit 1 Summerston Retail Park
Glasgow G23 5QG
Phone: 0141 945 5759

#464
Big Beat Promotions
Category: Wedding Dj's
Area: South Side
Address: 35 Bowden Drive
Glasgow G52 2LN
Phone: 0141 810 4109

#465
72 AD
Category: Event Management
Area: South Side
Address: 1994 Paisley Road West
Glasgow G52 3SY
Phone: 0141 882 2111

#466
Uniquity
Category: Art Gallery
Area: Giffnock, South Side
Address: 20 Merryton Avenue
Glasgow G46 6DT
Phone: 0141 585 3500

#467
Entertainment Direct
Category: Arcade
Area: Giffnock, South Side
Address: 14 Heathside Road
Glasgow G46 6HL
Phone: 0141 638 0724

#468
Harry Margolis
Category: Event Management
Area: Giffnock, South Side
Address: 14 Heathside Road
Glasgow G46 6HL
Phone: 0141 638 0724

#469
Youth Services
Category: Social Club
Area: Tollcross
Address: 150 Wellshot Road
Glasgow G32 7AX
Phone: 0141 778 5783

#470
Knights Of St Columba
Category: Social Club
Area: South Side
Address: 75 Hillington Road South
Glasgow G52 2AE
Phone: 0141 883 5700

#471
South West Arts & Music Project
Category: Social Club
Area: South Side
Address: 1 Barnbeth Road
Glasgow G53 5YR
Phone: 0141 891 5564

#472
Emerging Artists
Category: Art Gallery
Area: Giffnock, South Side
Address: 6 Burnfield Road
Glasgow G46 7QB
Phone: 0141 638 6552

#473
ScotlandArt
Category: Art Gallery
Area: Giffnock, South Side
Address: 6 Burnfield Road
Glasgow G46 7QB
Phone: 0141 638 1200

#474
Castlemilk Pensioners Action Centre
Category: Social Club
Area: South Side
Address: Dougrie Drive Lane
Glasgow G45 9AH
Phone: 0141 634 9301

#475
Cowglen Sports Club
Category: Social Club
Area: South Side
Address: Boydstone Road
Glasgow G58 1SB
Phone: 0141 632 0787

#476
Richard Fillingham Agency
Category: Event Management
Area: South Side, Clarkston
Address: 22 Williamwood Park West
Glasgow G44 3TE
Phone: 0141 633 2298

#477
Masonic Club
Category: Social Club
Area: Tollcross
Address: 25 Causewayside Street
Glasgow G32 8LU
Phone: 0141 778 7506

#478
North British Bowling Club
Category: Social Club
Area: Shettleston
Address: 42 Amulree Street
Glasgow G32 7UN
Phone: 0141 778 8011

#479
Tollcross Bowling Club
Category: Social Club
Area: Tollcross
Address: 157 Causewayside Street
Glasgow G32 8LP
Phone: 0141 778 6763

#480
Take Note Music
Category: Arcade
Area: Cambuslang
Address: 47 Stewarton Drive
Glasgow G72 8DQ
Phone: 0141 641 3365

#481
Savoy Bingo Club
Category: Social Club
Area: Cambuslang
Address: 52-58 Main Street
Glasgow G72 7EP
Phone: 0141 641 3558

#482
Cambuslang Karting
Category: Karting
Area: Cambuslang
Address: 91 Glasgow Road
Glasgow G72 7BT
Phone: 0141 641 0921

#483
Teelc Limited
Category: Tribute Entertainment
Area: Cambuslang
Address: 59D Main Street
Glasgow G72 7HB
Phone: 0843 289 4398

#484
The Wine Palate
Category: Wineries
Area: Charing Cross, City Centre
Address: 272 Bath Street
Glasgow G2 4JR
Phone: 0141 354 1638

#485
King Tut's Wah Wah Hut
Category: Pub, Music Venues
Area: City Centre
Address: 272 St Vincent Street
Glasgow G2 5RL
Phone: 0141 221 5279

#486
Glasgow Art Club
Category: Art Gallery, Music Venues
Area: City Centre
Address: 185 Bath Street
Glasgow G2 4HU
Phone: 0141 248 5210

#487
Sub Club Scotland
Category: Club, Music Venues
Area: City Centre
Address: 22 Jamaica Street
Glasgow G1 4QD
Phone: 0141 248 4600

#488
The Virginia Gallery
Category: Art Gallery
Area: City Centre, Merchant City
Address: 45 Virginia Street
Glasgow G1 1TS
Phone: 0141 552 5699

#489
Giffnock Theatre Players
Category: Social Club
Area: Giffnock, South Side
Address: 269 Fenwick Road
Glasgow G46 6JX
Phone: 0141 638 7719

#490
William King Bookmakers
Category: Social Club
Area: Giffnock, South Side
Address: 164 Fenwick Rd
East Renfrewshire G46 6XE
Phone: 0141 620 1387

#491
Hunterian Museum
Category: Museum
Area: Hillhead, West End
Address: University Avenue
Glasgow G12 8QQ
Phone: 0141 330 5431

#492
harleys skybar
Category: Music Venues
Area: Rutherglen
Address: 96-102 main street
Glasgow G73 2HZ
Phone: 0141 647 9070

#493
Ladbrokes
Category: Gambling
Area: South Side, Nitshill
Address: 5 Woodneuk Road
Glasgow G53 7QS
Phone: 0141 881 8409

#494
Gala Bingo
Category: Bingo
Area: South Side, Nitshill
Address: 12 Woodneuk Road
Glasgow G53 7RT
Phone: 0141 881 8118

#495
Masonic Lodge Nitshill No 1478
Category: Social Club
Area: South Side, Nitshill
Address: 11 Dove Street
Glasgow G53 7BS
Phone: 0141 881 9879

#496
Glasgow Museum Resource Centre
Category: Museum
Area: South Side, Nitshill
Address: 200 Woodhead Road
Glasgow G53 7NN
Phone: 0141 276 9300

#497
Mobile Disco Glasgow
Category: Music Venues
Area: Thornliebank, South Side
Address: 8 Hopeman Avenue Flat
Glasgow G46 8SG
Phone: 07886 356613

#498
Cabins Association
Category: Social Club
Area: Thornliebank, South Side
Address: 69 Kyleakin Road
Glasgow G46 8DE
Phone: 0141 638 8146

#499
Fab 'N' Funky Faces
Category: Arts, Crafts & Face Painting
Area: Tollcross
Address: 21 Strathord Street
Glasgow G32 7TD
Phone: 07910 009098

#500
Recoat Gallery
Category: Art Gallery
Area: West End
Address: 323 North Woodside Road
Glasgow G20 6ND
Phone: 0141 341 0069

TOP 500 NIGHTLIFE

The Most Recommended by Locals & Trevelers

(From #1 to #500)

#1
Barrowland Ballroom
Category: Arcade, Music Venues
Average price: Modest
Area: Gallowgate
Address: 244 Gallowgate
Glasgow G4 0TT
Phone: 0141 552 4601

#2
The Pot Still
Category: Pub
Average price: Modest
Area: City Centre
Address: 154 Hope Street
Glasgow G2 2TH
Phone: 0141 333 0980

#3
The Butchershop Bar & Grill
Category: Steakhouse, Wine Bar,
Breakfast & Brunch
Average price: Expensive
Area: SauchieHalls Street West
Address: 1055 SauchieHalls Street
Glasgow G3 7UD
Phone: 0141 339 2999

#4
Stereo
Category: Bar, Cafe
Average price: Inexpensive
Area: City Centre
Address: 20 Renfield Lane
Glasgow G2 6PH
Phone: 0141 222 2254

#5
King Tut's Wah Wah Hut
Category: Pub, Music Venues
Average price: Modest
Area: City Centre
Address: 272 St Vincent Street
Glasgow G2 5RL
Phone: 0141 221 5279

#6
BrewDog Glasgow
Category: Pub
Average price: Modest
Area: West End
Address: 1397 Argyle Street
Glasgow G3 8AN
Phone: 0141 334 7175

#7
The Tiki Bar & Kitsch Inn
Category: Bar, British, Thai
Average price: Expensive
Area: City Centre
Address: 214 Bath Street
Glasgow G2 4HW
Phone: 0141 332 1341

#8
Cocktail & Burger
Category: American, Cocktail Bar
Average price: Inexpensive
Area: SauchieHalls Street, City Centre
Address: 323 SauchieHalls Street
Glasgow G2 3HW
Phone: 0141 353 0953

#9
The 78
Category: Bar, Vegan
Average price: Inexpensive
Area: Finnieston, West End
Address: 10-14 Kelvinhaugh Street
Glasgow G3 8NU
Phone: 0141 576 5018

#10
Blythswood Square
Category: Champagne Bar, Cocktail Bar
Average price: Expensive
Area: City Centre
Address: 11 Blythswood Square
Glasgow G2 4AD
Phone: 0131 274 7450

#11
The Stand Comedy Club
Category: Comedy Club
Average price: Modest
Area: Woodlands, West End
Address: 333 Woodlands Road
Glasgow G3 6NG
Phone: 0844 335 8879

#12
Chinaski's
Category: Pub, Gastropub
Average price: Modest
Area: Charing Cross, SauchieHalls Street
West, West End
Address: 239 North Street
Glasgow G3 7DL
Phone: 0141 221 0061

#13
Nice N Sleazy
Category: Bar
Average price: Modest
Area: Charing Cross
Address: 421 SauchieHalls Street
Glasgow G2 3LG
Phone: 0141 333 0900

#14
Sub Club Scotland
Category: Club, Music Venues
Average price: Expensive
Area: City Centre
Address: 22 Jamaica Street
Glasgow G1 4QD
Phone: 0141 248 4600

#15
Tchai-Ovna House of Tea
Category: Tea Room, Hookah Bar
Average price: Modest
Area: West End
Address: 42 Otago Lane
Glasgow G11 9PB
Phone: 0141 357 4524

#16
Lebowskis
Category: Pub
Average price: Modest
Area: Finnieston, West End
Address: 1008 Argyle Street
Glasgow G3 8LX
Phone: 0141 564 7988

#17
Tennents Bar
Category: Pub
Average price: Inexpensive
Area: Byres Road, West End
Address: 191 Byres Road
Glasgow G12 8TN
Phone: 0141 339 7203

#18
The Flying Duck
Category: Bar, Club, Vegan
Average price: Inexpensive
Area: City Centre
Address: 142 Renfield Street
Glasgow G2 3AU
Phone: 0141 564 1450

#19
The Ben Nevis
Category: Pub
Average price: Modest
Area: Finnieston, West End
Address: 1147 Argyle Street
Glasgow G3 8TB
Phone: 0141 576 5204

#20
Dukes
Category: Pub
Average price: Inexpensive
Area: West End
Address: 41 Old Dumbarton Road
Glasgow G3 8RD
Phone: 0141 339 7821

#21
Firebird
Category: Italian, Pizza, Pub
Average price: Modest
Area: West End
Address: 1321 Argyle Street
Glasgow G3 8TL
Phone: 0141 334 0594

#22
Variety Bar
Category: Pub
Average price: Modest
Area: Charing Cross, SauchieHalls Street,
City Centre
Address: 401 SauchieHalls Street
Glasgow G2 3LG
Phone: 0141 332 4449

#23
The Old Fruitmarket
Category: Music Venues, Theatre
Average price: Modest
Area: City Centre, Merchant City
Address: Candleriggs
Glasgow G1 1NQ
Phone: 0141 353 8000

#24
Rogano
Category: Seafood, Champagne Bar
Average price: Exclusive
Area: City Centre
Address: 11 Exchange Place
Glasgow G1 3AN
Phone: 0141 248 4055

#25
The State Bar
Category: Pub
Average price: Modest
Area: SauchieHalls Street, City Centre
Address: 148-148a Holland Street
Glasgow G2 4NG
Phone: 0141 332 2159

#26
The Belle
Category: Pub
Average price: Modest
Area: Great Western Road, Hillhead
Address: 617 Great Western Road
Glasgow G12 8HX
Phone: 0141 339 2299

#27
McPhabbs
Category: Pub, British
Average price: Modest
Area: Charing Cross, West End
Address: 23 Sandyford Place
Glasgow G3 7NG
Phone: 0141 221 8176

#28
Wild Cabaret
Category: Bar, Cabaret, Club
Average price: Modest
Area: City Centre, Merchant City
Address: 18 Candleriggs
Glasgow G1 1LD
Phone: 0141 552 6165

#29
The Arches Nightclub
Category: Club
Average price: Modest
Area: City Centre
Address: 253 Argyle Street
Glasgow G2 8DL
Phone: 0141 565 1000

#30
Laurieston Bar
Category: Pub
Average price: Inexpensive
Area: South Side, Tradeston
Address: 58 Bridge Street
Glasgow G5 9HU
Phone: 0141 429 4528

#31
Reflex
Category: Bar, Club
Average price: Modest
Area: City Centre
Address: 110-114 W George St
Glasgow G2 1NF
Phone: 0141 332 9724

#32
The Glasgow Royal Concert Halls
Category: Music Venues
Average price: Modest
Area: Buchanan Street, City Centre
Address: 2 SauchieHalls Street
Glasgow G2 3NY
Phone: 0141 353 8000

#33
Inn Deep
Category: Pub
Average price: Modest
Area: Great Western Road, Kelvinbridge
Address: 445 Great Western Road
Glasgow G12 8HH
Phone: 0141 357 1075

#34
Ad Lib
Category: Bar, American
Average price: Modest
Area: City Centre
Address: 111 Hope Street
Glasgow G2 6LL
Phone: 0141 248 6645

#35
Slouch
Category: Lounge
Average price: Modest
Area: City Centre
Address: 203-205 Bath Street
Glasgow G2 4HZ
Phone: 0141 221 5518

#36
Oran Mor
Category: Pub, Scottish
Average price: Expensive
Area: Great Western Road, Hillhead
Address: 731 Great Western Road
Glasgow G12 8QX
Phone: 0141 357 6200

#37
Brel
Category: Belgian, Bar
Average price: Modest
Area: Hillhead, West End
Address: 39 Ashton Lane
Glasgow G12 8SJ
Phone: 0141 342 4966

#38
Park Bar
Category: Pub
Average price: Inexpensive
Area: Finnieston, West End
Address: 1202 Argyle Street
Glasgow G3 8TE
Phone: 0141 339 1715

#39
The Squid & Whale
Category: Pub, American, Mexican
Average price: Modest
Area: Great Western Road, West End
Address: 372-374 Great Western Road
Glasgow G4 9HT
Phone: 0141 339 5070

#40
Bloc+
Category: Pub
Average price: Modest
Area: City Centre
Address: 117 Bath Street
Glasgow G2 2SZ
Phone: 0141 574 6066

#41
The Curler's Rest
Category: Pub, Gastropub
Average price: Modest
Area: Byres Road, Hillhead, West End
Address: 256-260 Byres Road
Glasgow G12 8SH
Phone: 0141 341 0737

#42
The Arches Theatre
Category: Venues &Event Space
Average price: Modest
Area: City Centre
Address: 253 Argyle Street
Glasgow G2 8DL
Phone: 0141 585 1000

#43
Halt Bar
Category: Pub
Average price: Modest
Area: Woodlands, West End
Address: 160 Woodlands Road
Glasgow G3 6LF
Phone: 0141 111 1111

#44
The Sparkle Horse
Category: Pub
Average price: Modest
Area: Partick, West End
Address: 16 Dowanhill Street
Glasgow G11 5QS
Phone: 0141 562 3175

#45
Drum & Monkey
Category: Pub
Average price: Modest
Area: City Centre
Address: 91 St Vincent Street
Glasgow G2 5TF
Phone: 0141 221 6636

#46
Bar 91
Category: Pub
Average price: Modest
Area: City Centre, Merchant City
Address: 91 Candleriggs
Glasgow G1 1NP
Phone: 0141 552 5211

#47
Black Sparrow
Category: Pub
Average price: Modest
Area: Charing Cross, West End,
SauchieHalls Street West
Address: 241 North Street
Glasgow G3 7DL
Phone: 0141 221 5530

#48
Strata
Category: Pub
Average price: Modest
Area: City Centre
Address: 45 Queen Street
Glasgow G1 3EF
Phone: 0141 221 1888

#49
Vodka Wodka
Category: Pub, Lounge
Average price: Modest
Area: Hillhead, West End
Address: 31 Ashton Lane
Glasgow G12 8SJ
Phone: 0141 341 0669

#50
Buff Club
Category: Club, Bar, Cafe
Average price: Modest
Area: City Centre
Address: 142 Bath Lane
Glasgow G2 4RH
Phone: 0141 248 1777

#51
Merchant Square
Category: Local Flavour, Restaurants, Bars, Shopping Centre
Average price: Expensive
Area: City Centre, Merchant City
Address: Candleriggs
Glasgow G1 1LE
Phone: 0141 552 3452

#52
The Classic Grand
Category: Club, Music Venues
Average price: Modest
Area: City Centre
Address: 18 Jamaica St
Glasgow G1 4QD
Phone: 0141 847 0820

#53
The Polo Lounge
Category: Lounge
Average price: Inexpensive
Area: City Centre, Merchant City
Address: 84 Wilson Street
Glasgow G1 1UZ
Phone: 0845 659 5905

#54
SoHo On Miller Street
Category: Bar, Pizza
Average price: Modest
Area: City Centre, Merchant City
Address: 84 Miller Street
Glasgow G1 1DT
Phone: 0141 221 1568

#55
02 ABC
Category: Club, Music Venues, Bar
Average price: Modest
Area: City Centre
Address: 300 SauchieHalls St
Glasgow G2 3JA
Phone: 0141 332 2232

#56
The Griffin Bar
Category: Pub
Average price: Modest
Area: Charing Cross, City Centre
Address: 266 Bath Street
Glasgow G2 4JP
Phone: 0141 331 5170

#57
Clyde Auditorium
The Armadillo
Category: Music Venues, Theatre
Average price: Expensive
Area: Finnieston, West End
Address: Finnieston St
Glasgow G3 8YW
Phone: 0870 040 4000

#58
The Glasgow School of Art
Category: Club
Average price: Modest
Area: City Centre
Address: 167 Renfrew Street
Glasgow G3 6RQ
Phone: 0141 353 4500

#59
Waxy O'Connors
Category: Pub
Average price: Modest
Area: City Centre
Address: 44 W George Street
Glasgow G2 1DH
Phone: 0141 354 5154

#60
Tingle Bar
Category: Cocktail Bar
Average price: Modest
Area: City Centre
Address: 33 Mitchell Street
Glasgow G1 3LN
Phone: 0141 222 2000

#61
Barbarossa Restaurant
Category: Wine Bar, Italian
Average price: Expensive
Area: South Side
Address: 1/7 Clarkston Road
Glasgow G44 4EF
Phone: 0141 560 3898

#62
The Richmond Bar & Bistro
Category: Cocktail Bar, British
Average price: Modest
Area: Woodlands, West End
Address: 144 Park Road
Glasgow G4 9HB
Phone: 0141 334 3571

#63
Flat 0/1
Category: Club
Average price: Inexpensive
Area: Charing Cross, City Centre
Address: 162 Bath St
Glasgow G2 4TB
Phone: 0141 331 6227

#64
Munro's
Category: Pub
Average price: Modest
Area: Woodlands, Great Western Road
Address: 185 Great Western Road
Glasgow G4 9EB
Phone: 0141 332 0972

#65
Bunker Bar
Category: Pub
Average price: Modest
Area: City Centre
Address: 193-199 Bath Street
Glasgow G2 4HU
Phone: 0141 229 1427

#66
Vespbar
Category: Bar, Italian, Comedy Club
Average price: Modest
Area: City Centre
Address: 14 Drury Street
Glasgow G2 5AA
Phone: 0141 204 0060

#67
Mulberry Street
Category: Pub
Average price: Modest
Area: South Side
Address: 778 Pollokshaws Road
Glasgow G42 8
Phone: 0141 424 0858

#68
The Roxy 171
Category: Lounge, Pub
Average price: Modest
Area: Woodlands, Great Western Road
Address: 171 Great Western Road
Glasgow G4 9AW
Phone: 0141 311 1901

#69
The Black Rabbit
Category: Bar, Coffee & Tea
Average price: Modest
Area: Great Western Road, West End
Address: 526 Great Western Road
Glasgow G12 8EL
Phone: 0141 339 1199

#70
Scotia Bar
Category: Pub
Average price: Inexpensive
Area: City Centre, Merchant City
Address: 112 Stockwell Street
Glasgow G1 4LW
Phone: 0141 552 8681

#71
The Brass Monkey
Category: Pub
Average price: Modest
Area: Finnieston, West End
Address: 1004 Argyle Street
Glasgow G3 8LZ
Phone: 0141 243 2170

#72
O2 Academy Glasgow
Category: Music Venues
Average price: Modest
Area: South Side, Gorbals
Address: 121 Eglinton Street
Glasgow G5 9NT
Phone: 0870 0771 2000

#73
Pivo Pivo
Category: Pub
Average price: Modest
Area: City Centre
Address: 15 Waterloo Street
Glasgow G2 6AY
Phone: 0141 564 8100

#74
Little Urban Achievers Club
Category: Bar, Hot Dogs, Pizza
Average price: Modest
Area: Great Western Road, Kelvinbridge
Address: 508 Great Western Road
Glasgow G12 8EL
Phone: 0141 237 4040

#75
Gin 71
Category: Cocktail Bar
Average price:
Area: City Centre
Address: 71 Renfield Street
Glasgow G2 1LF
Phone: 0141 353 2959

#76
Ferry
Category: British, Music Venues
Average price: Modest
Area: Finnieston, West End
Address: 25 Anderston Quay
Glasgow G3 8BX
Phone: 0141 553 0606

#77
Bier Hallse
Category: Pub, Gastropub, Pizza
Average price: Modest
Area: City Centre
Address: 7-9 Gordon Street
Glasgow G1 3PL
Phone: 0141 204 0706

#78
Hillhead Bookclub
Category: Bar, Scottish
Average price: Modest
Area: Hillhead, West End
Address: 17 Vinicombe Street
Glasgow G12 8
Phone: 0141 576 1700

#79
Maggie May's
Category: Bar, Music Venues, Club
Average price: Modest
Area: City Centre, Merchant City
Address: 60 Trongate
Glasgow G1 5EP
Phone: 0141 548 1350

#80
Max's Bar & Grill
Category: American, Club, American
Average price: Modest
Area: City Centre
Address: 73 Queen Street
Glasgow G1 3BZ
Phone: 0141 221 1379

#81
Barca Tapas
Category: Spanish, Basque,
Champagne Bar
Average price: Modest
Area: City Centre
Address: 48 Buchanan Street
Glasgow G1 3JX
Phone: 0141 248 6555

#82
Bar 10
Category: Pub, Mediterranean
Average price: Modest
Area: City Centre
Address: 10 Mitchell Lane
Glasgow G1 3NU
Phone: 0141 572 1448

#83
Meat Bar
Category: Bar, Burgers, Steakhouse
Average price: Modest
Area: City Centre
Address: 142 West Regent Street
Glasgow G2 2RQ
Phone: 0141 204 3605

#84
The Arlington Bar
Category: Bar
Average price: Inexpensive
Area: Woodlands, West End
Address: 130 Woodlands Road
Glasgow G3 6
Phone: 0141 332 9782

#85
Revolution
Category: Bar
Average price: Expensive
Area: City Centre
Address: 67-69 Renfield Street
Glasgow G2 1LF
Phone: 0141 331 2614

#86
The Queen Margaret Union
Category: Music Venues
Average price: Modest
Area: Hillhead, West End
Address: University Gardens
Glasgow G12 8QN
Phone: 0141 339 9784

#87
The Finnieston
Category: Seafood, Bar
Average price: Modest
Area: Finnieston, West End
Address: 1125 Argyle Street
Glasgow G3 8ND
Phone: 0141 222 2884

#88
Rhoderick Dhu
Category: Pub
Average price: Modest
Area: City Centre
Address: 21-23 Waterloo Street
Glasgow G2 6BZ
Phone: 0141 221 5479

#89
The Lab
Category: Lounge
Average price: Modest
Area: City Centre
Address: 26 Springfield Court
Glasgow G1 3DQ
Phone: 0141 222 2116

#90
Brazen Head
Category: Pub
Average price: Modest
Area: South Side, Gorbals
Address: 1-3 Cathcart Road
Glasgow G42 7BE
Phone: 0141 420 1530

#91
Macsorley's
Category: Pub
Average price: Modest
Area: City Centre
Address: 42 Jamaica Street
Glasgow G1 4QG
Phone: 0141 248 8581

#92
Kelvingrove Café
Category: Cocktail Bar, Cafe
Average price: Modest
Area: Finnieston, West End
Address: 1163 Argyle Street
Glasgow G3 8TB
Phone: 0141 221 8988

#93
**The Scottish Exhibition
and Conference Centre**
Category: Music Venues
Average price: Expensive
Area: Finnieston, West End
Address: Finnieston Quay
Glasgow G3 8HN
Phone: 0870 040 4000

#94
The Counting House
Category: British, Pub
Average price: Inexpensive
Area: City Centre
Address: 2 St Vincent Place
Glasgow G1 2DH
Phone: 0141 225 0160

#95
Bar Gumbo
Category: Cajun/Creole, Bar, British
Average price: Modest
Area: Partick, Byres Road, West End
Address: 71-77 Byres Road
Glasgow G11 5HN
Phone: 0141 334 7132

#96
Rufus T Firefly
Category: Pub
Average price: Modest
Area: City Centre
Address: 207 Hope Street
Glasgow G2 2UW
Phone: 0141 332 1469

#97
The Garage
Category: Club
Average price: Modest
Area: Charing Cross
Address: 490 SauchieHalls Street
Glasgow G3 7UE
Phone: 0141 332 1120

#98
Bath Street Palomino
Category: Bar
Average price: Modest
Area: City Centre
Address: 207 Bath St
Glasgow G2 4HZ
Phone: 0141 221 9444

#99
Big Slope
Category: Gastropub
Average price: Modest
Area: SauchieHalls Street West
Address: 36a Kelvingrove Street
Glasgow G3 7SA
Phone: 0141 333 0869

#100
Red Onion
Category: Brasserie, Wine Bar
Average price: Modest
Area: City Centre
Address: 257 W Campbell Street
Glasgow G2 4TT
Phone: 0141 221 6000

#101
Urban Brasserie
Category: Bar, Brasserie
Average price: Expensive
Area: City Centre
Address: 23-25 St Vincent Place
Glasgow G1 2DT
Phone: 0141 248 5636

#102
Velvet Elvis
Category: Bar, American
Average price: Modest
Area: Partick, West End
Address: 566 Dumbarton Road
Glasgow G11 7
Phone: 0141 334 6677

#103
The SSE Hydro
Category: Music Venues
Average price: Modest
Area: Finnieston, West End
Address: Exhibition Way
Glasgow G3 8WY
Phone: 0141 248 3000

#104
Rockus
Category: Bar
Average price: Modest
Area: Finnieston, West End
Address: 1038 Argyle Street
Glasgow G3 8LX
Phone: 0141 204 5075

#105
The Drake
Category: Pub
Average price: Modest
Area: Woodlands, West End
Address: 1 Lynedoch Street
Glasgow G3 6EF
Phone: 0141 332 7363

#106
Cottier's
Category: Pub, American
Average price: Modest
Area: Partick, West End
Address: 93-95 Hyndland Street
Glasgow G11 5PX
Phone: 0141 357 5825

#107
Vroni's
Category: Wine Bar
Average price: Expensive
Area: City Centre
Address: 47 W Nile St
Glasgow G1 2PT
Phone: 0141 221 4677

#108
Brutti Compadres
Category: Bar, Tapas Bar, Mediterranean
Average price: Modest
Area: City Centre, Merchant City
Address: 3 Virginia Court
Glasgow G1 1TS
Phone: 0141 552 1777

#109
Hengler's Circus
Category: Pub
Average price: Inexpensive
Area: SauchieHalls Street, City Centre
Address: 361-363 SauchieHalls Street
Glasgow G2 3HU
Phone: 0141 331 9810

#110
Jackson's Drink Mongers
Category: Pub
Average price: Inexpensive
Area: City Centre
Address: 97 Cambridge Street
Glasgow G3 6RU
Phone: 0141 332 5298

#111
The Corinthian Club
Category: British, Lounge, Gastropub
Average price: Expensive
Area: City Centre, Merchant City
Address: 191 Ingram St
Glasgow G1 1DA
Phone: 0141 552 1101

#112
Booly Mardy's
Category: Gastropub, Cocktail Bar
Average price: Modest
Area: Byres Road, Hillhead, West End
Address: 28 Vinicombe Street
Glasgow G12 8BE
Phone: 0141 560 8004

#113
Alston Bar & Beef
Category: Steakhouse, Cocktail Bar
Average price: Modest
Area: City Centre
Address: 79 Gordon Street
Glasgow G1 3PE
Phone: 0141 221 7627

#114
The Cathouse
Category: Club, Music Venues
Average price: Modest
Area: City Centre
Address: 15 Union St
Glasgow G1 3RB
Phone: 0141 248 6606

#115
Mama San
Category: Asian Fusion,
Champagne Bar
Average price: Expensive
Area: City Centre
Address: 190 Bath Street
Glasgow G2 4HG
Phone: 0141 352 8800

#116
Crystal Palace
Category: Pub, Gastropub
Average price: Inexpensive
Area: City Centre
Address: 36 Jamaica St
Glasgow G1 4QD
Phone: 0141 221 2624

#117
Failte
Category: Pub
Average price: Inexpensive
Area: City Centre
Address: 79 St Vincent St
Glasgow G2 5TF
Phone: 0141 248 4989

#118
Centre For Contemporary Arts
Category: Art Gallery, Bar
Average price: Expensive
Area: City Centre
Address: 350 SauchieHalls Street
Glasgow G2 3JD
Phone: 0141 352 4900

#119
Bar Gandolfi
Category: Bar
Average price: Modest
Area: City Centre, Merchant City
Address: 64 Albion Street
Glasgow G1 1NY
Phone: 0141 552 6831

#120
Bothy Restaurant
Category: British, Scottish
Average price: Modest
Area: Byres Road, West End
Address: 11 Ruthven Lane
Glasgow G12 9BG
Phone: 0845 166 6032

#121
Jinty McGuinty's
Category: Pub
Average price: Modest
Area: Hillhead, West End
Address: 23 Ashton Lane
Glasgow G12 8SJ
Phone: 0141 339 0747

#122
The Social
Category: Bar, Gastropub
Average price: Modest
Area: City Centre
Address: 27 Royal Exchange Square
Glasgow G1 3AJ
Phone: 0845 166 6016

#123
Bamboo
Category: Club
Average price: Modest
Area: City Centre
Address: 51A W Regent Street
Glasgow G2 2AE
Phone: 0141 332 1067

#124
Horseshoe Bar
Category: Pub
Average price: Modest
Area: City Centre
Address: 17-19 Drury Street
Glasgow G2 5AE
Phone: 0141 229 5711

#125
Moskito
Category: Pub, Gastropub
Average price: Modest
Area: City Centre
Address: 198-200 Bath Street
Glasgow G2 4HG
Phone: 0141 331 1777

#126
The Arches Cafe Bar
Category: French, Bar
Average price: Modest
Area: City Centre
Address: 253 Argyle Street
Glasgow G2 8DL
Phone: 0141 565 1035

#127
The Auctioneers
Category: Pub
Average price: Inexpensive
Area: City Centre
Address: 6 North Court
Glasgow G1 2DP
Phone: 0141 222 2989

#128
O'Henry's
Category: Pub, British
Average price: Modest
Area: City Centre
Address: 14 Drury Street
Glasgow G2 5AA
Phone: 0141 248 3751

#129
Clutha Vaults
Category: Pub
Average price: Inexpensive
Area: City Centre, Merchant City
Address: 167 Stockwell Street
Glasgow G1 4SP
Phone: 0141 552 7520

#130
The Courtyard
Category: Pub
Average price: Modest
Area: City Centre
Address: 84 West Nile Street
Glasgow G1 2QH
Phone: 0141 332 5021

#131
Gallus
Category: Pub
Average price: Modest
Area: Partick, West End
Address: 80 Dumbarton Road
Glasgow G11 6NX
Phone: 0141 334 8012

#132
Glasgow University Union
Category: Club, Dive Bar, Local Flavour
Average price: Inexpensive
Area: Hillhead, West End
Address: 32 University Ave
Glasgow G12 8
Phone: 0141 339 8697

#133
The Butterfly and Pig West End
Category: Bar, British, Music Venues
Average price: Modest
Area: Partick, West End
Address: 2 Partickbridge Street
Glasgow G11 6PL
Phone: 0141 337 1200

#134
Old Smiddy
Category: Pub
Average price: Modest
Area: South Side
Address: 131 Old Castle Road
Glasgow G44 5TJ
Phone: 0141 637 3284

#135
Chaophraya
Category: Lounge, Thai
Average price: Expensive
Area: City Centre
Address: Nelson Mandela Place
Glasgow G1 2LL
Phone: 0141 332 0041

#136
Basement Bar
Category: Bar
Average price: Inexpensive
Area: Byres Road, West End
Address: 191 Byres Road
Glasgow G12 8
Phone: 0141 339 7203

#137
All Bar One
Category: Wine Bar
Average price: Expensive
Area: City Centre
Address: 56-72 St Vincent Street
Glasgow G2 5TS
Phone: 0141 229 6060

#138
Crosslands
Category: Pub
Average price: Modest
Area: West End
Address: 182 Queen Margaret Drive
Glasgow G20 8NX
Phone: 0141 576 0127

#139
The Hyndland Fox
Category: Cafe, Scottish, Bar
Average price: Modest
Area: West End
Address: 43 Clarence Drive
Glasgow G12 9QN
Phone: 0141 357 2909

#140
Common
Category: Club
Average price: Inexpensive
Area: City Centre
Address: 25 Royal Exchange Sq
Glasgow G1 3AG
Phone: 0141 204 0101

#141
Home
Category: Gastropub, Lounge, British
Average price: Modest
Area: City Centre, Merchant City
Address: 80 Albion Street
Glasgow G1 1NY
Phone: 0141 552 1734

#142
Shanghai Shuffle
Category: Karaoke, Chinese
Average price: Modest
Area: City Centre
Address: 256 Bath Street
Glasgow G2 4JW
Phone: 0141 572 0888

#143
Q Club
Category: Snooker & Pool Hallss, Pub
Average price: Inexpensive
Area: Charing Cross, Woodlands
Address: 101 ST Georges Road
Glasgow G3 6JA
Phone: 0141 333 9035

#144
The Old Hairdressers
Category: Music Venues, Pub
Average price: Modest
Area: City Centre
Address: 20-28 Renfield Lane
Glasgow G2 5AR
Phone: 0141 222 2254

#145
Snaffle Bit
Category: Pub
Average price: Inexpensive
Area: SauchieHalls Street West
Address: 979 SauchieHalls Street
Glasgow G3 7TQ
Phone: 0141 339 7163

#146
The Edward Wylie
Category: Pub
Average price: Inexpensive
Area: City Centre
Address: 107-109 Bothwell Street
Glasgow G2 7EE
Phone: 0141 229 5480

#147
Avant Garde
Category: Pub, Mediterranean, Gastropub
Average price: Modest
Area: City Centre, Merchant City
Address: 34-44 King Street
Glasgow G1 5QT
Phone: 0141 552 7123

#148
Viper
Category: Club
Average price: Inexpensive
Area: Great Western Road, West End
Address: 500 Great Western Road
Glasgow G12 8EN
Phone: 0845 659 5906

#149
Underground Glasgow Bar
Category: Pub
Average price: Modest
Area: City Centre, Merchant City
Address: 6a John Street
Glasgow G1 1JQ
Phone: 0141 553 2456

#150
Committee Room No. 9
Category: Wine Bar, Gastropub
Average price: Inexpensive
Area: City Centre, Merchant City
Address: 18 John Street
Glasgow G1 1JQ
Phone: 0845 166 6035

#151
University Of Strathclyde Students Union
Category: Club
Average price: Modest
Area: City Centre, Merchant City
Address: 90 John Street
Glasgow G1 1JH
Phone: 0141 567 5000

#152
Arta
Category: Mediterranean, Bar, Spanish, Basque
Average price: Modest
Area: City Centre, Merchant City
Address: 62 Albion Street
Glasgow G1 1PA
Phone: 0845 166 6018

#153
The Aragon
Category: Pub
Average price: Exclusive
Area: Partick, Byres Road, West End
Address: 131 Byres Road
Glasgow G12 8TT
Phone: 0141 339 3252

#154
The Ark
Category: Pub
Average price: Inexpensive
Area: City Centre, Merchant City
Address: 42-46 N Frederick St
Glasgow G1 2BS
Phone: 0141 559 4331

#155
West End Festival Glasgow
Category: Local Flavour, Music Venues
Average price: Inexpensive
Area: Partick, West End
Address: 50 Havelock Street
Glasgow G11 5JE
Phone: 0141 341 0844

#156
The Burrell
Category: Pub, British
Average price: Modest
Area: South Side
Address: 1534 Pollokshaws Road
Glasgow G43 1RF
Phone: 0141 632 0161

#157
Molly Malones
Category: Pub
Average price: Modest
Area: City Centre
Address: 224 Hope Street
Glasgow G2 2UG
Phone: 0141 332 2757

#158
The Admiral
Category: Pub
Average price: Modest
Area: City Centre
Address: 72a Waterloo Street
Glasgow G2 7DA
Phone: 0141 221 7705

#159
Boteco Do Brasil
Category: Bar, Brazilian, Tapas Bar
Average price: Modest
Area: City Centre, Merchant City
Address: 62 Trongate
Glasgow G1 5EP
Phone: 0141 548 1330

#160
Hummingbird
Category: Bar, British
Average price: Modest
Area: City Centre
Address: 186 Bath St
Glasgow G2 4HG
Phone: 0141 332 8513

#161
Bar Soba
Category: Bar, Asian Fusion
Average price: Modest
Area: Byres Road, West End
Address: 116-122 Byres Road
Glasgow G12 8TB
Phone: 0141 357 5482

#162
Skinny's
Category: Pub, Burgers
Average price: Modest
Area: West End
Address: 61 Otago Street
Glasgow G12 8PQ
Phone: 0141 339 8455

#163
Firewater
Category: Pub, Club
Average price: Modest
Area: SauchieHalls Street, City Centre
Address: 319 SauchieHalls Street
Glasgow G2 3HW
Phone: 0141 354 0350

#164
Delmonicas
Category: Pub, Gay Bar
Average price: Inexpensive
Area: City Centre, Merchant City
Address: 68 Virginia Street
Glasgow G1 1TX
Phone: 0141 552 4803

#165
Atholl Arms
Category: Pub
Average price: Modest
Area: City Centre
Address: 134 Renfield Street
Glasgow G2 3AU
Phone: 0141 332 2541

#166
October
Category: Club, Wine Bar
Average price: Modest
Area: Buchanan Street, City Centre
Address: Princes Square
Glasgow G1 3JN
Phone: 0845 166 6014

#167
Winterfest George Square
Category: Local Flavour, Music Venues
Average price: Inexpensive
Area: City Centre, Merchant City
Address: George Sq
Glasgow G1 1DU
Phone: 0141 302 2845

#168
Court Bar
Category: Pub
Average price: Modest
Area: City Centre, Merchant City
Address: 69 Hutcheson Street
Glasgow G1 1SH
Phone: 0141 552 2463

#169
Solid Rock Cafe
Category: Pub
Average price: Modest
Area: City Centre
Address: 19 Hope Street
Glasgow G2 6AB
Phone: 0141 221 1105

#170
The Gate
Category: Pub
Average price: Modest
Area: City Centre, Merchant City
Address: 62 Trongate
Glasgow G1 5ET
Phone: 0141 548 1330

#171
Gilmorehill G12 Theatre
Category: Theatre, Music Venues
Average price: Modest
Area: Kelvingrove, West End
Address: 9-11 University Ave
Glasgow G12 8QQ
Phone: 0141 330 5522

#172
Carnarvon Bar
Category: Pub
Average price: Modest
Area: Woodlands, West End
Address: 129 ST. Georges Road
Glasgow G3 6JA
Phone: 0141 332 5125

#173
Press Bar
Category: Pub, Dive Bar
Average price: Inexpensive
Area: City Centre, Merchant City
Address: 199 Albion Street
Glasgow G1 1RU
Phone: 0141 552 5142

#174
Fiddlers Bar
Category: Pub
Average price: Inexpensive
Area: Partick, West End
Address: 10 Fortrose Street
Glasgow G11 5NS
Phone: 0141 339 7406

#175
Linen 1906
Category: Wine Bar, Music Venues
Average price: Modest
Area: South Side, Shawlands
Address: 1110 Pollokshaws Road
Glasgow G41 2HG
Phone: 0141 649 3815

#176
The Libertine
Category: Bar
Average price: Modest
Area: City Centre, Merchant City
Address: 45-47 Bell Street
Glasgow G1 1NX
Phone: 0141 552 3539

#177
The Rock
Category: Pub, Gastropub
Average price: Inexpensive
Area: Partick, West End
Address: 205 Hyndland Rd
Glasgow G12 9HE
Phone: 0141 334 6977

#178
Driftwood
Category: Pub
Average price: Inexpensive
Area: Charing Cross, City Centre
Address: 2 St Georges Road
Glasgow G3 6UJ
Phone: 0141 332 7000

#179
The Waverley Tea Room
Category: Bar, Italian, British
Average price: Modest
Area: South Side
Address: 18 Moss Side Road
Glasgow G41 3TN
Phone: 0845 659 5903

#180
Tunnel
Category: Club, Bar
Average price: Modest
Area: City Centre
Address: 84 Mitchell Street
Glasgow G1 3NA
Phone: 0141 204 1000

#181
O'Couture
Category: Club, British
Average price: Modest
Area: SauchieHalls Street, City Centre
Address: 373-377 SauchieHalls Street
Glasgow G2 3HU
Phone: 0141 333 3940

#182
Lloyds No.1
Category: Pub, Gastropub
Average price: Modest
Area: City Centre
Address: 151 West George Street
Glasgow G2 2JJ
Phone: 0141 229 7560

#183
The Cabin
Category: Irish, Karaoke
Average price: Expensive
Area: Partick
Address: 998 Dumbarton Road
Glasgow G14 9UJ
Phone: 0141 569 1036

#184
The Dolphin
Category: Pub
Average price: Modest
Area: Partick, West End
Address: 157 Dumbarton Road
Glasgow G11 6PT
Phone: 0141 576 0175

#185
The Islay Inn
Category: Pub
Average price: Modest
Area: Finnieston, West End
Address: 1256-1260 Argyle Street
Glasgow G3 8TJ
Phone: 0141 334 7774

#186
Bar Square
Category: British, Bar
Average price: Expensive
Area: City Centre, Merchant City
Address: 5 Bell St
Glasgow G1 1NU
Phone: 0141 552 3232

#187
Dram!
Category: Pub
Average price: Modest
Area: Woodlands, West End
Address: 232-246 Woodlands Rd
Glasgow G3 6ND
Phone: 0141 332 1622

#188
O'Neills
Category: Pub
Average price: Modest
Area: Charing Cross, SauchieHalls
Street, City Centre
Address: 457 SauchieHalls Street
Glasgow G2 3LG
Phone: 0141 332 9482

#189
Glasgow Art Club
Category: Art Gallery, Music Venues
Average price: Modest
Area: City Centre
Address: 185 Bath Street
Glasgow G2 4HU
Phone: 0141 248 5210

#190
Broadcast
Category: Music Venues, Pub
Average price: Modest
Area: Charing Cross, SauchieHalls
Street, City Centre
Address: 427 SauchieHalls Street
Glasgow G2 3LG
Phone: 0141 332 7304

#191
Moda
Category: Bar
Average price: Modest
Area: City Centre, Merchant City
Address: 58 Virginia Street
Glasgow G1 1TX
Phone: 0141 553 2553

#192
One Up
Category: Pub
Average price: Modest
Area: City Centre
Address: 23 Royal Exchange Square
Glasgow G1 3AJ
Phone: 0141 225 5612

#193
Jellyhill
Category: Bar
Average price: Modest
Area: West End
Address: 195 Hyndland Rd
Glasgow G12 9HT
Phone: 0141 341 0125

#194
The Two Figs
Category: Pub, Cafe
Average price: Modest
Area: Partick, Byres Road, West End
Address: 5 and 9 Byres Road
Glasgow G11 5RD
Phone: 0141 334 7277

#195
The Sanctuary
Category: Club, Lounge
Average price: Modest
Area: Partick, West End
Address: 59 Dumbarton Road
Glasgow G11 6PD
Phone: 0141 334 0770

#196
Stanley Bar
Category: Pub
Average price: Modest
Area: South Side, Kinning Park
Address: 69 Stanley Street
Glasgow G41 1JA
Phone: 0141 429 1806

#197
The Ruag Function Suite
Category: Wine Bar
Average price: Modest
Area: City Centre
Address: 21-23 Waterloo Street
Glasgow G2 6BZ
Phone: 0141 221 7824

#198
Kuta
Category: Bar, Asian Fusion
Average price: Modest
Area: City Centre
Address: 104 Bath Street
Glasgow G2 2EN
Phone: 0141 332 6678

#199
Otis B Driftwood
Category: Dive Bar, Music Venues
Average price: Modest
Area: SauchieHalls Street, City Centre
Address: 201 Hope Street
Glasgow G2 2UW
Phone: 0141 332 1469

#200
Westering Winds
Category: Pub
Average price: Modest
Area: City Centre
Address: 123 Bridgegate
Glasgow G1 5HY
Phone: 0141 552 3674

#201
The Winchester Club
Category: Club
Average price: Modest
Area: City Centre, Merchant City
Address: 45 Bell Street
Glasgow G1 1NX
Phone: 0141 552 3586

#202
Bar 67
Category: Pub
Average price: Inexpensive
Area: Gallowgate
Address: 257-259 Gallowgate
Glasgow G4 0TP
Phone: 0141 564 1967

#203
The Maltman
Category: Pub
Average price: Modest
Area: City Centre
Address: 59-63 Renfield Street
Glasgow G2 1LF
Phone: 0141 331 0299

#204
Speakeasy
Category: Gay Bar
Average price: Modest
Area: City Centre, Merchant City
Address: 10 John St
Glasgow G1 1HP
Phone: 0845 166 6036

#205
Hetherington Research Club
Category: Club, Bar
Average price: Modest
Area: West End
Address: University of Glasgow
Glasgow G12 8QQ
Phone: 0141 330 4503

#206
McChuills Public House
Category: Pub
Average price: Inexpensive
Area: Merchant City
Address: 40 High Street
Glasgow G1 1NL
Phone: 0141 552 2135

#207
Hyde Bar & Dining
Category: Lounge, Cocktail Bar
Average price: Modest
Area: Partick, West End
Address: 9-17 Partick Bridge Street
Glasgow G11 6PN
Phone: 0141 334 9568

#208
The Wee Pub at the Chip
Category: Bar
Average price: Modest
Area: Hillhead, West End
Address: 8-12 Ashton Lane
Glasgow G12 8SJ
Phone: 0141 334 5007

#209
The Hill
Category: Bar, British
Average price: Modest
Area: Partick, Byres Road, West End
Address: 94 Byres Road
Glasgow G12 8TB
Phone: 0141 339 8558

#210
Three Craws
Category: Pub
Average price: Expensive
Area: West End
Address: 501 Crow Road
Glasgow G11 7DN
Phone: 0141 958 1221

#211
Esquire House
Category: Pub
Average price: Inexpensive
Area: Great Western Road, Anniesland
Address: 1487 Great Western Road
Glasgow G12 0AU
Phone: 0141 341 1130

#212
Saint Judes
Category: Bar
Average price: Exclusive
Area: City Centre
Address: 190 Bath Street
Glasgow G2 4HG
Phone: 0141 352 8800

#213
The Piper
Category: British, Pub
Average price: Modest
Area: City Centre, Merchant City
Address: 57 Cochrane Street
Glasgow G1 1HL
Phone: 0141 552 1740

#214
Nude
Category: Pub
Average price: Modest
Area: Hillhead, West End
Address: 46 Ashton Lane
Glasgow G12 8SJ
Phone: 0845 166 6011

#215
Walkabout
Category: Pub, Sports Bar, Australian
Average price: Modest
Area: City Centre
Address: 128 Renfield Street
Glasgow G2 3AL
Phone: 0141 332 8209

#216
The Howlin' Wolf
Category: Bar, Music Venues
Average price: Modest
Area: City Centre
Address: 100 Bath St
Glasgow G2 2EN
Phone: 0141 333 3333

#217
Ivory Blacks
Category: Music Venues
Average price: Modest
Area: City Centre
Address: 56 Oswald St
Glasgow G1 4PL
Phone: 0141 248 4114

#218
Clockwork Beer Co.
Category: Pub, Gastropub
Average price: Expensive
Area: South Side, Mount Florida
Address: 1153-1155 Cathcart Road
Glasgow G42 9HB
Phone: 0141 649 0184

#219
The Record Factory
Category: Dive Bar
Average price: Modest
Area: Partick, Byres Road, West End
Address: 17 Byres Road
Glasgow G11 5RD
Phone: 0141 334 8888

#220
Iron Horse
Category: Pub
Average price: Modest
Area: SauchieHalls Street, City Centre
Address: 115 West Nile Street
Glasgow G1 2SB
Phone: 0141 332 2215

#221
The Junction Bar
Category: Pub
Average price: Modest
Area: City Centre
Address: 14 - 16 West George Street
Glasgow G2 1DA
Phone: 0141 353 6082

#222
Braehead Arena
Category: Music Venues
Average price:
Area: City Centre
Address: Unit 25 Braehead Shopping
Centre, Glasgow G51 4BN
Phone: 0141 885 4600

#223
The Riding Room
Category: Bar, Club
Average price: Modest
Area: City Centre, Merchant City
Address: 58 Virginia Street
Glasgow G1 1TX
Phone: 0845 659 5904

#224
The Bank
Category: Pub, Gastropub
Average price: Modest
Area: South Side
Address: 443 Clarkston Rd
Glasgow G44 3LL
Phone: 0141 637 8461

#225
Heraghty's Bar
Category: Pub
Average price: Modest
Area: South Side
Address: 708 Pollokshaws Road
Glasgow G41 2AD
Phone: 0141 423 0380

#226
Allison Arms
Category: Pub
Average price: Expensive
Area: South Side
Address: 720 Pollokshaws Road
Glasgow G41 2AD
Phone: 0141 423 1661

#227
Strathmore Bar
Category: Pub
Average price: Modest
Area: West End
Address: 775 Maryhill Road
Glasgow G20 7TL
Phone: 0141 946 8114

#228
The Lane
Category: Bar
Average price: Expensive
Area: Hillhead, West End
Address: Ashton Ln
Glasgow G12 8SJ
Phone: 0845 166 6028

#229
Collage Bar
Category: Bar
Average price: Modest
Area: City Centre
Address: 301 Argyle Street
Glasgow G2 8DL
Phone: 0141 225 2046

#230
Toby Jug
Category: Pub
Average price: Modest
Area: City Centre
Address: 8 Waterloo Street
Glasgow G2 6DA
Phone: 0141 221 4159

#231
The Berkeley Suite
Category: Pub
Average price: Expensive
Area: Charing Cross, West End
Address: 237 North Street
Glasgow G3 7DL
Phone: 0141 237 3235

#232
The Society Room
Category: Pub
Average price: Modest
Area: City Centre
Address: 151 W George Street
Glasgow G2 2JJ
Phone: 0141 229 7560

#233
Swing
Category: Cocktail Bar
Average price: Modest
Area: City Centre
Address: 183A Hope Street
Glasgow G2 2UL
Phone: 0141 332 2147

#234
Creation Studio
Category: Music Venues
Average price: Modest
Area: City Centre, Merchant City
Address: 16 Trongate
Glasgow G1 5EU
Phone: 0141 237 7653

#235
The Old Schoolhouse
Category: Bar
Average price: Inexpensive
Area: Woodlands, West End
Address: 311 Woodlands Rd
Glasgow G3 6NG
Phone: 0141 337 1790

#236
Millenium Platter
Category: Buffet, Asian Fusion, Bar
Average price: Modest
Area: Partick, West End
Address: 120 Dumbarton Rd
Glasgow G11 6NY
Phone: 0141 339 2068

#237
The Box
Category: Dive Bar, Music Venues
Average price: Inexpensive
Area: City Centre
Address: 431 SauchieHalls Street
Glasgow G2 3LG
Phone: 0141 332 5059

#238
Savoy Disco
Category: Club
Average price: Exclusive
Area: City Centre
Address: 140 SauchieHalls Street
Glasgow G2 3DH
Phone: 0141 332 0751

#239
Citation Taverne & Restaurant
Category: Pub, Gastropub
Average price: Expensive
Area: City Centre, Merchant City
Address: 40 Wilson Street
Glasgow G1 1HD
Phone: 0141 559 6799

#240
Corona Bar
Category: Pub
Average price: Modest
Area: South Side, Shawlands
Address: 1039 Pollokshaws Road
Glasgow G41 3YF
Phone: 0141 632 6230

#241
The Lee
Category: Pub, Gastropub
Average price: Inexpensive
Area: City Centre
Address: 100 ST James Road
Glasgow G4 0PS
Phone: 0141 564 1973

#242
A Little Taste of Italy
Category: Bar
Average price: Modest
Area: Charing Cross, City Centre
Address: 61 Elmbank Street
Glasgow G2 4PQ
Phone: 0141 332 3565

#243
Curry Karaoke
Category: Karaoke, Indian
Average price: Modest
Area: City Centre
Address: 100 Stobcross Road
Glasgow G3 8QQ
Phone: 0141 221 0313

#244
Rock Lobster
Category: British, Seafood, Wine Bar
Average price: Modest
Area: City Centre, Merchant City
Address: Unit 1/4 43 Virginia Ct
Glasgow G1
Phone: 0141 553 2326

#245
Bar Bliss
Category: Pub
Average price: Expensive
Area: City Centre
Address: 1 Cowgate
Glasgow G66 1HW
Phone: 0141 776 0988

#246
Intermezzo Bar Public House
Category: Pub
Average price: Modest
Area: City Centre
Address: 22 Renfrew Street
Glasgow G2 3BW
Phone: 0141 332 6288

#247
Ceroc Scotland Glasgow
Category: Music Venues,
Dance Studio, Jazz & Blues
Average price: Inexpensive
Area: City Centre
Address: 292 SauchieHalls Street
Glasgow G2 3JA
Phone: 07528 694901

#248
Brechin Bar
Category: Pub
Average price: Modest
Area: South Side, Govan
Address: 803 Govan Road
Glasgow G51 3DJ
Phone: 0141 445 1349

#249
FHQ
Category: Bar
Average price: Modest
Area: City Centre, Merchant City
Address: 10 John Street
Glasgow G1 1JQ
Phone: 0845 166 6037

#250
The Merchant
Category: Pub
Average price: Modest
Area: City Centre
Address: 134-136 West George Street
Glasgow G2 2HG
Phone: 0141 353 3926

#251
Gala Casino
Category: Gambling
Average price: Modest
Area: Charing Cross, City Centre
Address: 528 SauchieHalls Street
Glasgow G2 3LW
Phone: 0141 332 8171

#252
Manhattans Bar Diner
Category: American, Bar
Average price: Modest
Area: South Side
Address: 235 St Andrews Road
Glasgow G41 1PD
Phone: 0141 429 4657

#253
Bargo Public House
Category: Pub
Average price: Expensive
Area: City Centre, Merchant City
Address: Albion Street
Glasgow G1 1NY
Phone: 0141 553 4771

#254
Pourhouse
Category: Pub
Average price: Modest
Area: Finnieston, West End
Address: 1038-1042 Argyle Street
Glasgow G3 8LX
Phone: 0141 221 4449

#255
Victoria Bar
Category: Pub
Average price: Modest
Area: South Side
Address: 400 Victoria Road
Glasgow G42 8YS
Phone: 0141 423 3303

#256
Jumpin Jaks
Category: Pub, Club
Average price: Modest
Area: SauchieHalls Street, City Centre
Address: 299 SauchieHalls Street
Glasgow G2 3HQ
Phone: 0844 891 0850

#257
Kelly's Bar
Category: Pub
Average price: Modest
Area: South Side
Address: 686-688 Pollokshaws Road
Glasgow G41 2QB
Phone: 0141 423 1387

#258
Deoch an Dorus
Category: Bar
Average price: Modest
Area: Partick, West End
Address: 427-429 Dumbarton Road
Glasgow G11 6DD
Phone: 0141 357 2644

#259
The Rosevale Tavern
Category: Pub
Average price: Modest
Area: Partick, West End
Address: 483 Dumbarton Road
Glasgow G11 6BE
Phone: 0141 337 2877

#260
Miso
Category: Pub
Average price: Modest
Area: City Centre
Address: 53-57 West Regent Street
Glasgow G2 2AE
Phone: 0141 333 0133

#261
The Pacific
Category: Bar, Thai, Mexican
Average price: Modest
Area: Partick, West End
Address: 562 Dumbarton Road
Glasgow G11 6RH
Phone: 0141 334 9000

#262
The Shed
Category: Club
Average price: Modest
Area: South Side, Shawlands
Address: 26 Langside Avenue
Glasgow G41 2QS
Phone: 0141 649 5020

#263
Minnesota Fats
Category: Snooker & Pool Halls
Average price: Modest
Area: South Side, Mount Florida
Address: 1055 Cathcart Road
Glasgow G42 9AF
Phone: 0141 649 0558

#264
Lauders
Category: Pub
Average price: Modest
Area: SauchieHalls Street, City Centre
Address: 76 SauchieHalls Street
Glasgow G2 3DE
Phone: 0141 332 9690

#265
Times Square
Category: Pub
Average price: Inexpensive
Area: City Centre
Address: 46-48 St Enoch Square
Glasgow G1 4DH
Phone: 0141 221 6579

#266
Thomsons Public House
Category: Pub
Average price: Modest
Area: Springburn
Address: 275 Springburn Way
Glasgow G21 1JX
Phone: 0141 557 5819

#267
NYC
Category: Bar
Average price: Modest
Area: City Centre
Address: 185 Hope Street
Glasgow G2
Phone: 0141 353 2913

#268
Yates
Category: Pub, Gastropub
Average price: Inexpensive
Area: City Centre
Address: 134-136 W George Street
Glasgow G2 2HG
Phone: 0141 353 3926

#269
The Halls
Category: Pub
Average price: Inexpensive
Area: Charing Cross, SauchieHalls
Street, City Centre
Address: 457 SauchieHalls St
Glasgow G2 3LG
Phone: 0141 352 7970

#270
Sportsman Bar
Category: Pub
Average price: Expensive
Area: Rutherglen
Address: 73
Glasgow Road
Glasgow G73 1LJ
Phone: 0141 647 1262

#271
McMillans Emporium
Category: Delis, Wine Bar
Average price: Modest
Area: Partick, West End
Address: 6-8 Norby Road
Glasgow G11 7BN
Phone: 0141 337 6988

#272
Diamond Dolls
Category: Adult Entertainment
Average price: Exclusive
Area: City Centre
Address: 39 Mitchell Street
Glasgow G1 3LN
Phone: 0141 226 3490

#273
The Mini Bar
Category: Pub, Scottish, British
Average price: Modest
Area: City Centre
Address: 244a Bath Street
Glasgow G2 4JW
Phone: 0141 332 2732

#274
Baby Grand
Category: Bar, Brasserie
Average price: Modest
Area: Charing Cross, City Centre
Address: 3 - 7 Elmbank Gardens
Glasgow G2 4NQ
Phone: 0141 248 4942

#275
Lakota
Category: Lounge
Average price: Inexpensive
Area: City Centre
Address: 110-114 W George Street
Glasgow G2 1NF
Phone: 0141 332 9724

#276
Zebra Bar & Cafe
Category: Bar, Music Venues
Average price: Inexpensive
Area: City Centre, Merchant City
Address: 32-34 Queen Street
Glasgow G1 3DX
Phone: 0141 221 8954

#277
AXM
Category: Gay Bar
Average price: Modest
Area: City Centre, Merchant City
Address: 80 Glassford Street
Glasgow G1 1UR
Phone: 0141 552 5761

#278
Mcconnells Bar
Category: Pub
Average price: Inexpensive
Area: City Centre
Address: 335 Hope St
Glasgow G2 3PT
Phone: 0141 333 9844

#279
The Grove
Category: Pub
Average price: Inexpensive
Area: Finnieston, West End
Address: 8 Kelvingrove St
Glasgow G3 7RX
Phone: 0141 243 2565

#280
Gala Casino
Category: Gambling
Average price: Modest
Area: City Centre, Merchant City
Address: 16-18 Glassford Street
Glasgow G1 1UL
Phone: 0141 553 5410

#281
Muse
Category: Pub, Gastropub
Average price: Inexpensive
Area: City Centre
Address: 35 - 41 Queen Street
Glasgow G1 3EF
Phone: 0141 221 1779

#282
The Bellrock
Category: Pub
Average price: Inexpensive
Area: South Side, Kinning Park
Address: 4-6 Cornwall St
Glasgow G41 1AH
Phone: 0141 427 7712

#283
Finlays Bar
Category: Pub, Food
Average price: Modest
Area: South Side, Shawlands
Address: 137-139 Kilmarnock Road
Glasgow G41 3YT
Phone: 0141 636 4440

#284
Orchard Park Hotel
Category: Hotel, Bar
Average price: Modest
Area: Giffnock, South Side
Address: 2 Park Road
Glasgow G46 7LY
Phone: 0141 638 1044

#285
Metropolitan
Category: Lounge, Champagne Bar
Average price: Expensive
Area: City Centre, Merchant City
Address: 60 Candleriggs
Glasgow G1 1LE
Phone: 0141 553 1488

#286
Pewter Pot
Category: Pub
Average price: Inexpensive
Area: Kelvinbridge, West End
Address: 392 N Woodside Road
Glasgow G20 6NF
Phone: 0141 341 1030

#287
Victoria Bar
Category: Bar, Gastropub
Average price: Modest
Area: Partick, West End
Address: 336 Dumbarton Rd
Glasgow G11 6TG
Phone: 0141 339 1000

#288
The Common Room
Category: Pub
Average price: Modest
Area: Partick, Byres Road, West End
Address: 71-77 Byres Rd
Glasgow G11 5HN
Phone: 0141 334 7132

#289
BoBar
Category: Brasserie, Cocktail Bar
Average price: Modest
Area: Byres Road, Great Western Road
Address: 383 Byres Road
Glasgow G12 8AU
Phone: 0141 341 6516

#290
Beechings Public House
Category: Pub
Average price: Expensive
Area: South Side
Address: 34 Clarkston Road
Glasgow G44 3QH
Phone: 0141 633 3585

#291
The Alpen Lodge
Category: Pub
Average price: Inexpensive
Area: City Centre
Address: 25a Hope Street
Glasgow G2 6AB
Phone: 0141 221 4648

#292
Arc Studio
Category: Theatre, Music Venues
Average price: Modest
Area: South Side, Tradeston
Address: 65 Commerce Street
Glasgow G5 8AD
Phone: 0141 418 0818

#293
The Golf Lounge
Category: Pub
Average price: Modest
Area: City Centre
Address: 221 West George Street
Glasgow G2 2ND
Phone: 0141 248 1611

#294
Highlight
Category: Comedy Club, Music Venues
Average price: Modest
Area: City Centre
Address: 11 Renfrew St
Glasgow G2 3AB
Phone: 0844 844 0044

#295
Carlton Studio
Category: Music Venues, Theatre
Average price: Modest
Area: South Side, Gorbals
Address: 54 Carlton Pl
Glasgow G5 9TW
Phone: 0141 429 5723

#296
Drouthy's
Category: Pub
Average price: Modest
Area: City Centre
Address: 157 Queen Street
Glasgow G1 3BJ
Phone: 0141 243 2964

#297
Sharkeys Bar
Category: Pub
Average price: Inexpensive
Area: South Side, Gorbals
Address: 51 Old Rutherglen Road
Glasgow G5 9DT
Phone: 0141 429 3944

#298
Katie's Bar Glasgow
Category: Gay Bar
Average price:
Area: City Centre, Merchant City
Address: Glasgow G1 1HP
Phone: 0141 237 3030

#299
Bilberry Cocktail Bar
Category: Cocktail Bar
Average price: Modest
Area: SauchieHalls Street West
Address: 923 SauchieHalls Street
Glasgow G3 7TQ
Phone: 0141 330 1550

#300
The White Elephant
Category: Pub
Average price: Modest
Area: South Side
Address: 128 Merrylee Road
Glasgow G44 3DL
Phone: 0141 637 5774

#301
McKinnon's Bar
Category: Pub
Average price: Modest
Area: Gallowgate
Address: 48 Gallowgate
Glasgow G1 5AB
Phone: 0141 552 3525

#302
The Pandora
Category: Pub
Average price: Modest
Area: South Side
Address: 349 Victoria Road
Glasgow G42 7SA
Phone: 0141 423 7017

#303
The Pines
Category: Pub
Average price: Modest
Area: South Side
Address: 210 Crookston Road
Glasgow G52 3NF
Phone: 0141 810 8751

#304
The Vale
Category: Pub
Average price: Inexpensive
Area: City Centre
Address: 5 Dundas Street
Glasgow G1 2AH
Phone: 0141 333 0946

#305
The Waterloo Bar
Category: Gay Bar
Average price: Modest
Area: City Centre
Address: 306 Argyle Street
Glasgow G2 8LY
Phone: 0141 248 7216

#306
Kudos
Category: Pub
Average price: Modest
Area: City Centre
Address: 29 Waterloo Street
Glasgow G2 6BZ
Phone: 0141 221 1066

#307
Bacchus Cafe Bar
Category: Pub, British, Lounge
Average price: Inexpensive
Area: City Centre, Merchant City
Address: 80 Glassford Street
Glasgow G1 1UR
Phone: 0141 572 0080

#308
O'Neill's Irish Bar
Category: Pub, Irish
Average price: Inexpensive
Area: City Centre
Address: 155 Queen Street
Glasgow G1 3BJ
Phone: 0141 229 5871

#309
Saracens Head
Category: Pub
Average price: Modest
Area: Dennistoun, Gallowgate
Address: 209 Gallowgate
Glasgow G1 5DX
Phone: 0141 552 9306

#310
Stirling Castle Bar
Category: Pub, Gastropub
Average price: Modest
Area: West End
Address: 90 Old Dumbarton Road
Glasgow G3 8PZ
Phone: 0141 339 8132

#311
Bank Street Bar Kitchen
Category: Bar, British
Average price: Modest
Area: Hillhead, West End
Address: 52 Bank Street
Glasgow G12
Phone: 0141 334 4343

#312
O'Neill's
Category: Pub
Average price: Modest
Area: City Centre, Merchant City
Address: 71 -73 Albion Street
Glasgow G1 1NY
Phone: 0141 552 0822

#313
Victoria Bar
Category: Pub
Average price: Inexpensive
Area: Rutherglen
Address: 55 Farmeloan Road
Glasgow G73 1DN
Phone: 0141 647 4898

#314
Drop
Category: Bar, Club, British
Average price: Modest
Area: City Centre
Address: 17 Waterloo Street
Glasgow G2 6AY
Phone: 04414 1248 8878

#315
Berkeley 2
Category: Music Venues
Average price: Modest
Area: Finnieston, West End
Address: 93 Lancefield Street
Glasgow G3 8HZ
Phone: 0141 248 1822

#316
Bar Budda
Category: Bar
Average price: Modest
Area: City Centre
Address: 142 St Vincent Street
Glasgow G2 5LA
Phone: 0141 221 5660

#317
Morrison's Bar
Category: Pub
Average price: Modest
Area: City Centre
Address: 220 Clyde Street
Glasgow G1 4JH
Phone: 0141 248 5329

#318
Candy Bar
Category: Bar
Average price: Modest
Area: City Centre
Address: 185 Hope St
Glasgow G2 2UL
Phone: 0141 353 7420

#319
The Abode Glasgow
Category: Hotel, Bar
Average price: Modest
Area: City Centre
Address: 129 Bath Street
Glasgow G2 2SZ
Phone: 0141 572 6000

#320
One Ten Grill
Category: Bar, British
Average price: Modest
Area: City Centre
Address: 110 Bath Street
Glasgow G2 2EN
Phone: 0141 353 0800

#321
Barbushka
Category: Bar, Gastropub
Average price: Inexpensive
Area: SauchieHalls Street, City Centre
Address: 426-430 SauchieHalls Street
Glasgow G2 3JD
Phone: 0141 353 6715

#322
The Sauchiehaugh
Category: Pub
Average price: Inexpensive
Area: City Centre
Address: 410 SauchieHalls Street
Glasgow G2 3JD
Phone: 0141 333 1138

#323
Yates
Category: Wine Bar, Pub
Average price: Inexpensive
Area: City Centre
Address: 292 SauchieHalls Street
Glasgow G2 3JA
Phone: 0141 332 5457

#324
Cairns
Category: Gastropub, Pub
Average price: Modest
Area: City Centre, Merchant City
Address: 5-15 Miller Street
Glasgow G1 1EA
Phone: 0141 248 5007

#325
Walkabout Inn
Category: Pub
Average price: Modest
Area: City Centre
Address: 11 Renfrew Street
Glasgow G2 3AB
Phone: 0141 332 8209

#326
The Shimmy Club
Category: Club
Average price: Modest
Area: City Centre
Address: 25 Royal Exchange Square
Glasgow G1 3AJ
Phone: 0141 204 0101

#327
The Gallery
Category: Gay Bar
Average price: Modest
Area: City Centre, Merchant City
Address: 101 Brunswick Street
Glasgow G1 1BT
Phone: 0141 552 6310

#328
Georgics Bar
Category: Lounge
Average price: Modest
Area: City Centre, Merchant City
Address: George Square
Glasgow G2 1DS
Phone: 0141 332 6711

#329
The Bay Horse
Category: Pub, Coffee & Tea
Average price: Modest
Area: City Centre
Address: 87 Renfield St
Glasgow G2 1LP
Phone: 0141 332 7861

#330
Dows Public House
Category: Pub, Dive Bar
Average price: Modest
Area: City Centre
Address: 9 Dundas Street
Glasgow G1 2AH
Phone: 0141 332 7935

#331
The Gallery
Category: Pub
Average price: Modest
Area: Buchanan Street, City Centre
Address: 203 Buchanan Street
Glasgow G1 2JZ
Phone: 0141 332 1187

#332
Sweeney's On The Park
Category: Pub, Music Venues
Average price: Modest
Area: South Side, Queen's Park
Address: 958 Pollokshaws Road
Glasgow G41 2ET
Phone: 0141 632 6741

#333
Empire Bar
Category: Pub
Average price: Inexpensive
Area: City Centre, Merchant City
Address: 66 Saltmarket
Glasgow G1 5LD
Phone: 0141 552 0844

#334
District Bar
Category: Pub
Average price: Inexpensive
Area: South Side, Kinning Park
Address: 252 Paisley Road West
Glasgow G51 1BS
Phone: 0141 427 5151

#335
Old College Bar
Category: Pub
Average price: Modest
Area: City Centre, Merchant City
Address: 219-221 High Street
Glasgow G1 1PP
Phone: 0141 548 6710

#336
Collage Corner Bar
Category: Bar
Average price: Modest
Area: City Centre
Address: 91 Oswald Street Glasgow
Phone: 0141 225 2407

#337
Madness Theatre Of Fun
Category: Bar
Average price: Modest
Area: City Centre
Address: 30 Bothwell Street
Glasgow G2 7JT
Phone: 0141 204 5999

#338
Tall Cranes
Category: Pub
Average price: Modest
Area: South Side, Govan
Address: 10 Craigton Road
Glasgow G51 3TB
Phone: 0141 445 2751

#339
The Stadium Bar
Category: Pub
Average price: Inexpensive
Area: South Side, Ibrox
Address: 111-119 Copland Road
Glasgow G51 2JE
Phone: 0141 445 3645

#340
Play
Category: Club
Average price: Modest
Area: City Centre
Address: 7 Renfield Street
Glasgow G2 5EZ
Phone: 0845 166 6029

#341
BarMc and Grill
Category: Bar
Average price: Modest
Area: City Centre
Address: 129 Bath Street
Glasgow G2 2SZ
Phone: 0141 572 6014

#342
Orwell's Bar
Category: Pub
Average price: Modest
Area: Charing Cross, West End
Address: 70 Elderslie Street
Glasgow G3 7AL
Phone: 0141 221 4439

#343
Cask & Still
Category: Pub
Average price: Modest
Area: City Centre
Address: 185 Hope Street
Glasgow G2 2UL
Phone: 0141 353 7420

#344
Drummond's Public House
Category: Pub
Average price: Modest
Area: City Centre
Address: 4a West Regent Street
Glasgow G2 1RW
Phone: 0141 332 2217

#345
The Whistlin' Kirk
Category: Pub
Average price: Modest
Area: Gallowgate
Address: 5 Greendyke St
Glasgow G1 5PU
Phone: 0141 552 7851

#346
Byblos
Category: Club
Average price: Modest
Area: City Centre, Merchant City
Address: 71 - 73 Albion St
Glasgow G1 1NY
Phone: 0141 552 3895

#347
Star Bar
Category: Pub
Average price: Inexpensive
Area: South Side
Address: 537-539 Eglinton Street
Glasgow G5 9RN
Phone: 0141 429 2520

#348
The Titwood Bar
Category: Bar
Average price: Modest
Area: South Side
Address: 52-58 Nithsdale Road
Glasgow G41 2AN
Phone: 0141 424 5081

#349
Hurdy Gurdy
Category: Pub
Average price: Modest
Area: City Centre
Address: 83-85 Lister Street
Glasgow G4 0BZ
Phone: 0141 552 3951

#350
The Woodside Inn
Category: Pub
Average price: Modest
Area: West End
Address: 239 Maryhill Rd
Glasgow G20 7YB
Phone: 0141 332 8639

#351
Nico's
Category: Pub
Average price: Inexpensive
Area: SauchieHalls Street, City Centre
Address: 375-379 SauchieHalls Street
Glasgow G2 3HU
Phone: 0141 332 7438

#352
Criterion
Category: Bar, Italian
Average price: Modest
Area: Partick, West End
Address: 568 Dumbarton Road
Glasgow G11 7
Phone: 0141 334 1964

#353
The Millhouse
Category: Pub
Average price: Exclusive
Area: Partick, West End
Address: 2 Partick Bridge Street
Glasgow G11 6PN
Phone: 0141 337 1200

#354
Three Judges
Category: Pub
Average price: Modest
Area: Partick, West End
Address: 141 Dumbarton Road
Glasgow G11 6PR
Phone: 0141 337 3055

#355
Clyde Valley
Category: Pub
Average price: Modest
Area: Partick, West End
Address: 243 Dumbarton Road
Glasgow G11 6AB
Phone: 0141 576 0020

#356
Hayburn Vaults
Category: Pub, Dive Bar
Average price: Modest
Area: Partick, West End
Address: 427-429 Dumbarton Rd
Glasgow G11 6DD
Phone: 0141 339 1240

#357
The Social South Side
Category: Bar, British
Average price: Modest
Area: South Side, Shawlands
Address: 28-30 Kilmarnock Road
Glasgow G41 3NH
Phone: 0845 659 5902

#358
Armstrong's
Category: Pub
Average price: Modest
Area: South Side, Mount Florida
Address: 136 Battlefield Road
Glasgow G42 9
Phone: 0141 636 9229

#359
The Thornwood
Category: Pub
Average price: Inexpensive
Area: Partick, West End
Address: 724 Dumbarton Road
Glasgow G11 6RB
Phone: 0141 334 5059

#360
Sloans
Category: Bar, American
Average price: Modest
Area: City Centre
Address: 62 Argyll Arcade
Glasgow G2 8BG
Phone: 0141 221 8886

#361
The Florida Park
Category: Pub
Average price: Modest
Area: South Side, Mount Florida
Address: 318 Battlefield Road
Glasgow G42 9JD
Phone: 0141 649 8045

#362
The Partick Brewing Company
Category: Pub
Average price: Expensive
Area: Partick, West End
Address: 163 Dumbarton Road
Glasgow G11 6AA
Phone: 0141 339 7571

#363
Campus
Category: Club, Bar
Average price: Inexpensive
Area: SauchieHalls Street, City Centre
Address: 332 SauchieHalls Street
Glasgow G2 3JD
Phone: 0141 332 5388

#364
Spirit
Category: Pub
Average price: Inexpensive
Area: Gallowgate
Address: 30 London Road
Glasgow G1 5NB
Phone: 0141 552 9245

#365
The Kensington
Category: Pub
Average price: Inexpensive
Area: South Side, Kinning Park
Address: 408 Paisley Rd W
Glasgow G51 1BE
Phone: 0141 427 3328

#366
Finlays
Category: Pub
Average price: Modest
Area: Cambuslang
Address: 230 Main Street
Glasgow G72 7EG
Phone: 0141 646 3411

#367
Croft Bar
Category: Pub
Average price: Inexpensive
Area: South Side, Rutherglen
Address: 22 Lugar Place
Glasgow G44 5HB
Phone: 0141 633 5791

#368
Quarter Gill
Category: Pub
Average price: Modest
Area: City Centre
Address: 42 Oswald Street
Glasgow G1 4PL
Phone: 0141 221 0654

#369
Sea Nightclub
Category: Club
Average price: Exclusive
Area: City Centre
Address: 18 Cambridge St
Glasgow G2 3DZ
Phone: 0141 353 6555

#370
Lauries Acoustic Music Bar
Category: Bar
Average price: Modest
Area: City Centre, Merchant City
Address: 34 King Street
Glasgow G1 5QT
Phone: 0141 552 7123

#371
The Lismore
Category: Pub
Average price: Modest
Area: Partick, West End
Address: 206 Dumbarton Road
Glasgow G11 6UN
Phone: 0141 576 0103

#372
Stumps Bar
Category: Pub
Average price: Modest
Area: Partick, West End
Address: 7 Peel St
Glasgow G11 5LL
Phone: 0141 334 7737

#373
Ross's Original Bar
Category: Pub
Average price: Modest
Area: City Centre
Address: 78 Mitchell Street
Glasgow G1 3NA
Phone: 0141 221 5050

#374
Taste Good Inn
Category: Pub
Average price: Modest
Area: Cambuslang
Address: 7 Burn Place
Glasgow G72 7DS
Phone: 0141 569 1101

#375
The V Club
Category: Club
Average price: Modest
Area: SauchieHalls Street, City Centre
Address: 375 SauchieHalls Street
Glasgow G2 3HU
Phone: 0141 333 9919

#376
Station Bar
Category: Pub
Average price: Inexpensive
Area: City Centre, Cowcaddens
Address: 55 Port Dundas Road
Glasgow G4 0HF
Phone: 0141 332 3117

#377
Merchant Pride
Category: Pub
Average price: Inexpensive
Area: City Centre, Merchant City
Address: 20 Candleriggs
Glasgow G1 1LD
Phone: 0141 564 1285

#378
Crystal Bell
Category: Pub
Average price: Modest
Area: Dennistoun, Gallowgate
Address: 31 Gallowgate
Glasgow G1 5AA
Phone: 0141 552 2690

#379
The Strathduie Bar
Category: Pub
Average price: Modest
Area: City Centre, Merchant City
Address: 5 Blackfriars St
Glasgow G1 1PG
Phone: 0141 572 0935

#380
Strathies
Category: Pub
Average price: Modest
Area: South Side
Address: 657 Pollockshaws Road
Glasgow G41 2AB
Phone: 0141 424 3220

#381
Munns Vaults
Category: Pub
Average price: Modest
Area: West End
Address: 610 Maryhill Road
Glasgow G20 7ED
Phone: 0141 946 0706

#382
The Bay Horse
Category: Pub
Average price: Modest
Area: South Side, Queen's Park
Address: 962 Pollokshaws Rd
Glasgow G41 2ET
Phone: 0141 636 4430

#383
Toby Jug
Category: Pub
Average price: Modest
Area: City Centre
Address: 97 Hope Street
Glasgow G2 6LL
Phone: 0141 221 7121

#384
Mint & Lime
Category: Bar
Average price: Modest
Area: City Centre
Address: 77 Jamaica street
Glasgow G1
Phone: 0141 222 1098

#385
Rufus T Firefly
Category: Pub
Average price: Modest
Area: City Centre
Address: 207 Hope Street
Glasgow G2 2UW
Phone: 0141 332 1469

#386
Guru
Category: Club
Average price: Modest
Area: SauchieHalls Street, City Centre
Address: 520 SauchieHalls Street
Glasgow G2 3LW
Phone: 0141 332 0755

#387
KOKOMO
Category: Cocktail Bar, Club, American
Average price: Modest
Area: City Centre
Address: 51 W Regent Street
Glasgow G2 2AE
Phone: 0141 353 1152

#388
Cova
Category: Cocktail Bar
Average price: Inexpensive
Area: City Centre
Address: 53 West Regent Street
Glasgow G2 2AE
Phone: 0141 237 2367

#389
Archaos
Category: Club
Average price: Modest
Area: City Centre
Address: 25-37 Queen Street
Glasgow G1 3EF
Phone: 0141 204 3189

#390
Edward
Category: Pub
Average price: Modest
Area: City Centre
Address: 410 SauchieHalls Street
Glasgow G2 3JD
Phone: 0141 333 1138

#391
Club 520
Category: Club
Average price: Modest
Area: Charing Cross, SauchieHalls
Street, City Centre
Address: 520 SauchieHalls Street
Glasgow G2 3LW
Phone: 0141 332 0755

#392
GLC Cafe Bar
Category: Pub
Average price: Modest
Area: City Centre
Address: 11 Dixon Street
Glasgow G1 4AL
Phone: 0141 226 5050

#393
The Vale Lounge
Category: Club
Average price: Modest
Area: City Centre
Address: 5 Dundas Street
Glasgow G1 2AH
Phone: 0141 332 4928

#394
Gallery Bar
Category: Lounge
Average price: Modest
Area: Finnieston, West End
Address: 1038-1042 Argyle Street
Glasgow G3
Phone: 0141 221 4449

#395
54 Below
Category: Pub
Average price: Modest
Area: Finnieston, West End
Address: 1106 Argyle Street
Glasgow G3 8TD
Phone: 0141 357 5454

#396
The Old Ship Bank
Category: Pub
Average price: Modest
Area: City Centre
Address: 164-166 Saltmarket
Glasgow G1 5LA
Phone: 0141 552 8458

#397
El Barrio Latino Bar & Club
Category: Bar, Club
Average price: Modest
Area: City Centre, Merchant City
Address: 69 Albion Street
Glasgow G1 1NY
Phone: 0141 552 1212

#398
Visge Beatha
Category: Pub
Average price: Modest
Area: Woodlands, West End
Address: 242 Woodlands Road
Glasgow G3 6ND
Phone: 0141 564 1596

#399
Thirsty Scholar
Category: Pub
Average price: Modest
Area: West End
Address: 67 Old Dumbarton Road
Glasgow G3
Phone: 0141 339 6244

#400
The Portland Arms
Category: Pub
Average price: Modest
Area: Shettleston
Address: 1169 Shettleston Road
Glasgow G32 7NB
Phone: 0141 778 6657

#401
Ladywell Bar
Category: Pub
Average price: Modest
Area: Dennistoun
Address: 139 Barrack Street
Glasgow G4 0UE
Phone: 0141 552 1600

#402
New Regent Bar
Category: Pub
Average price: Modest
Area: South Side
Address: 752 Pollokshaws Road
Glasgow G41 2AE
Phone: 0141 423 1176

#403
The Drover
Category: Pub
Average price: Modest
Area: Dennistoun, Gallowgate
Address: 447 Gallowgate
Glasgow G40 2DX
Phone: 0141 554 1540

#404
Chapmans Bar
Category: Pub
Average price: Exclusive
Area: Rutherglen
Address: 251 Main Street
Glasgow G73 2HN
Phone: 0141 647 1987

#405
Quarter Gill
Category: Pub
Average price: Modest
Area: Partick, West End
Address: 232 Dumbarton Road
Glasgow G11 6TU
Phone: 0141 576 0018

#406
Alfredos Public House
Category: Pub
Average price: Modest
Area: SauchieHalls Street, City Centre
Address: 146 West Nile Street
Glasgow G1 2RQ
Phone: 0141 564 1270

#407
Craigpark Masters
Category: Snooker & Pool Halls
Average price: Modest
Area: Dennistoun
Address: 164 Craigpark
Glasgow G31 2HE
Phone: 0141 554 4204

#408
Reardons Southside
Category: Snooker & Pool Halls
Average price: Modest
Area: South Side, Shawlands
Address: 1060 Pollokshaws Road
Glasgow G41 3YG
Phone: 0141 632 0007

#409
Mills Bar
Category: Pub
Average price: Modest
Area: Duke Street, Dennistoun
Address: 380 Duke Street
Glasgow G31 2
Phone: 0141 551 9581

#410
Jam
Category: Bar
Average price: Modest
Area: South Side, Shawlands
Address: 28-30 Kilmarnock Road
Glasgow G41 3NH
Phone: 0845 659 5902

#411
Sir John Stirling Maxwell
Category: Pub
Average price: Modest
Area: South Side, Shawlands
Address: 140 Kilmarnock Road
Glasgow G41 3NN
Phone: 0141 636 9024

#412
Crown Creighton
Category: Pub
Average price: Modest
Area: Duke Street, Dennistoun
Address: 476-480 Duke Street
Glasgow G31 1QF
Phone: 0141 554 5690

#413
JAYZ Bar & Restaurant
Category: Bar, British
Average price: Modest
Area: South Side, Shawlands
Address: 87 Kilmarnock Road
Glasgow G41 3YR
Phone: 0141 387 9046

#414
Mansion House
Category: Lounge
Average price: Expensive
Area: City Centre, Merchant City
Address: 20 Glassford St
Glasgow G1 1UL
Phone: 0141 553 4888

#415
Montford Bar
Category: Pub
Average price: Expensive
Area: South Side
Address: 23-27 Curtis Avenue
Glasgow G44 4QD
Phone: 0141 569 1113

#416
Kerrydale Bar
Category: Sports Bar
Average price: Modest
Area: Parkhead
Address: Celtic Park
Glasgow G40 3RE
Phone: 0871 226 1888

#417
The Bank
Category: Pub
Average price: Modest
Area: Parkhead
Address: 1450 Gallowgate
Glasgow G31 4ST
Phone: 0141 550 8999

#418
Dr Gormans
Category: Pub
Average price: Modest
Area: Rutherglen
Address: 33 Queen Street
Glasgow G73 1JP
Phone: 0141 647 5155

#419
Seventh Heaven
Category: Club
Average price: Modest
Area: Charing Cross, City Centre
Address: 15 Elmbank Gardens
Glasgow G2 4NQ
Phone: 0141 221 2772

#420
Mint and Lime
Category: Sports Bar
Average price: Modest
Area: City Centre
Address: 318 Clyde Street
Glasgow G1 4NR
Phone: 0141 222 2828

#421
The Souwester Inn
Category: Pub
Average price: Inexpensive
Area: South Side, Tradeston
Address: 24 Bridge Street
Glasgow G5 9HU
Phone: 0141 429 7062

#422
The Lane Bar & Restaurant
Category: Bar
Average price: Modest
Area: City Centre
Address: 57-59 SauchieHalls Lane
Glasgow G2 4AB
Phone: 0141 332 8899

#423
Independent Bar & Kitchen
Category: Bar, Diners
Average price: Modest
Area: City Centre, Merchant City
Address: Queen Street Glasgow
Phone: 0141 221 1779

#424
Destiny
Category: Club
Average price: Modest
Area: City Centre
Address: 18 Cambridge Street
Glasgow G2 3DZ
Phone: 0141 353 6555

#425
Oriental Bar
Category: Bar
Average price: Modest
Area: City Centre, Merchant City
Address: 11-13 Hutcheson St
Glasgow G1 1SL
Phone: 0141 553 1500

#426
The New Blane Valley Bar
Category: Pub
Average price: Modest
Area: City Centre, Merchant City
Address: 76 Glassford Street
Glasgow G1 1UP
Phone: 0141 552 4286

#427
Genting Casino
Category: Casino
Average price: Modest
Area: Charing Cross, SauchieHalls Street
West, Woodlands, West End
Address: 506 - 516 SauchieHalls
Street Glasgow G2 3LW
Phone: 0141 332 0992

#428
Scotch Corner
Category: Pub
Average price: Expensive
Area: City Centre, Merchant City
Address: Bridgegate
Glasgow G1 5HY
Phone: 0141 552 7520

#429
The Cambridge
Category: Pub
Average price: Modest
Area: City Centre
Address: Cambridge St
Glasgow G3 6QX
Phone: 0141 276 1830

#430
Black Bull
Category: Pub
Average price: Modest
Area: City Centre, Merchant City
Address: 111 High Street
Glasgow G1 1PH
Phone: 0141 572 0532

#431
Wintersgills Bar
Category: Pub
Average price: Modest
Area: Great Western Road, West End
Address: 226 Great Western Rd
Glasgow G4 9EJ
Phone: 0141 332 3532

#432
Alfies Bar
Category: Bar
Average price: Modest
Area: West End
Address: 67 Old Dumbarton Road
Glasgow G3 8RF
Phone: 0141 339 5315

#433
Kimberley
Category: Pub
Average price: Modest
Area: Tollcross
Address: 1137 Tollcross Road
Glasgow G32 8HB
Phone: 0141 778 5685

#434
The Attic Restaurant & Bar
Category: Pub
Average price: Expensive
Area: City Centre
Address: Dundas St
Glasgow G1 2AQ
Phone: 0141 353 6040

#435
The Lord Nelson
Category: Pub
Average price: Inexpensive
Area: South Side, Tradeston
Address: 123 Nelson Street
Glasgow G5 8DZ
Phone: 0141 429 1783

#436
Old Stag Inn
Category: Pub
Average price: Modest
Area: South Side
Address: 12 Greenview Street
Glasgow G43 1SN
Phone: 0141 632 0209

#437
Beechwood Tavern
Category: Pub
Average price: Inexpensive
Area: South Side
Address: 156-164 Ardmay Crescent
Glasgow G44 4PP
Phone: 0141 632 5476

#438
Denholms
Category: Pub
Average price: Inexpensive
Area: City Centre
Address: 17 Hope Street
Glasgow G2 6AB
Phone: 0141 221 9641

#439
Club 30
Category: Club
Average price: Modest
Area: City Centre
Address: 26 Cambridge Street
Glasgow G2 3DZ
Phone: 0141 332 3437

#440
Rams Head
Category: Pub
Average price: Modest
Area: Maryhill
Address: 1971 Maryhill Road
Glasgow G20 0BT
Phone: 0141 946 4044

#441
Hoops Public House
Category: Pub
Average price: Inexpensive
Area: Gallowgate
Address: 283 Gallowgate
Glasgow G4 0TR
Phone: 0141 552 4995

#442
Tir Chonaill
Category: Pub
Average price: Modest
Area: South Side
Address: 506 Victoria Road
Glasgow G42 8PQ
Phone: 0141 423 0064

#443
Cotters Bar
Category: Pub
Average price: Modest
Area: Parkhead
Address: 498 Tollcross Road
Glasgow G31 4XX
Phone: 0141 550 4903

#444
Reardons Pool & Snooker Club
Category: Snooker & Pool Halls
Average price: Modest
Area: City Centre
Address: 26 Hope Street
Glasgow G2 6AA
Phone: 0141 221 4646

#445
Malones Irish Bar
Category: Sports Bar, Irish
Average price: Modest
Area: City Centre
Address: 57-59 SauchieHalls Lane
Glasgow G2 4AB
Phone: 0141 375 1200

#446
The Bristol Bar
Category: Dive Bar
Average price: Modest
Area: Duke Street, Dennistoun
Address: 600 Duke St
Glasgow G31 1JX
Phone: 0141 554 7890

#447
The Quaich
Category: Pub
Average price: Expensive
Area: South Side, Shawlands
Address: 52 Coustonholm Road
Glasgow G43 1UF
Phone: 0141 632 9003

#448
Stirrup Cup
Category: Pub
Average price: Inexpensive
Area: Rutherglen
Address: 183 Main Street
Glasgow G73 2HG
Phone: 0141 647 6731

#449
B J's
Category: Pub
Average price: Modest
Area: Great Western Road, Anniesland
Address: 828 Crow Road
Glasgow G13 1HA
Phone: 0141 959 7789

#450
Maryhill Burgh Halls
Category: Music Venues
Average price: Modest
Area: West End
Address: 10-24 Gairbraid Avenue
Glasgow G20 8YE
Phone: 0845 860 1891

#451
Ivy
Category: Bar
Average price: Modest
Area: Charing Cross, West End
Address: 1102-1106 Argyle Street
Glasgow G3 7RX
Phone: 0141 221 1144

#452
Bunker
Category: Bar
Average price: Modest
Area: City Centre
Address: 193-199 Bath Street
Glasgow G2 4HU
Phone: 0141 229 1427

#453
Milan
Category: Club
Average price: Modest
Area: City Centre, Merchant City
Address: 42 Queen St
Glasgow G1 3DX
Phone: 0141 221 2452

#454
Victoria's
Category: Club
Average price: Modest
Area: SauchieHalls Street, City Centre
Address: 98 SauchieHalls Street
Glasgow G2 3DE
Phone: 0141 332 1444

#455
Entertainment Guides
Category: Event Management
Average price: Modest
Area: City Centre, Merchant City
Address: 229 George Street
Glasgow G1 1QU
Phone: 07523 244108

#456
Victoria Bar
Category: Pub
Average price: Modest
Area: City Centre, Merchant City
Address: 159 Bridgegate
Glasgow G1 5HZ
Phone: 0141 552 6040

#457
Milk
Category: Bar
Average price: Modest
Area: City Centre, Merchant City
Address: 17 John Street
Glasgow G1 1HP
Phone: 0141 552 2237

#458
The Grapes Bar
Category: Pub
Average price: Inexpensive
Area: South Side, Kinning Park
Address: 218 Paisley Road West
Glasgow G51 1BU
Phone: 0141 427 2932

#459
Curry Karaoke
Category: Karaoke
Average price: Modest
Area: Finnieston, West End
Address: 100 Stobcross Road
Glasgow G3 8QQ
Phone: 0141 248 1485

#460
The Sanctuary
Category: Bar
Average price: Modest
Area: Partick, West End
Address: 59 Dumbarton Road
Glasgow G11 6PD
Phone: 0141 334 0770

#461
Treble Two Bar
Category: Pub
Average price: Inexpensive
Area: Gallowgate
Address: 222 Abercromby Street
Glasgow G40 2BZ
Phone: 0141 554 3491

#462
13th Note
Category: Bar, Music Venues, Vegan
Average price: Modest
Area: City Centre, Merchant City
Address: 50-60 King Street
Glasgow G1 5QT
Phone: 0141 553 1638

#463
Ajs-Sauna
Category: Gay Bar
Average price: Modest
Area: City Centre
Address: 41b York street
Glasgow G2 8JQ
Phone: 0141 237 3011

#464
AJ's Male Only Sauna
Category: Adult Entertainment
Average price: Modest
Area: City Centre
Address: 41b York street
Glasgow G2 8JQ
Phone: 0141 237 3011

#465
Red Leaf Bar
Category: Bar
Average price: Modest
Area: South Side, Kinning Park
Address: Springfield Quay Paisley Road
Glasgow G5 8NP
Phone: 0141 555 6100

#466
Osmosis
Category: Lounge
Average price: Modest
Area: City Centre
Address: 77 Jamaica St
Glasgow G1 4NR
Phone: 0141 222 2828

#467
Groove Bar
Category: Pub
Average price: Modest
Area: City Centre
Address: 8 Kelvingrove Street
Glasgow G3 7RX
Phone: 0141 243 2565

#468
Fantoosh Shisha Cafe
Category: Hookah Bar
Average price: Modest
Area: South Side, Tradeston
Address: 90 Commerce St
Glasgow G5 8DG
Phone: 0141 429 1780

#469
The Truffle Club
Category: Sports Club, Club
Average price: Modest
Area: City Centre
Address: 24 Drury Street
Glasgow G2 5AA
Phone: 0141 229 0714

#470
Finnegans Wake
Category: Pub
Average price: Modest
Area: City Centre
Address: 79 St Vincent Street
Glasgow G2 5TF
Phone: 0141 248 4989

#471
BarCo
Category: Pub
Average price: Modest
Area: Charing Cross, Finnieston
Address: 512 St Vincent Street
Glasgow G3 8XZ
Phone: 0141 248 2223

#472
Bar Bia
Category: Pub
Average price: Modest
Area: City Centre
Address: 142 West Regent Street
Glasgow G2 2RQ
Phone: 0141 572 4041

#473
Black Ice Bar&Club
Category: Wine Bar
Average price: Modest
Area: SauchieHalls Street, City Centre
Address: 437 SauchieHalls Street
Glasgow G2 3LG
Phone: 0141 332 3050

#474
Sola Bar
Category: Bar
Average price: Modest
Area: City Centre, Merchant City
Address: 18 John Street
Glasgow G1 1JQ
Phone: 0141 552 3801

#475
Duke Bar
Category: Pub
Average price: Modest
Area: Duke Street, Dennistoun
Address: 631 Duke Street
Glasgow G31 1QA
Phone: 0141 554 2461

#476
The West Bar
Category: Pub
Average price: Modest
Area: West End
Address: 1397-1403 Argyle Street
Glasgow G3 8AN
Phone: 0141 357 4328

#477
Quo Vadis
Category: Pub
Average price: Modest
Area: South Side
Address: 1860 Paisley Road West
Glasgow G52 3TN
Phone: 0141 883 6538

#478
Radio
Category: Lounge
Average price: Modest
Area: Hillhead, West End
Address: 44-46 Ashton Lane
Glasgow G12 8SJ
Phone: 0845 166 6011

#479
Bar Soba
Category: Pub, Japanese
Average price: Modest
Area: City Centre
Address: 11 Mitchell Lane
Glasgow G1 3NU
Phone: 0141 204 2404

#480
Distill
Category: Music Venues, Cocktail Bar
Average price: Modest
Area: Finnieston, West End
Address: 1102-1106 Argyle Street
Glasgow G3 7RX
Phone: 0141 337 3006

#481
Church On The Hill
Category: Pub
Average price: Modest
Area: South Side, Shawlands
Address: 16 Algie Street
Glasgow G41 3DJ
Phone: 0141 636 9171

#482
Café Source
Category: Pub, Gastropub
Average price: Modest
Area: Gallowgate
Address: 1 St Andrews Square
Glasgow G1 5PP
Phone: 0141 548 6020

#483
The Granary
Category: Pub, Gastropub
Average price: Modest
Area: South Side, Shawlands
Address: 10 Kilmarnock Rd
Glasgow G41 3NH
Phone: 0141 649 0594

#484
Hielan Jessie
Category: Pub
Average price: Inexpensive
Area: Gallowgate
Address: 374 Gallowgate
Glasgow G4 0TX
Phone: 0141 552 0753

#485
Bon Accord
Category: Pub
Average price: Modest
Area: Charing Cross, West End
Address: 153 North Street
Glasgow G3 7DA
Phone: 0141 248 4427

#486
Kushion
Category: Club
Average price: Modest
Area: City Centre
Address: 158-166 Bath St
Glasgow G2 4TB
Phone: 0845 166 6031

#487
Blue Dog
Category: Wine Bar, Cocktail Bar,
Champagne Bar
Average price: Expensive
Area: City Centre
Address: 151 West George Street
Glasgow G2 1JJ
Phone: 0141 229 0707

#488
Buddy's Bar Diner Grill
Category: American, Barbeque, Bar
Average price: Inexpensive
Area: South Side
Address: 677-681 Pollokshaws Road
Glasgow G41 2AB
Phone: 0141 423 9988

#489
Thistle Bar
Category: Pub
Average price: Modest
Area: Cambuslang
Address: 70 Main Street
Glasgow G72 7EP
Phone: 0141 771 1457

#490
Beer Café
Category: Pub
Average price: Modest
Area: City Centre, Merchant City
Address: 78 Candleriggs
Glasgow G1 1TS
Phone: 0141 552 9815

#491
The Doublet
Category: Pub
Average price: Modest
Area: Woodlands, West End
Address: 74 Park Road
Glasgow G4 9JF
Phone: 0141 334 1982

#492
Blackfriars
Category: Pub
Average price: Modest
Area: City Centre, Merchant City
Address: 36 Bell Street
Glasgow G1 1LG
Phone: 0141 552 5924

#493
Royale Snooker Club
Category: Snooker & Pool Halls
Average price: Modest
Area: Rutherglen
Address: 96 Main Street
Glasgow G73 2HZ
Phone: 0141 647 9070

#494
Rab Ha's
Category: Hotel, Pub
Average price: Modest
Area: City Centre, Merchant City
Address: 83 Hutcheson Street
Glasgow G1 1SH
Phone: 0141 572 0400

#495
Bannisters
Category: Pub
Average price: Modest
Area: Finnieston, West End
Address: 956 Argyle Street
Glasgow G3 8LU
Phone: 0141 564 1062

#496
The Arrol
Category: Pub, Dive Bar
Average price: Modest
Area: Dennistoun
Address: Glasgow Central Station
Glasgow G1 3SL
Phone: 0141 226 3730

#497
Sir John Stirling Maxwell
Category: Pub
Average price: Inexpensive
Area: South Side, Shawlands
Address: 136 Kilmarnock Road
Glasgow G41 3NN
Phone: 0141 636 9024

#498
Queen's Park Café
Category: Pub
Average price: Inexpensive
Area: South Side
Address: 530 Victoria Road
Glasgow G42 8BG
Phone: 0141 424 1374

#499
Mono
Category: Bar, Vegan
Average price: Modest
Area: City Centre, Merchant City
Address: 12 Kings Court
Glasgow G1 5RB
Phone: 0141 553 2400

#500
The Steps Bar
Category: Pub
Average price: Modest
Area: City Centre, Merchant City
Address: 62 Glassford Street
Glasgow G1 1UP
Phone: 0141 552 3059

CPSIA information can be obtained
at www.ICGtesting.com
Printed in the USA
BVHW091805120223
658375BV00026B/600